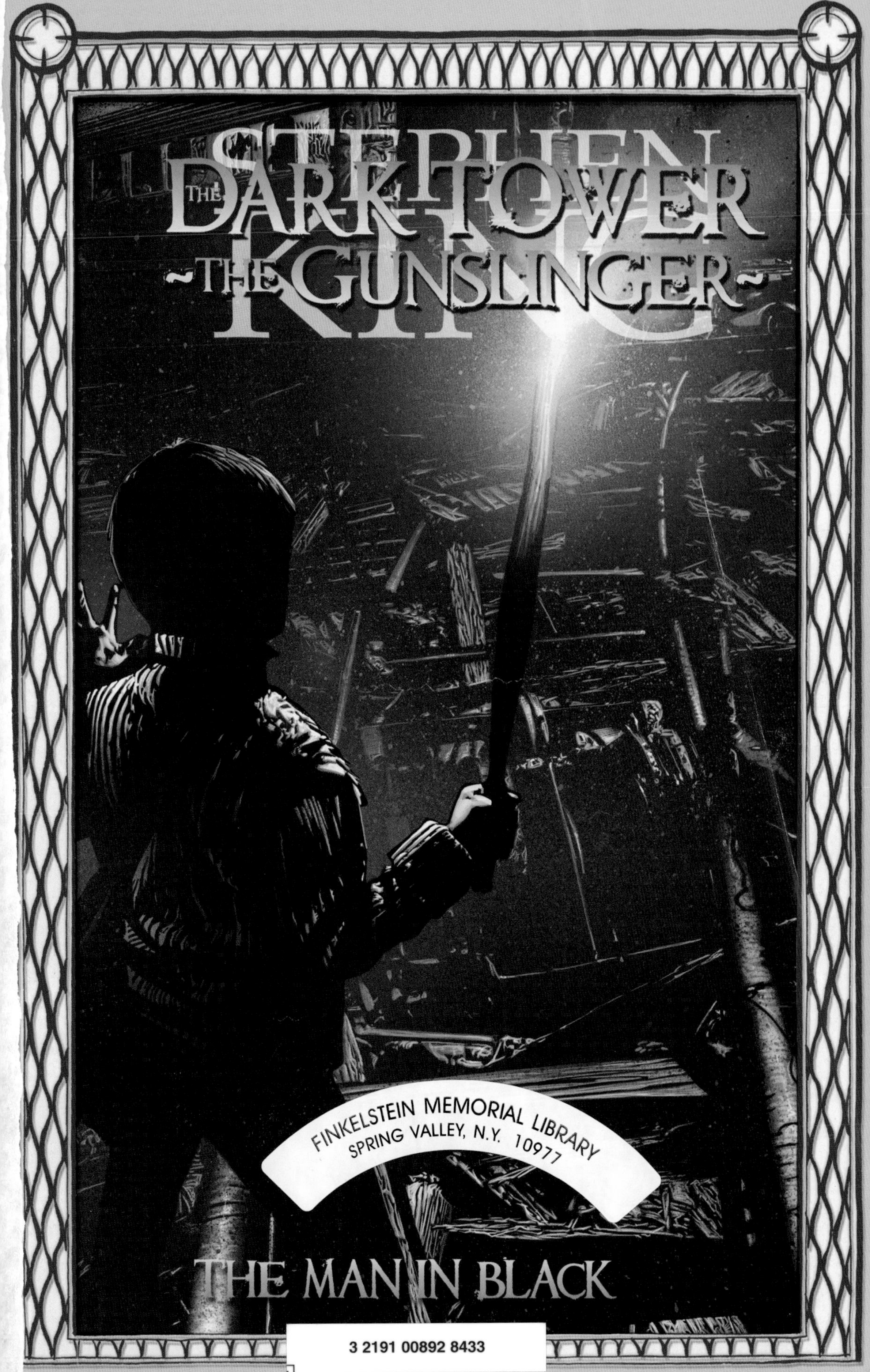
STEPHEN KING
THE DARK TOWER
~THE GUNSLINGER~
THE MAN IN BLACK

THE DARK TOWER
~THE GUNSLINGER~
THE MAN IN BLACK

CREATIVE DIRECTOR AND EXECUTIVE DIRECTOR
STEPHEN KING

PLOTTING AND CONSULTATION
ROBIN FURTH

SCRIPT
PETER DAVID

ARTIST
ALEX MALEEV

COLOR ART
RICHARD ISANOVE

LETTERING
VC'S JOE SABINO

PRODUCTION
MAYELA GUTIERREZ & IDETTE WINECOOR

COVER ART
ALEX MALEEV

DARK TOWER: THE GUNSLINGER — THE MAN IN BLACK. Contains material originally published in magazine form as DARK TOWER: THE GUNSLINGER — THE MAN IN BLACK #1-5. First printing 2013. ISBN# 978-0-7851-4937-8. Published by MARVEL WORLDWIDE, INC., a subsidiary of MARVEL ENTERTAINMENT, LLC. OFFICE OF PUBLICATION: 135 West 50th Street, New York, NY 10020. Copyright © Stephen King. All rights reserved. $24.99 per copy in the U.S. and $27.99 in Canada (GST #R127032852); Canadian Agreement #40668537. All characters featured in this issue and the distinctive names and likenesses thereof, and all related indicia are trademarks of Stephen King. No similarity between any of the names, characters, persons, and/or institutions in this magazine with those of any living or dead person or institution is intended, and any such similarity which may exist is purely coincidental. Marvel and its logos are TM & © Marvel Characters, Inc. **Printed in the U.S.A.** ALAN FINE, EVP - Office of the President, Marvel Worldwide, Inc. and EVP & CMO Marvel Characters B.V.; DAN BUCKLEY, Publisher & President - Print, Animation & Digital Divisions; JOE QUESADA, Chief Creative Officer; TOM BREVOORT, SVP of Publishing; DAVID BOGART, SVP of Operations & Procurement, Publishing; RUWAN JAYATILLEKE, SVP & Associate Publisher, Publishing; C.B. CEBULSKI, SVP of Creator & Content Development; DAVID GABRIEL, SVP of Publishing Sales & Circulation; MICHAEL PASCIULLO, SVP of Brand Planning & Communications; JIM O'KEEFE, VP of Operations & Logistics; DAN CARR, Executive Director of Publishing Technology; SUSAN CRESPI, Editorial Operations Manager; ALEX MORALES, Publishing Operations Manager; STAN LEE, Chairman Emeritus. For information regarding advertising in Marvel Comics or on Marvel.com, please contact Niza Disla, Director of Marvel Partnerships, at ndisla@marvel.com. For Marvel subscription inquiries, please call 800-217-9158. **Manufactured between 10/29/2012 and 12/17/2012 by R.R. DONNELLEY, INC., SALEM, VA, USA.**

10 9 8 7 6 5 4 3 2 1

ASSISTANT EDITOR
ELLIE PYLE

CONSULTING EDITOR
RALPH MACCHIO

EDITOR
SANA AMANAT

COLLECTION EDITOR
MARK D. BEAZLEY

ASSISTANT EDITORS
NELSON RIBEIRO & ALEX STARBUCK

EDITOR, SPECIAL PROJECTS
JENNIFER GRÜNWALD

SENIOR EDITOR, SPECIAL PROJECTS
JEFF YOUNGQUIST

SENIOR VICE PRESIDENT OF SALES
DAVID GABRIEL

SVP OF BRAND PLANNING & COMMUNICATIONS
MICHAEL PASCIULLO

ASSOCIATE PUBLISHER & SVP, PRINT, ANIMATION & DIGITAL MEDIA
RUWAN JAYATILLEKE

BOOK DESIGN
PATRICK McGRATH

EDITOR IN CHIEF
AXEL ALONSO

CHIEF CREATIVE OFFICER
JOE QUESADA

PUBLISHER
DAN BUCKLEY

SPECIAL THANKS TO
CHUCK VERRILL, MARSHA DEFILIPPO, BARBARA ANN McINTYRE, BRIAN STARK,
JIM NAUSEDAS, JIM McCANN, ARUNE SINGH, JEFF SUTER, JOHN BARBER, LAUREN
SANKOVITCH, MIKE HORWITZ, CHARLIE BECKERMAN & CHRIS ELIOPOULOS

Dear Fellow Constant Readers,

When I think about differences between the novels and the comics—and there are many of them—I always keep in mind Jake Chambers' famous phrase, "there are other worlds than these." *The Dark Tower* contains many levels, and within those levels are parallel worlds which mirror each other, but which are not exactly alike.

I always view the *Dark Tower* comics as existing in one of these parallel worlds. If the *Dark Tower* novels exist in Tower Keystone, or the central world of the *Dark Tower* universe, then the *Dark Tower* comics exist in a spinoff world, one which is very similar to, but not exactly the same as, the one where *The Gunslinger, The Drawing of the Three, The Waste Lands, Wizard and Glass*, and the rest of the *Dark Tower* novels take place. When you think about it, this idea of parallel worlds isn't so very different from contemporary theories in quantum physics. According to these theories, every time we make a decision and follow a certain path in life, *another* reality is born where we make a *different* decision and follow a *different* life path. For example, imagine that you are walking down the street. You come to a crossroad. You have a decision to make—you can either turn left and go home or you can turn right and go to the shop and buy a lottery ticket. You tell yourself that buying a lottery ticket is stupid, so you go home and take a nap. However in a parallel reality, a *different* version of you turned right and bought a lottery ticket . . . and won! (But don't be too sad that in this *where* and *when* you didn't buy that lottery ticket. On another level of the Tower, you were hit by a van before you even reached the store.)

As you will see when you read this collection, our present tale is not *exactly* like the one recounted in *The Gunslinger*, though the characters, the energy, and our end point, are the same. As in the original version of the tale, Roland and Jake have just met the Man in Black, a story recounted at the end of *The Way Station*. During that interchange, Roland's nemesis announced that he and Roland would meet on the other side of the mountains and hold palaver . . . alone. In both Stephen King's original tale and our version of the story, the Man in Black succeeds in making Jake suspect Roland's honesty, and in making Roland doubt himself. But at this particular point in the narrative, our story (recounted in the present comic), and Steve King's tale, diverge. In Stephen King's original version, Roland and Jake enter the mountain tunnels *together*, and they do so *immediately*. In our version of the story, Roland and Jake set up camp, the Man in Black appears as a fire demon, tempting Roland to betray his young companion, and then Roland journeys into the mountain alone, seemingly abandoning Jake.

It might seem strange that I chose to alter the original tale, but as always my goal was to create an atmosphere which exists in the books but which is expressed only through nuance and internal dialogue. I hoped that by expanding this section of Roland and Jake's journey, I could emphasize the complicated emotions—love, suspicion, self-doubt, self-hatred, fear of betrayal and abandonment—which weave their way through Roland and Jake's relationship.

Throughout "The Slow Mutants" (part of which is adapted here) there is a tremendous tension in Roland and Jake's relationship. Roland is coming to love Jake as a son, but there is still a part of him that is completely and ruthlessly devoted to his quest, and which is willing to sacrifice anything to reach the Tower. In King's tale, this coldness is described very vividly, but in a way that is very difficult to portray in comics. When Jake says that he does not want to follow Roland beneath the mountains, Roland's response is surprisingly chilly. "Come with me or stay," he says impassively. But though Roland's words seem to lack emotion, in his mind, something dangerous is taking place. Roland is beginning to see Jake not as a vulnerable young boy, but as a potential pawn in the game he plays with the Man in Black: "That was the moment at which the small figure before him ceased to be Jake and became only the boy, an impersonality to be moved and used."

Since the book you now hold in your hands is a new graphic tale, I wanted to remind readers of the Man in Black's corrupting influence upon Roland (what happened at the end of *The Way Station*), but I also wanted to draw a subliminal connection between the Man in Black and the evil devils that dance in devil grass fires—little demons that twist men's minds and drive them mad. Hence, I decided to make the Man in Black into a flame-creature.

By temporarily separating Roland and Jake, I wanted to emphasize something which is extremely apparent in the book: Jake does not completely trust Roland, and for good reason. However, the gifts Roland gives to his young companion—his compass, his flint and steel, and one torch—are signs that our gunslinger still has a heart, and his heart contains affection for Jake, no matter how complicated that affection might be. (And by the way, bringing in Roland's compass was an excellent excuse to introduce the fact that in Mid-World, directions no longer hold true!)

Plotting Jake's solitary adventure was not easy. I wanted to make sure that I didn't move too far away from King territory, so for Jake's lonely trek I turned to Larry's and Rita's horrible journey through the Lincoln Tunnel in *The Stand*, and Jack Sawyer's solitary journey through the Oatley Tunnel in *The Talisman*. And as for the rats? Well, I'd recently reread "Graveyard Shift," and rats were on my mind. As for Jake's encounter with an act of terrorism, I'd also recently reread "The Things They Left Behind," and so couldn't help but think about the ruthless acts of cruelty we humans commit in the name of politics or religious causes.

Until next time—

Long Days and Pleasant Nights!

Robin Furth

Previously...

Roland Deschain is the last gunslinger in the line of Arthur Eld. His quest is the pursuit of the elusive Man in Black and Roland will not stop until he brings him to the Dark Tower itself.

An immeasurable amount of time has passed since Roland began his expedition. Since then he's escaped murderers and marauders, the bewitched and the demonic, all in the name of a promise he once made. After meeting Jake, a young boy from another earth where cars roam streets and clothes are sold on mannequins, Roland learns he's closer to his prey than ever before.

For Jake is the gateway to the Man in Black.

STEPHEN KING

THE DARK TOWER ~THE GUNSLINGER~

THE MAN IN BLACK

CHAPTER ONE

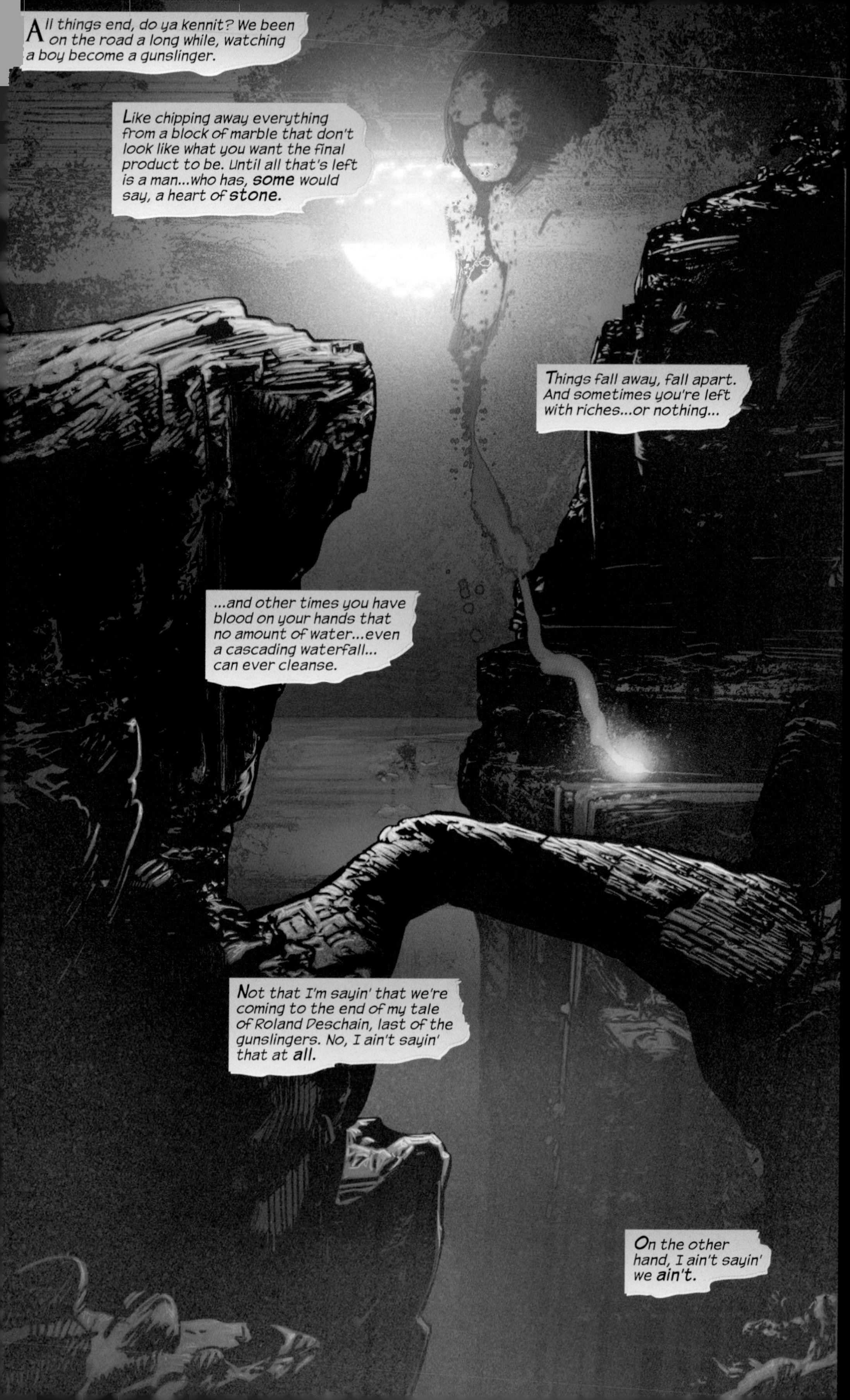
All things end, do ya kennit? We been on the road a long while, watching a boy become a gunslinger.
Like chipping away everything from a block of marble that don't look like what you want the final product to be. Until all that's left is a man...who has, some would say, a heart of stone.
Things fall away, fall apart. And sometimes you're left with riches...or nothing...
...and other times you have blood on your hands that no amount of water...even a cascading waterfall... can ever cleanse.
Not that I'm sayin' that we're coming to the end of my tale of Roland Deschain, last of the gunslingers. No, I ain't sayin' that at all.
On the other hand, I ain't sayin' we ain't.

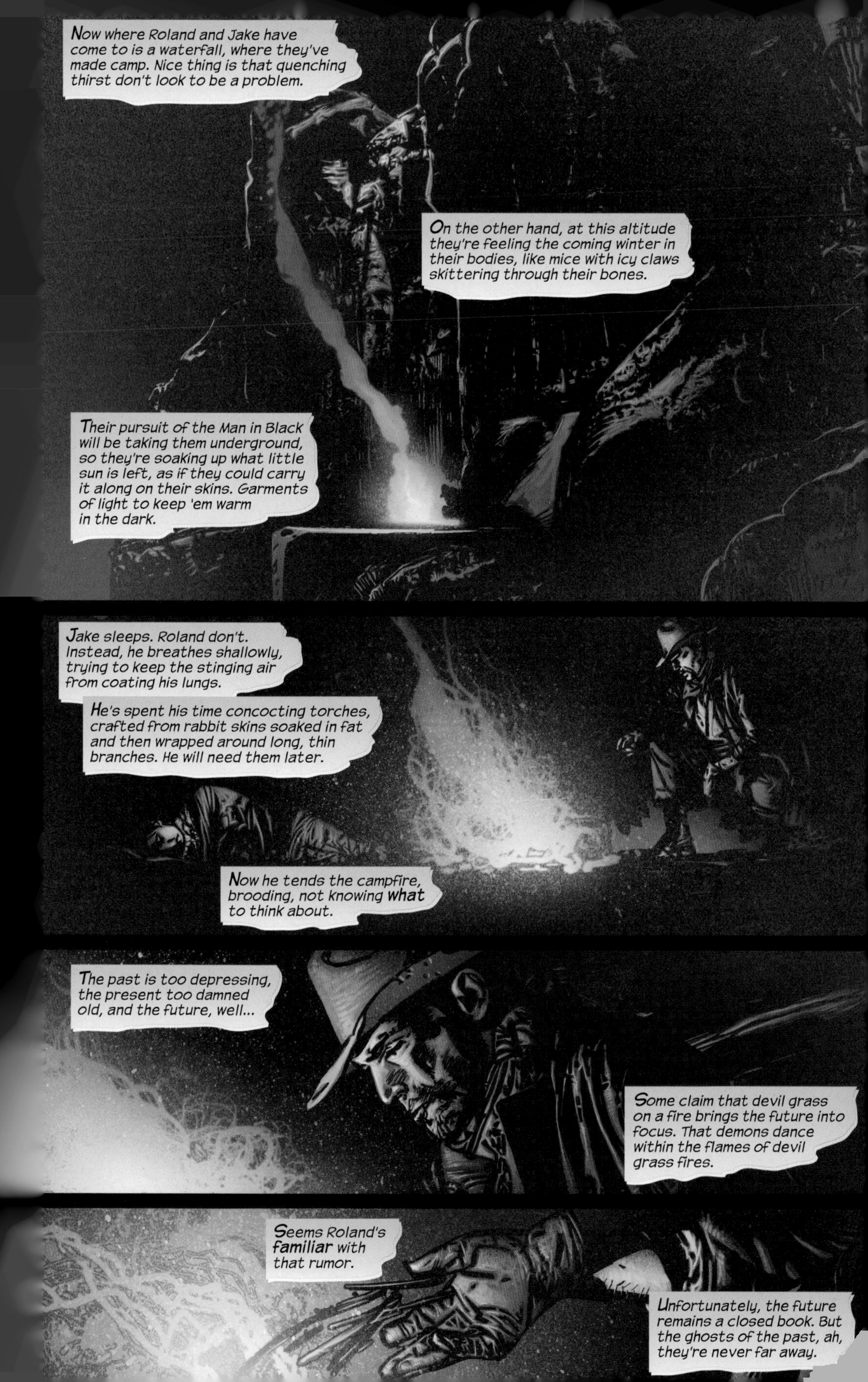
Now where Roland and Jake have come to is a waterfall, where they've made camp. Nice thing is that quenching thirst don't look to be a problem.
On the other hand, at this altitude they're feeling the coming winter in their bodies, like mice with icy claws skittering through their bones.
Their pursuit of the Man in Black will be taking them underground, so they're soaking up what little sun is left, as if they could carry it along on their skins. Garments of light to keep 'em warm in the dark.
Jake sleeps. Roland don't. Instead, he breathes shallowly, trying to keep the stinging air from coating his lungs.
He's spent his time concocting torches, crafted from rabbit skins soaked in fat and then wrapped around long, thin branches. He will need them later.
Now he tends the campfire, brooding, not knowing **what** to think about.
The past is too depressing, the present too damned old, and the future, well...
Some claim that devil grass on a fire brings the future into focus. That demons dance within the flames of devil grass fires.
Seems Roland's **familiar** with that rumor.
Unfortunately, the future remains a closed book. But the ghosts of the past, ah, they're never far away.

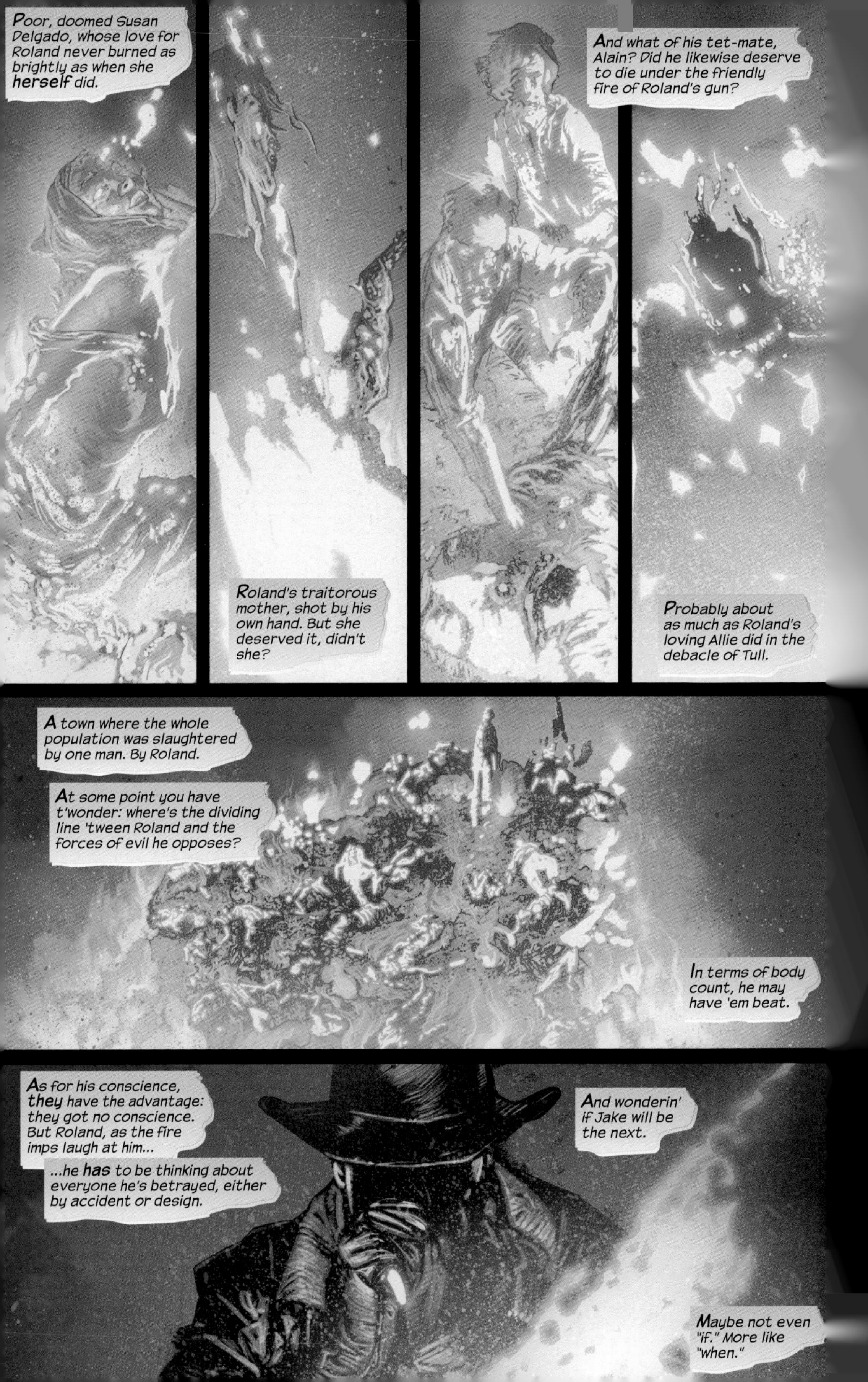
Poor, doomed Susan Delgado, whose love for Roland never burned as brightly as when she **herself** did.
Roland's traitorous mother, shot by his own hand. But she deserved it, didn't she?
And what of his tet-mate, Alain? Did he likewise deserve to die under the friendly fire of Roland's gun?
Probably about as much as Roland's loving Allie did in the debacle of Tull.
A town where the whole population was slaughtered by one man. By Roland.
At some point you have t'wonder: where's the dividing line 'tween Roland and the forces of evil he opposes?
In terms of body count, he may have 'em beat.
As for his conscience, **they** have the advantage: they got no conscience. But Roland, as the fire imps laugh at him...
...he **has** to be thinking about everyone he's betrayed, either by accident or design.
And wonderin' if Jake will be the next.
Maybe not even "if." More like "when."

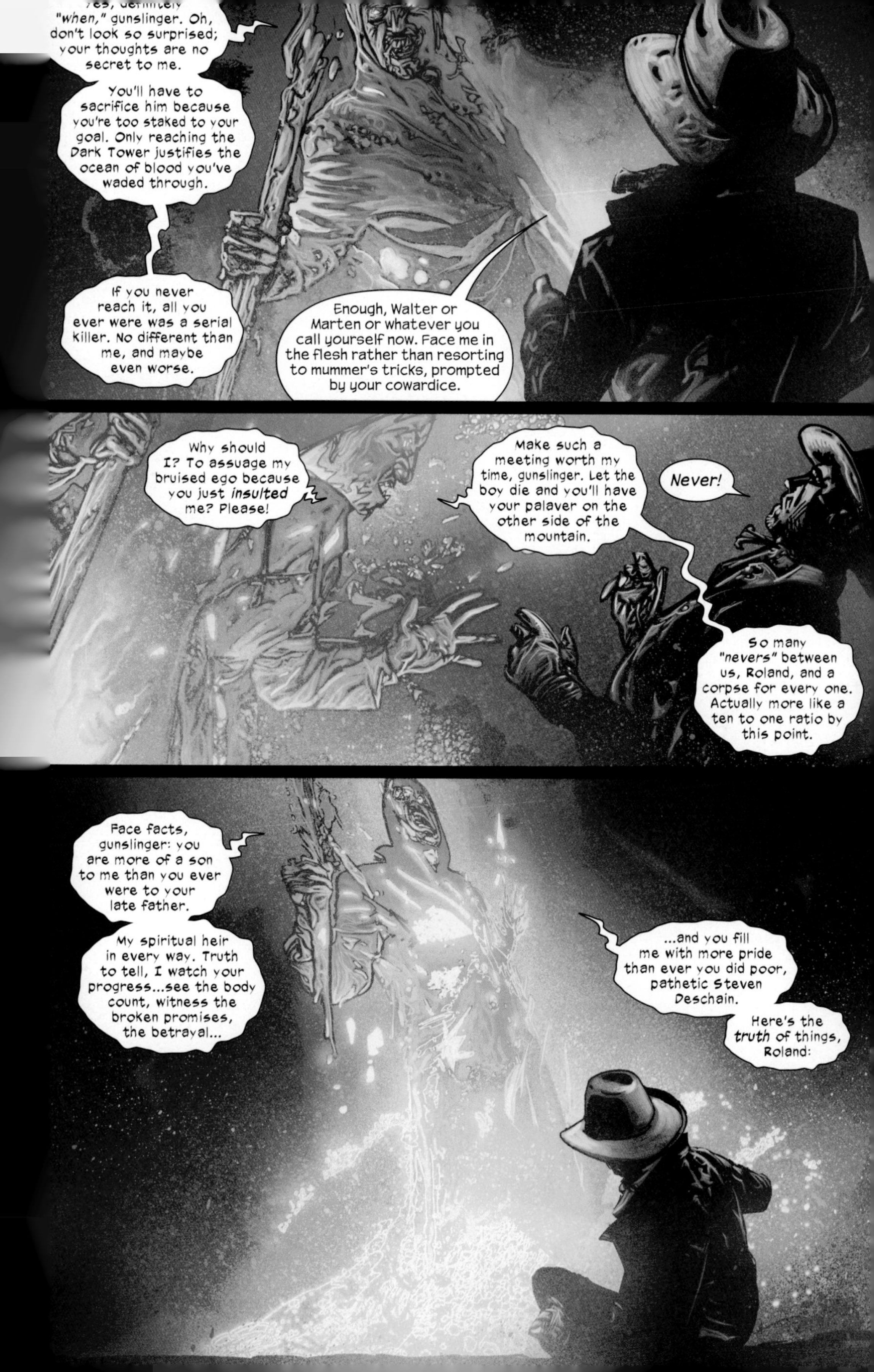
"*when*," gunslinger. Oh, don't look so surprised; your thoughts are no secret to me.
You'll have to sacrifice him because you're too staked to your goal. Only reaching the Dark Tower justifies the ocean of blood you've waded through.
If you never reach it, all you ever were was a serial killer. No different than me, and maybe even worse.
Enough, Walter or Marten or whatever you call yourself now. Face me in the flesh rather than resorting to mummer's tricks, prompted by your cowardice.
Why should *I*? To assuage my bruised ego because you just *insulted* me? Please!
Make such a meeting worth my time, gunslinger. Let the boy die and you'll have your palaver on the other side of the mountain.
Never!
So many *"nevers"* between us, Roland, and a corpse for every one. Actually more like a ten to one ratio by this point.
Face facts, gunslinger: you are more of a son to me than you ever were to your late father.
My spiritual heir in every way. Truth to tell, I watch your progress...see the body count, witness the broken promises, the betrayal...
...and you fill me with more pride than ever you did poor, pathetic Steven Deschain.
Here's the *truth* of things, Roland:

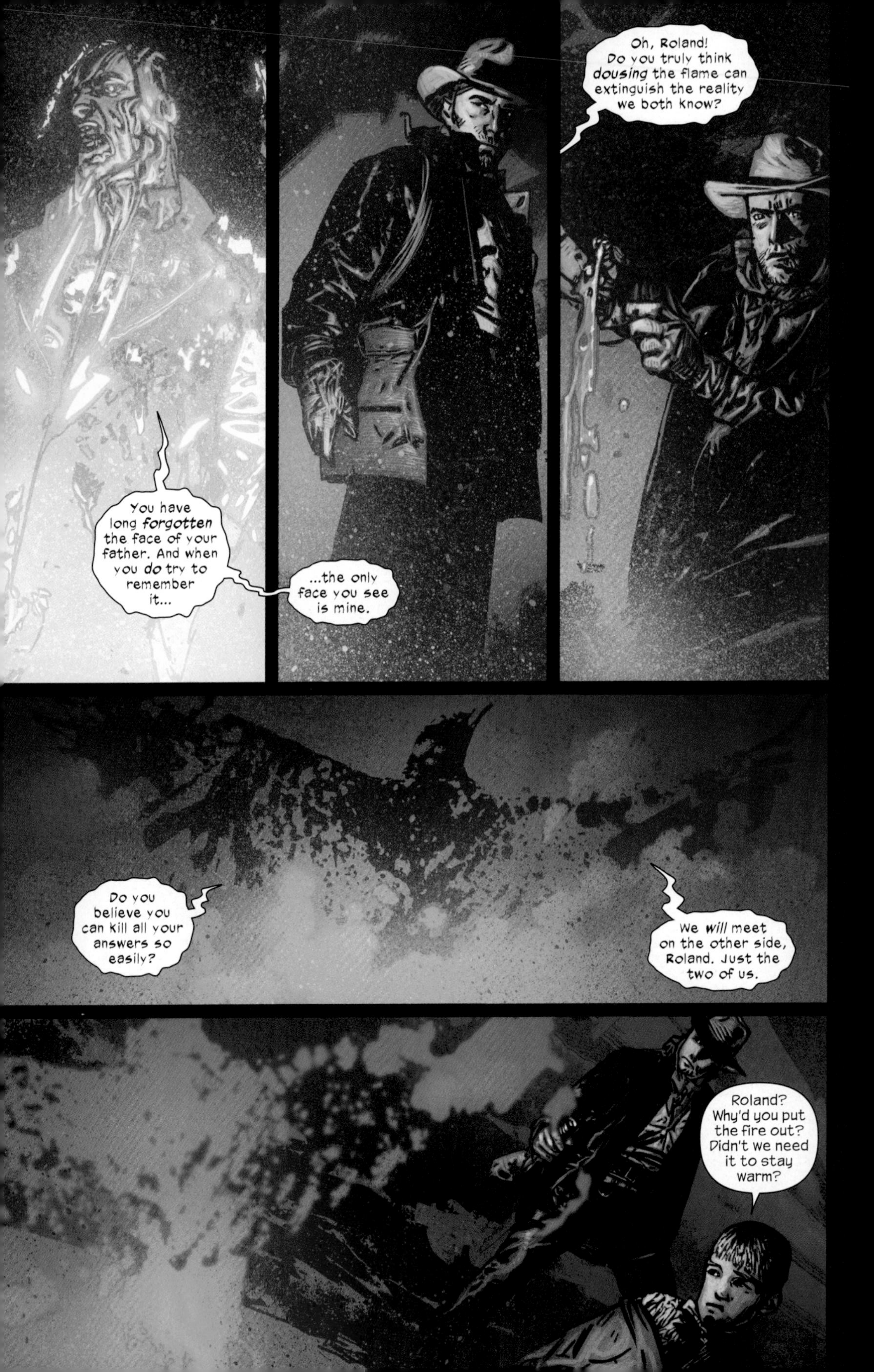
You have long *forgotten* the face of your father. And when you *do* try to remember it...
...the only face you see is mine.
Oh, Roland! Do you truly think *dousing* the flame can extinguish the reality we both know?
Do you believe you can kill all your answers so easily?
We *will* meet on the other side, Roland. Just the two of us.
Roland? Why'd you put the fire out? Didn't we need it to stay warm?

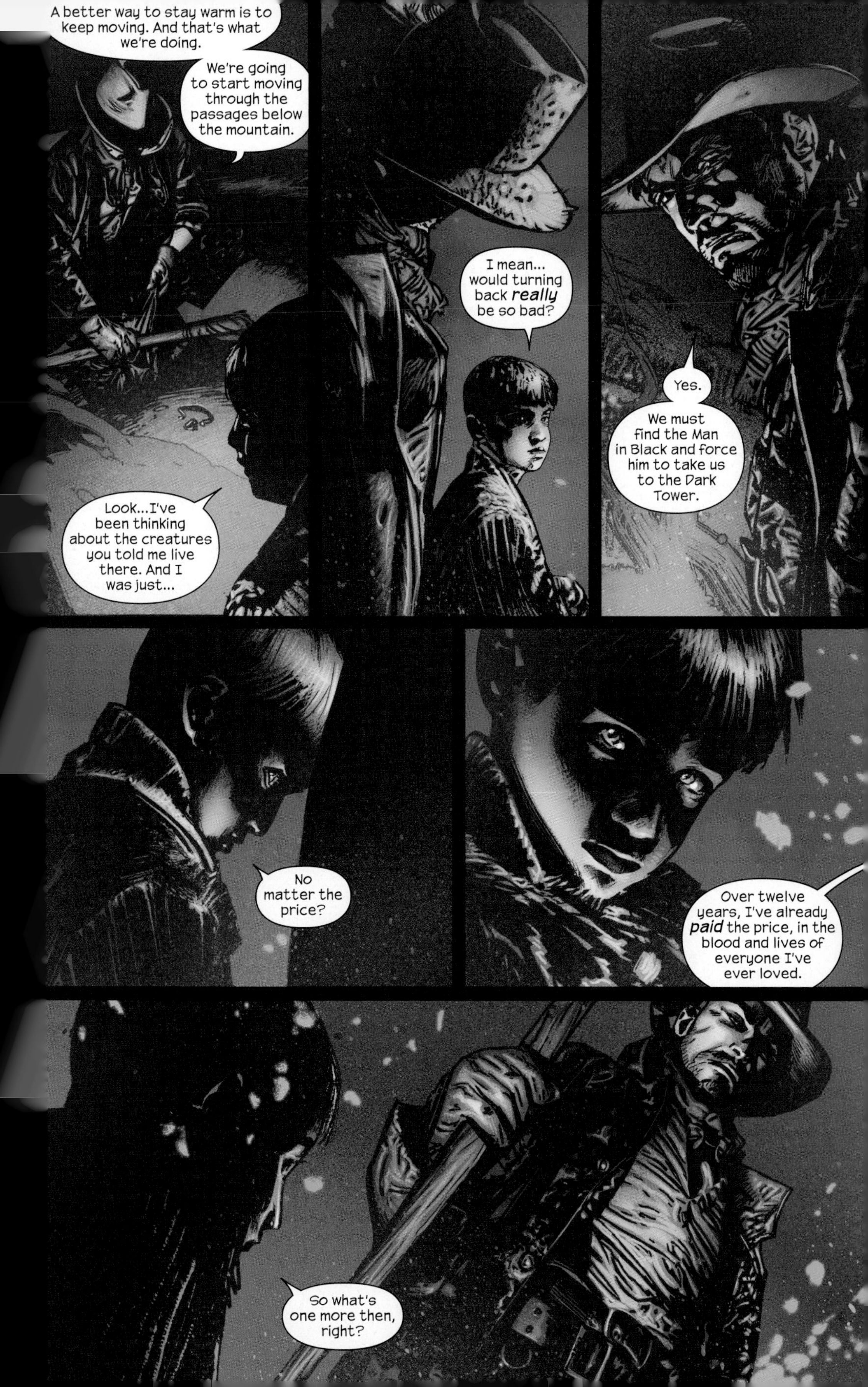

A better way to stay warm is to keep moving. And that's what we're doing.
We're going to start moving through the passages below the mountain.
Look...I've been thinking about the creatures you told me live there. And I was just...
I mean... would turning back really be so bad?
Yes.
We must find the Man in Black and force him to take us to the Dark Tower.
No matter the price?
Over twelve years, I've already paid the price, in the blood and lives of everyone I've ever loved.
So what's one more then, right?

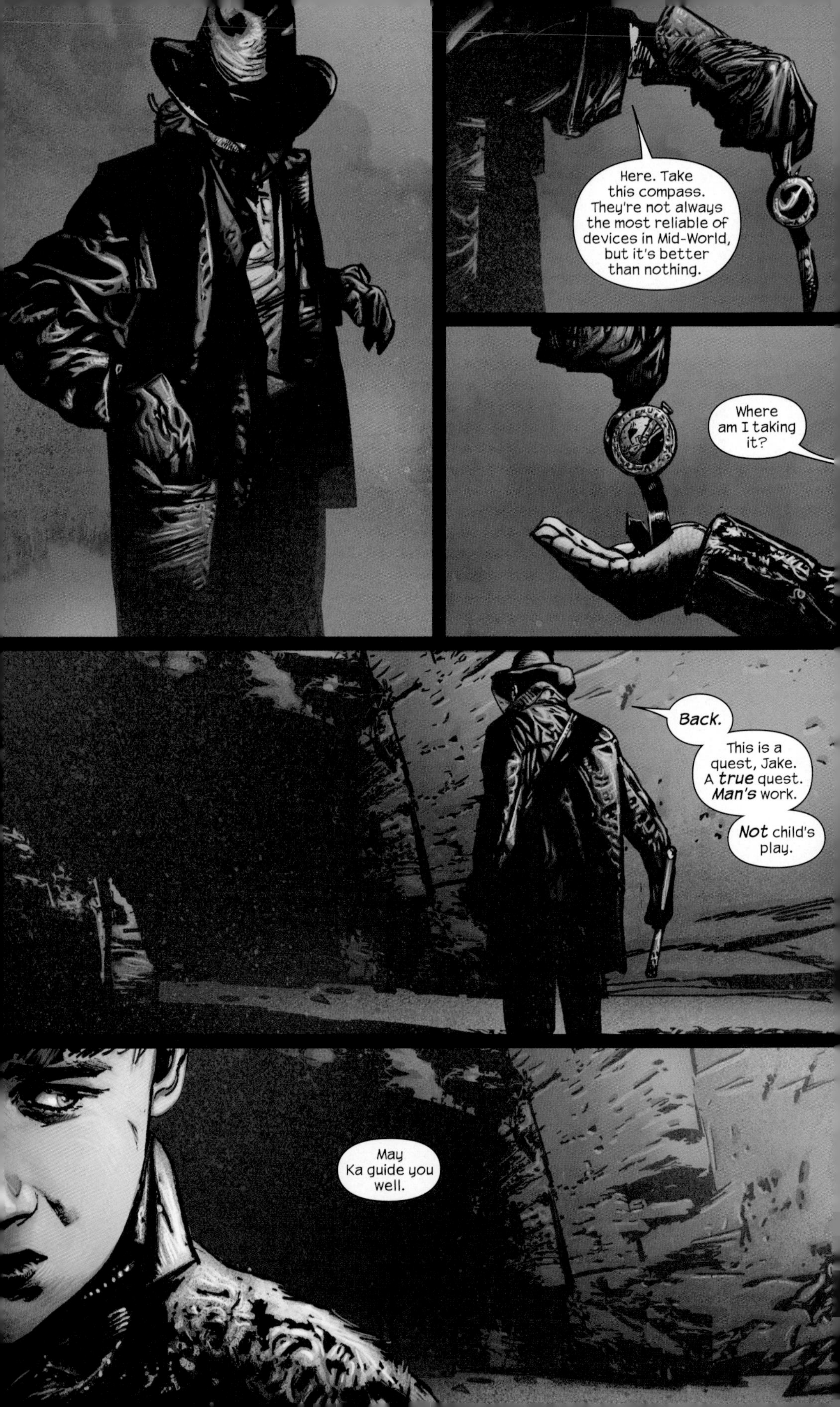
Here. Take this compass. They're not always the most reliable of devices in Mid-World, but it's better than nothing.
Where am I taking it?
Back.
This is a quest, Jake. A *true* quest. *Man's* work.
Not child's play.
May Ka guide you well.

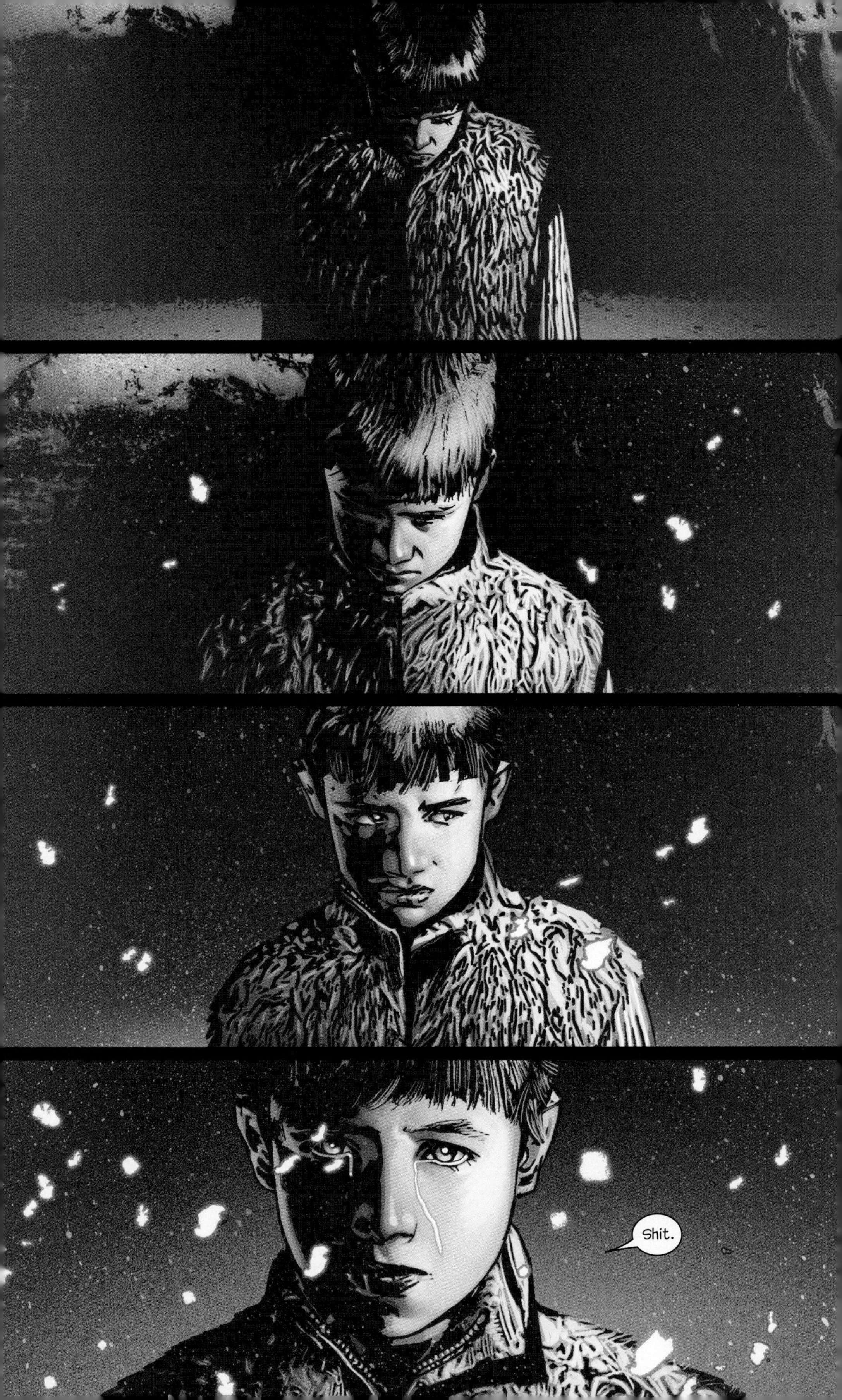
Shit.

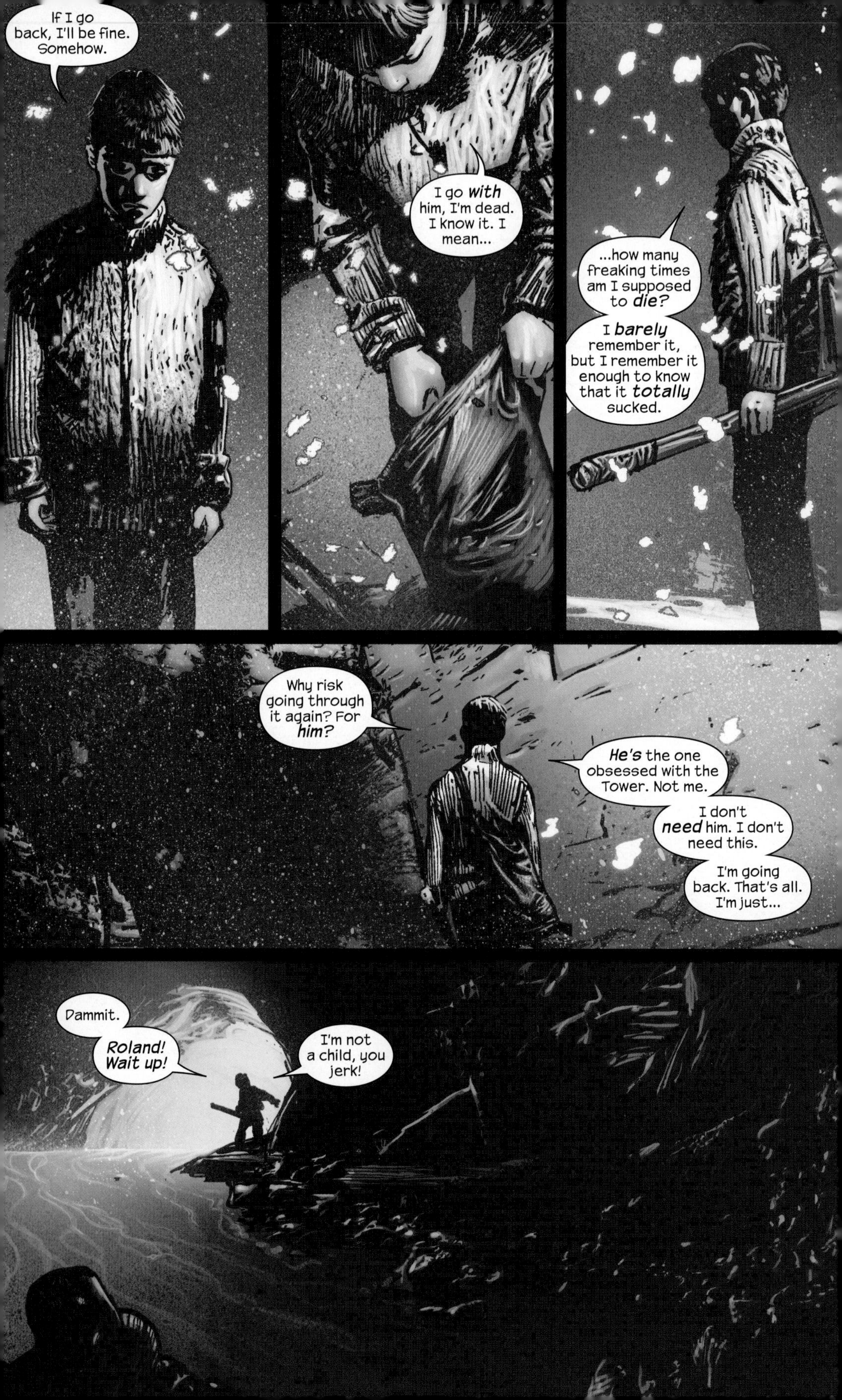
If I go back, I'll be fine. Somehow.
I go *with* him, I'm dead. I know it. I mean...
...how many freaking times am I supposed to *die?*
I *barely* remember it, but I remember it enough to know that it *totally* sucked.
Why risk going through it again? For *him?*
He's the one obsessed with the Tower. Not me.
I don't *need* him. I don't need this.
I'm going back. That's all. I'm just...
Dammit.
Roland! Wait up!
I'm not a child, you jerk!

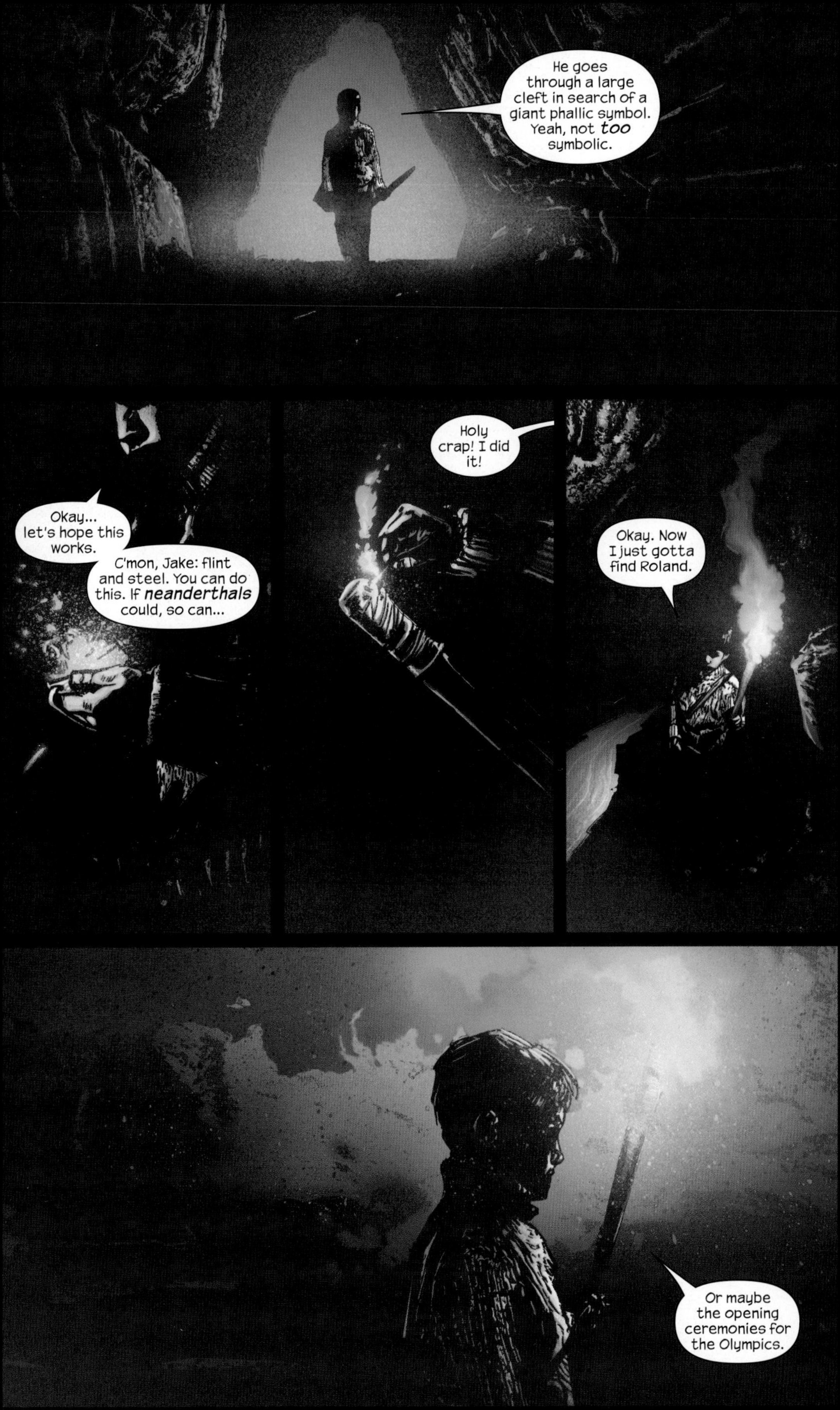
He goes through a large cleft in search of a giant phallic symbol. Yeah, not *too* symbolic.
Okay... let's hope this works.
C'mon, Jake: flint and steel. You can do this. If *neanderthals* could, so can...
Holy crap! I did it!
Okay. Now I just gotta find Roland.
Or maybe the opening ceremonies for the Olympics.

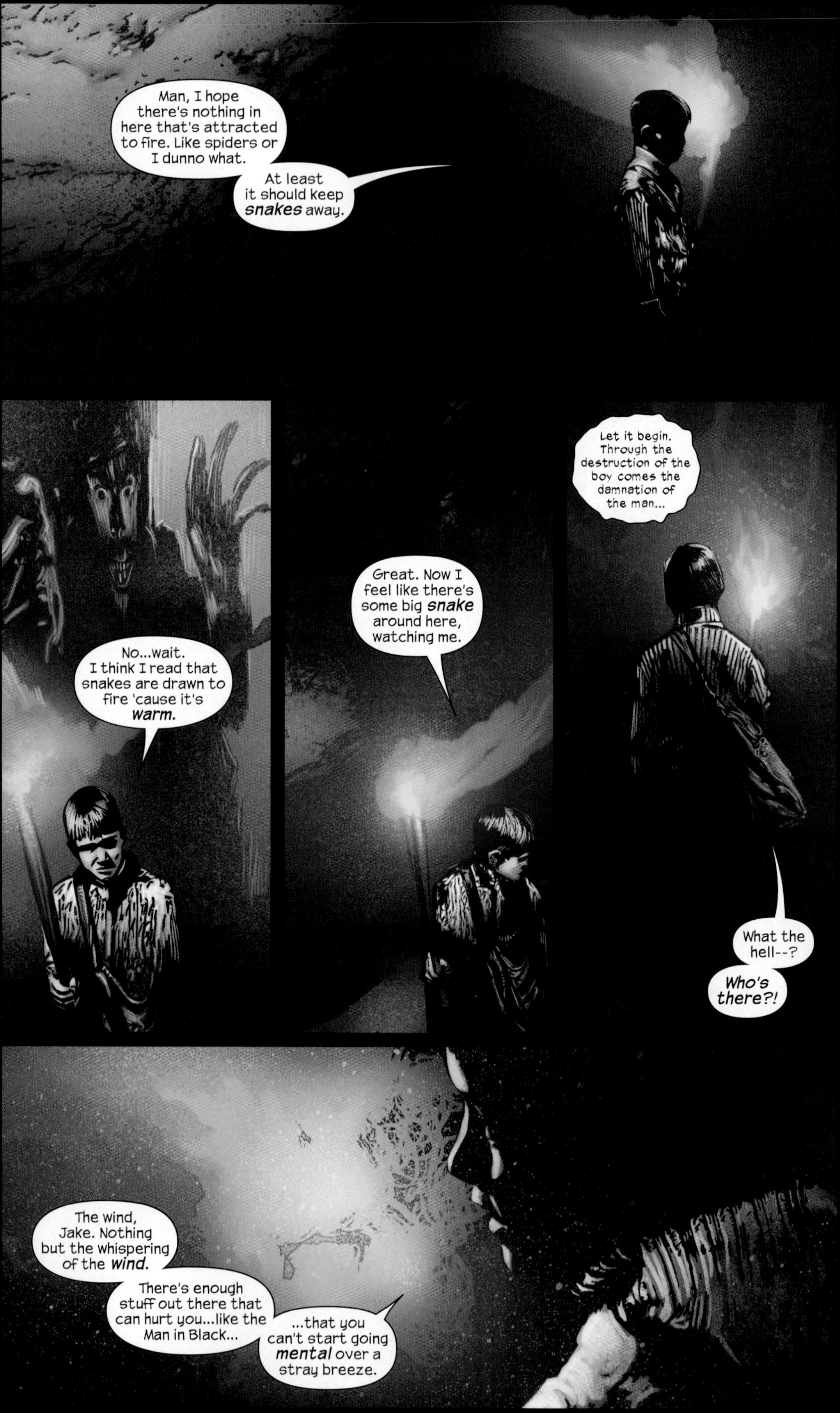
Man, I hope there's nothing in here that's attracted to fire. Like spiders or I dunno what.
At least it should keep *snakes* away.
No...wait. I think I read that snakes are drawn to fire 'cause it's *warm.*
Great. Now I feel like there's some big *snake* around here, watching me.
Let it begin. Through the destruction of the boy comes the damnation of the man...
What the hell--?
Who's there?!
The wind, Jake. Nothing but the whispering of the *wind.*
There's enough stuff out there that can hurt you...like the Man in Black...
...that you can't start going *mental* over a stray breeze.

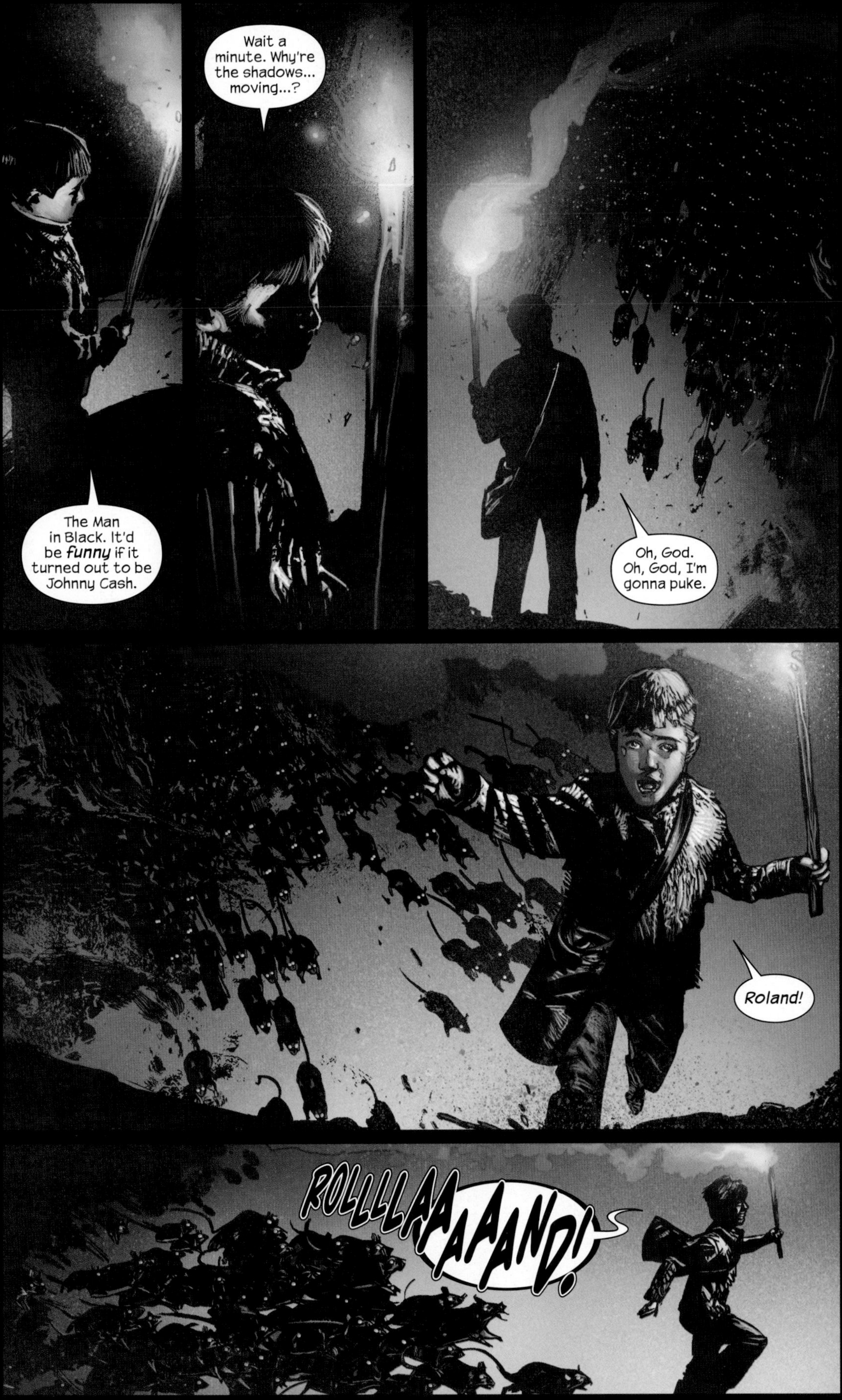
The Man in Black. It'd be *funny* if it turned out to be Johnny Cash.
Wait a minute. Why're the shadows... moving...?
Oh, God. Oh, God, I'm gonna puke.
Roland!
ROLLLLAAAAAND!

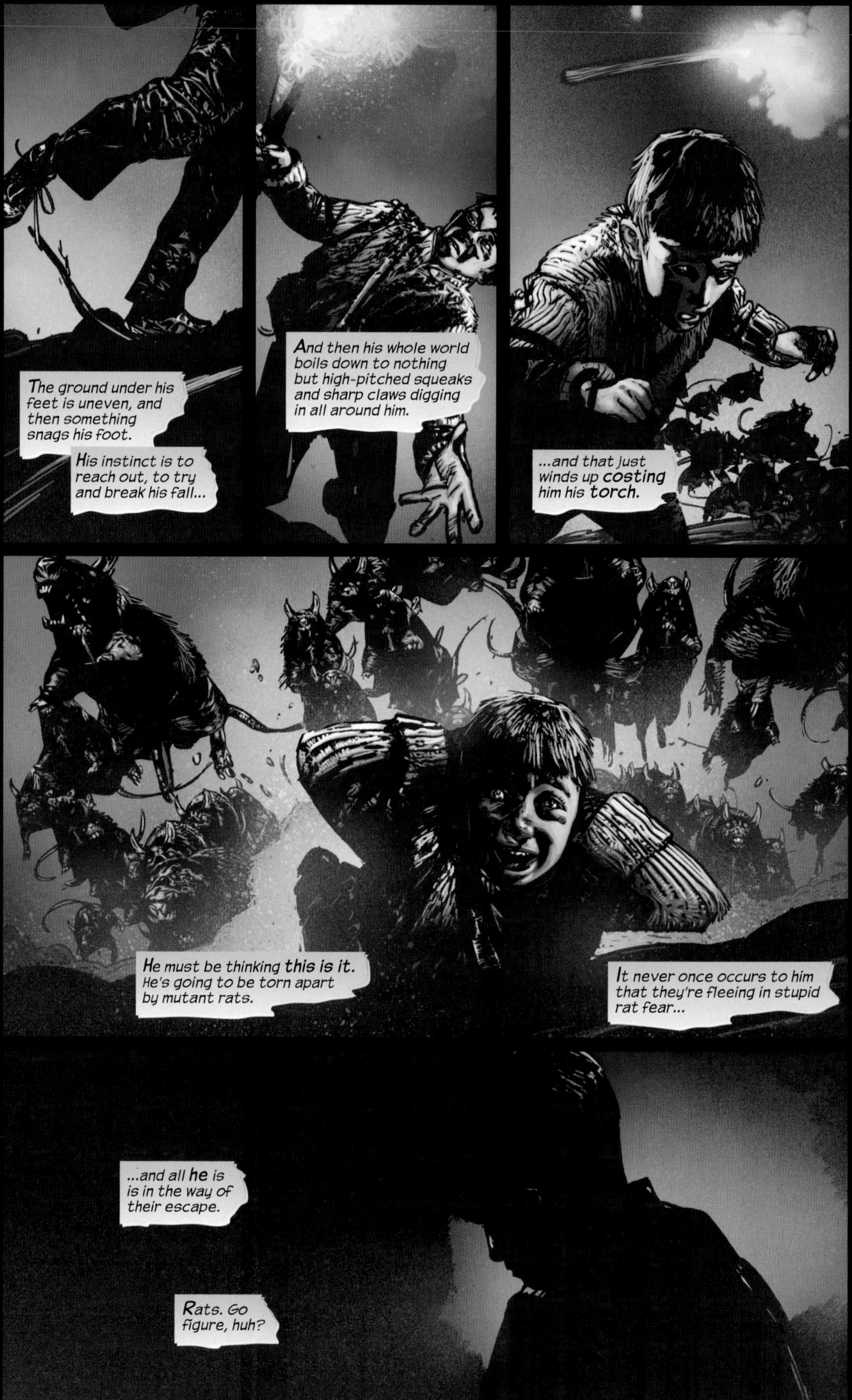

The ground under his feet is uneven, and then something snags his foot.
His instinct is to reach out, to try and break his fall...
And then his whole world boils down to nothing but high-pitched squeaks and sharp claws digging in all around him.
...and that just winds up costing him his torch.
He must be thinking this is it. He's going to be torn apart by mutant rats.
It never once occurs to him that they're fleeing in stupid rat fear...
...and all he is is in the way of their escape.
Rats. Go figure, huh?

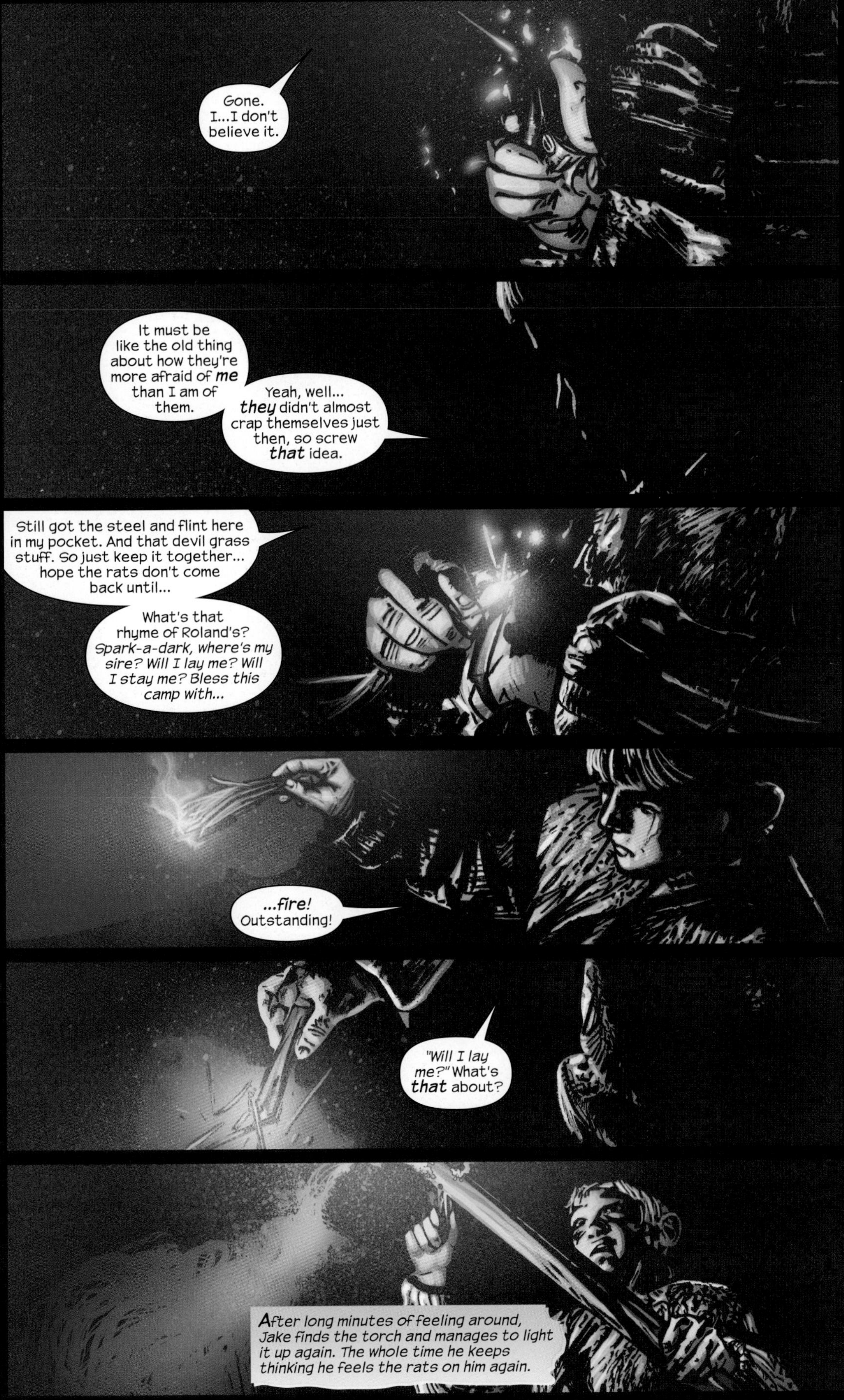
Gone. I...I don't believe it.
It must be like the old thing about how they're more afraid of *me* than I am of them.
Yeah, well... *they* didn't almost crap themselves just then, so screw *that* idea.
Still got the steel and flint here in my pocket. And that devil grass stuff. So just keep it together... hope the rats don't come back until...
What's that rhyme of Roland's? *Spark-a-dark, where's my sire? Will I lay me? Will I stay me? Bless this camp with...*
...fire! Outstanding!
"Will I lay me?" What's *that* about?
After long minutes of feeling around, Jake finds the torch and manages to light it up again. The whole time he keeps thinking he feels the rats on him again.

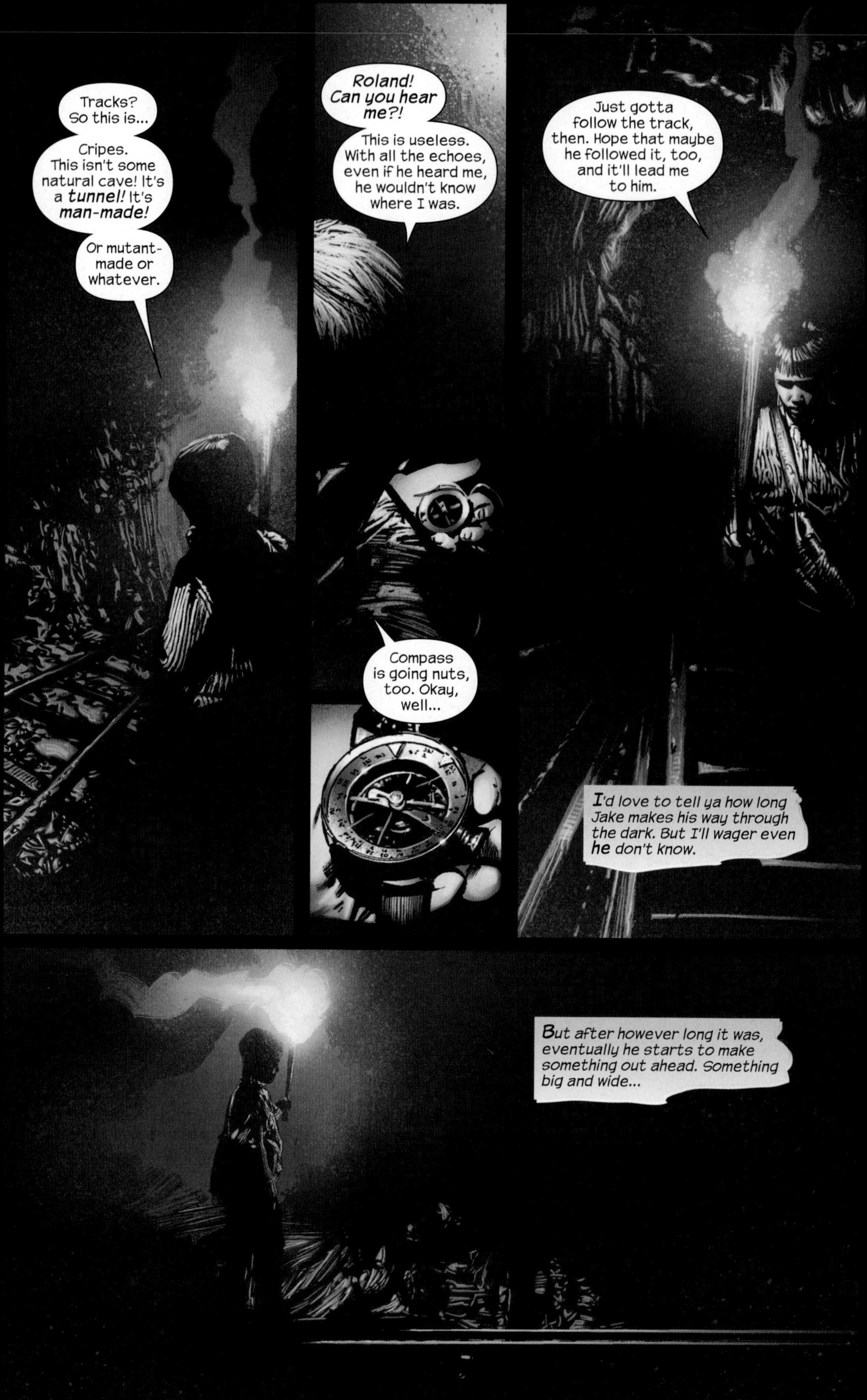
Tracks? So this is...
Cripes. This isn't some natural cave! It's a tunnel! It's man-made!
Or mutant-made or whatever.
Roland! Can you hear me?!
This is useless. With all the echoes, even if he heard me, he wouldn't know where I was.
Compass is going nuts, too. Okay, well...
Just gotta follow the track, then. Hope that maybe he followed it, too, and it'll lead me to him.
I'd love to tell ya how long Jake makes his way through the dark. But I'll wager even he don't know.
But after however long it was, eventually he starts to make something out ahead. Something big and wide...

...and filled with death.
Bits of human skeletons scattered all over, some of which look to have been gnawed on by something very, very...
...big.
And if you're thinking that maybe the rats ran from Jake, not because of the fire, but because they thought he was something else...something truly terrifying...
...well, that prob'ly occurred to Jake as well.

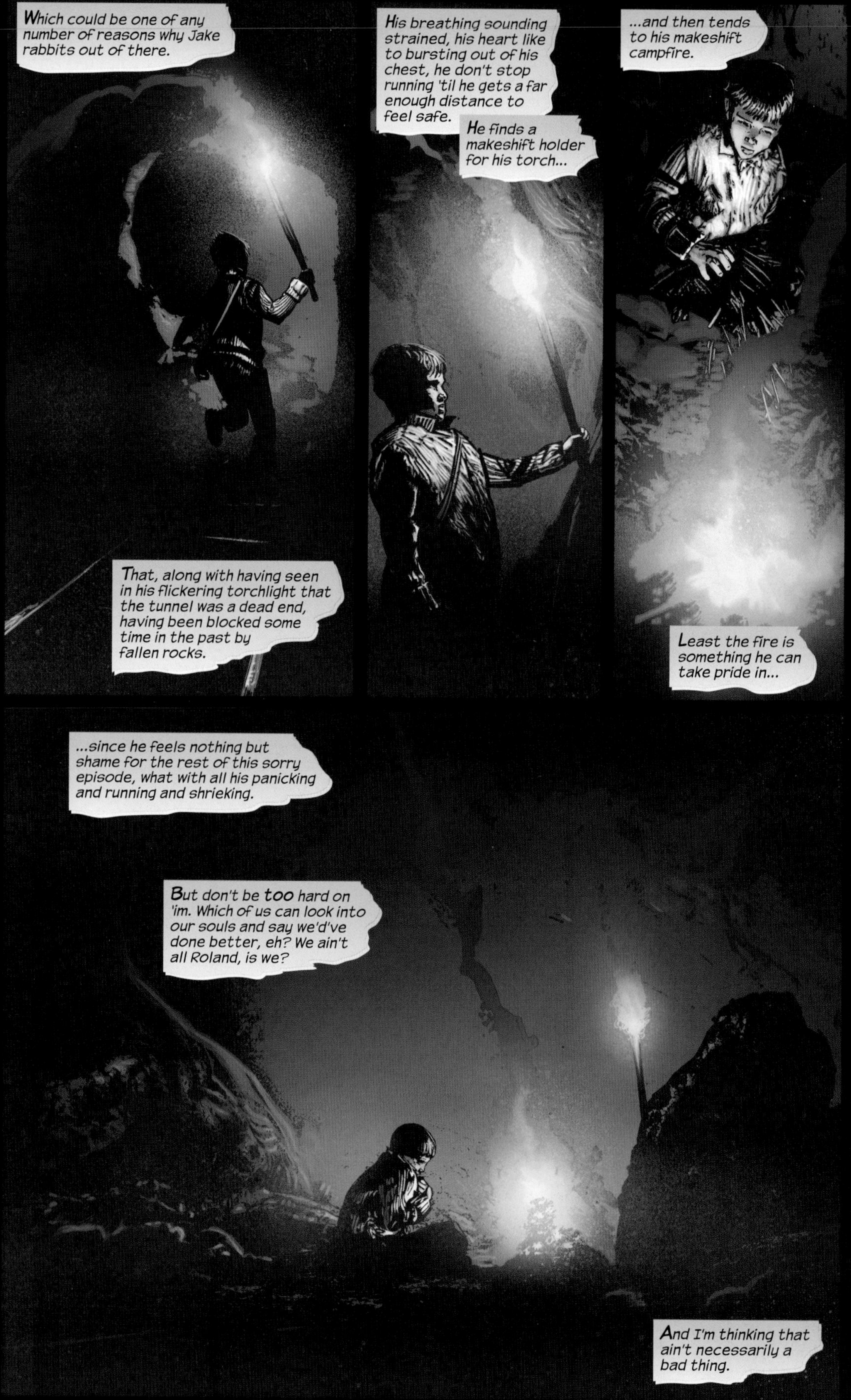
Which could be one of any number of reasons why Jake rabbits out of there.
That, along with having seen in his flickering torchlight that the tunnel was a dead end, having been blocked some time in the past by fallen rocks.
His breathing sounding strained, his heart like to bursting out of his chest, he don't stop running 'til he gets a far enough distance to feel safe.
He finds a makeshift holder for his torch...
...and then tends to his makeshift campfire.
Least the fire is something he can take pride in...
...since he feels nothing but shame for the rest of this sorry episode, what with all his panicking and running and shrieking.
But don't be too hard on 'im. Which of us can look into our souls and say we'd've done better, eh? We ain't all Roland, is we?
And I'm thinking that ain't necessarily a bad thing.

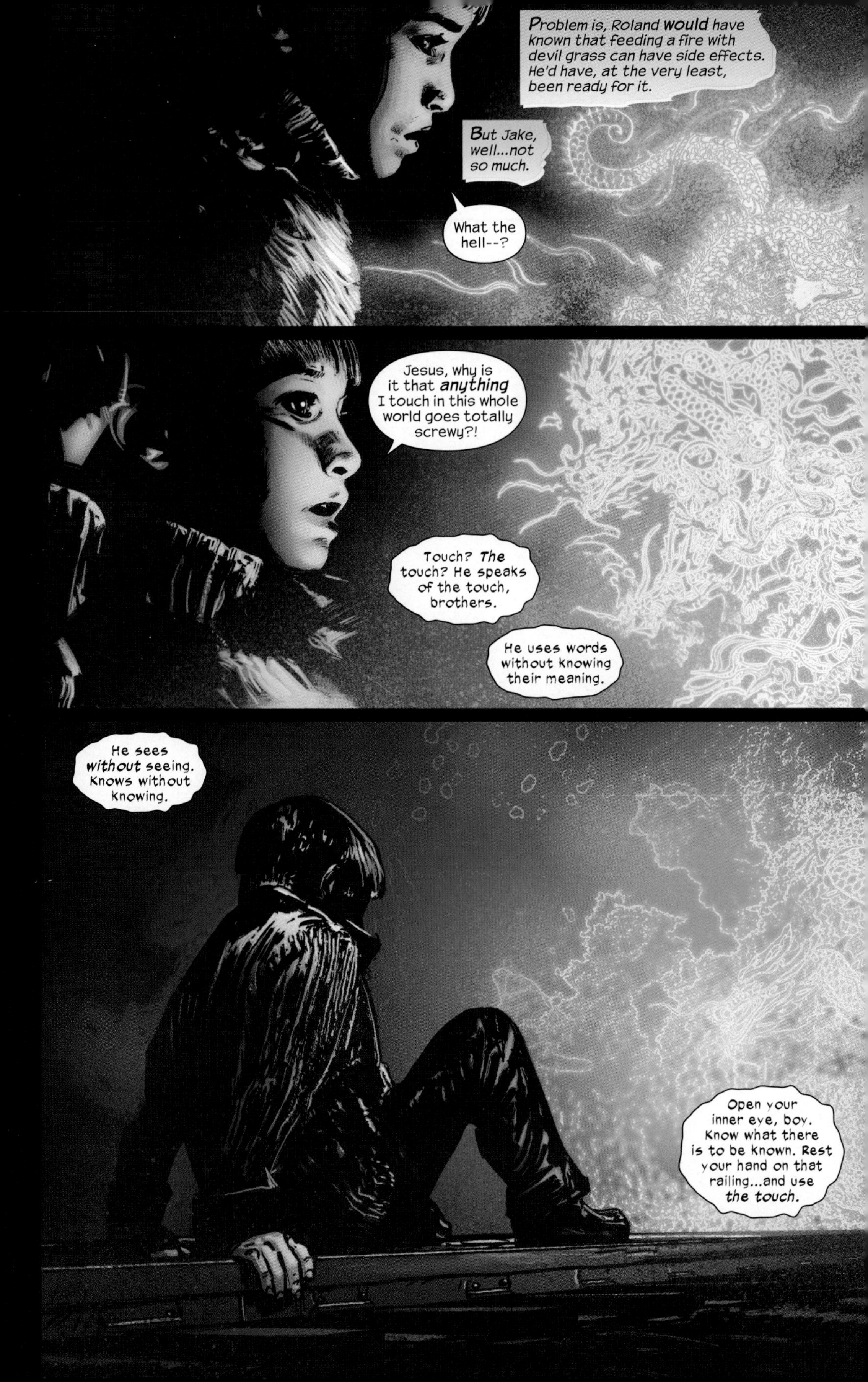

Problem is, Roland **would** have known that feeding a fire with devil grass can have side effects. He'd have, at the very least, been ready for it.
But Jake, well...not so much.
What the hell--?
Jesus, why is it that ***anything*** I touch in this whole world goes totally screwy?!
Touch? ***The*** touch? He speaks of the touch, brothers.
He uses words without knowing their meaning.
He sees ***without*** seeing. Knows without knowing.
Open your inner eye, boy. Know what there is to be known. Rest your hand on that railing...and use ***the touch.***

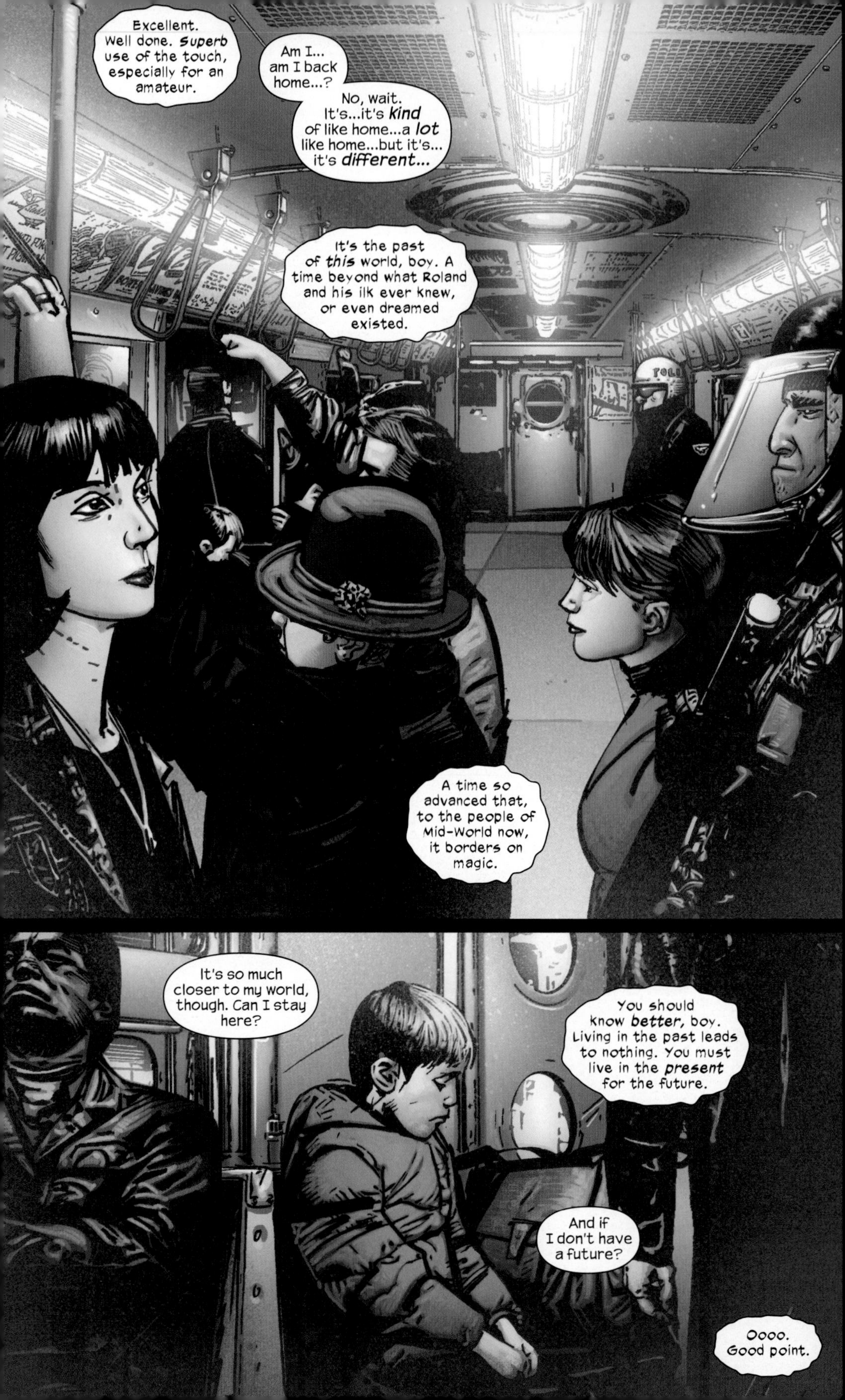
Excellent. Well done. Superb use of the touch, especially for an amateur.
Am I... am I back home...?
No, wait. It's...it's kind of like home...a lot like home...but it's... it's different...
It's the past of this world, boy. A time beyond what Roland and his ilk ever knew, or even dreamed existed.
A time so advanced that, to the people of Mid-World now, it borders on magic.
It's so much closer to my world, though. Can I stay here?
You should know better, boy. Living in the past leads to nothing. You must live in the present for the future.
And if I don't have a future?
Oooo. Good point.

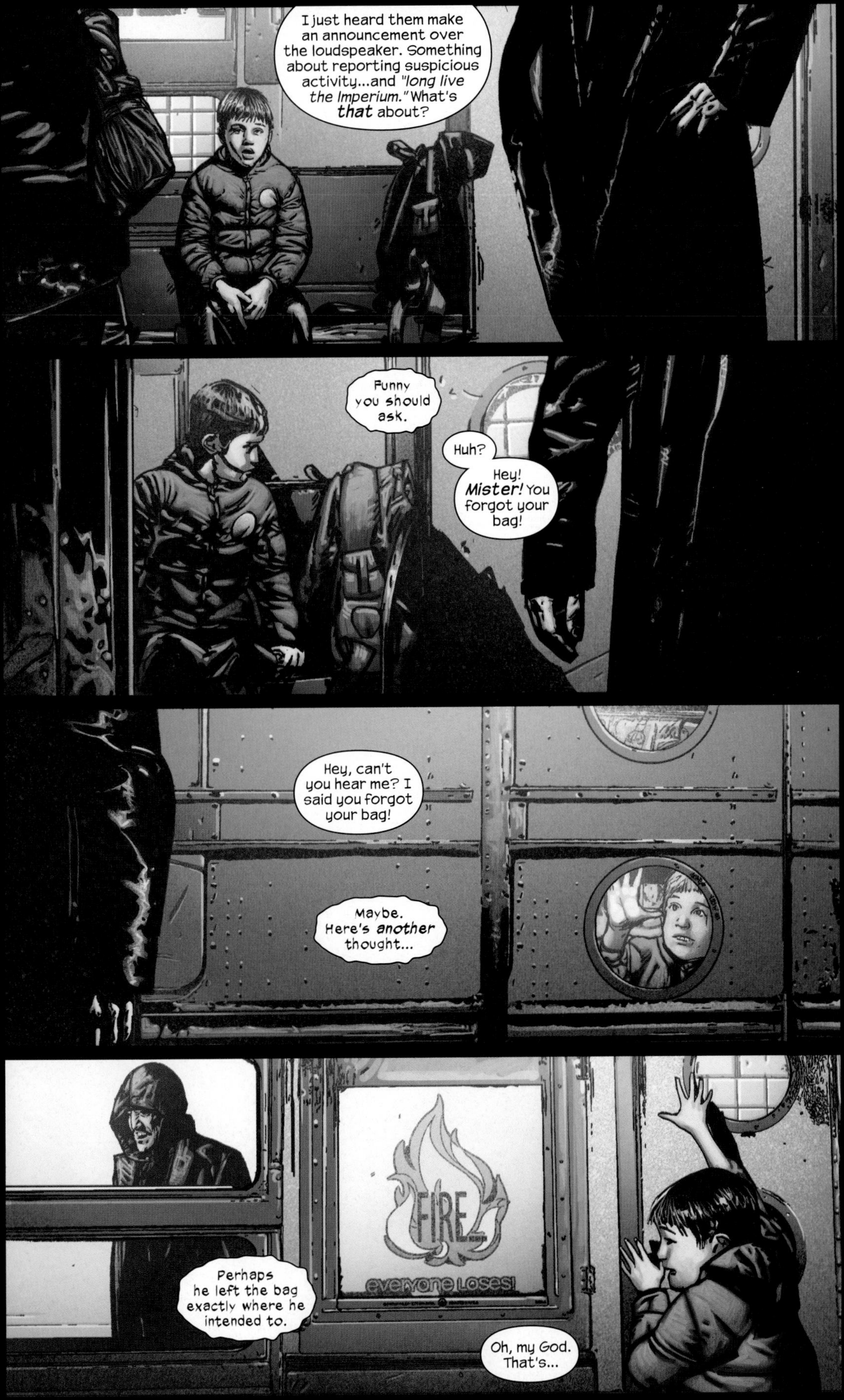
I just heard them make an announcement over the loudspeaker. Something about reporting suspicious activity...and "long live the Imperium." What's that about?
Funny you should ask.
Huh?
Hey! Mister! You forgot your bag!
Hey, can't you hear me? I said you forgot your bag!
Maybe. Here's another thought...
FIRE everyone loses!
Perhaps he left the bag exactly where he intended to.
Oh, my God. That's...

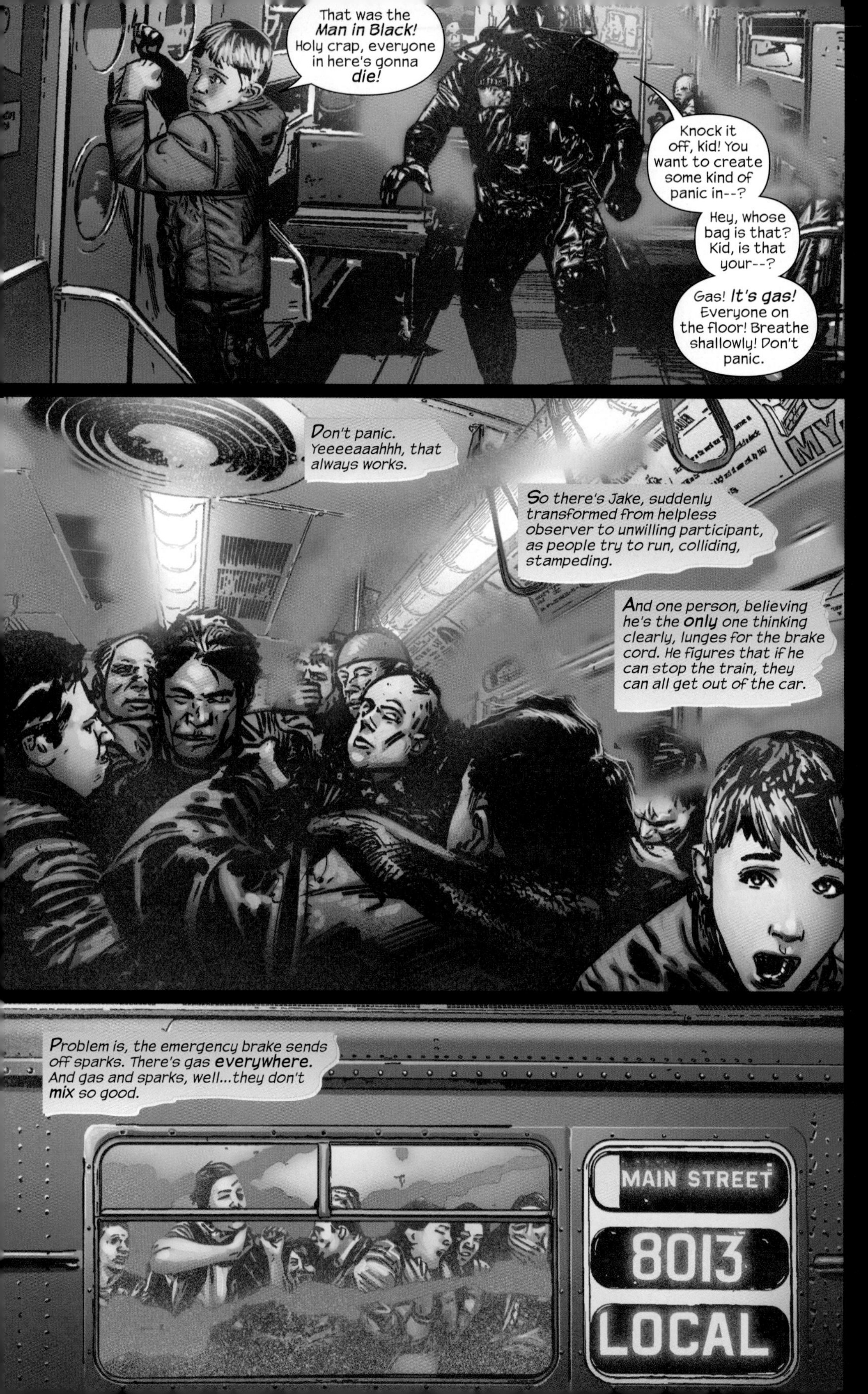
That was the *Man in Black!* Holy crap, everyone in here's gonna *die!*
Knock it off, kid! You want to create some kind of panic in--?
Hey, whose bag is that? Kid, is that your--?
Gas! *It's gas!* Everyone on the floor! Breathe shallowly! Don't panic.
Don't panic. Yeeeeaaahhh, that always works.
So there's Jake, suddenly transformed from helpless observer to unwilling participant, as people try to run, colliding, stampeding.
And one person, believing he's the **only** one thinking clearly, lunges for the brake cord. He figures that if he can stop the train, they can all get out of the car.
Problem is, the emergency brake sends off sparks. There's gas **everywhere.** And gas and sparks, well...they don't **mix** so good.
MAIN STREET
8013
LOCAL

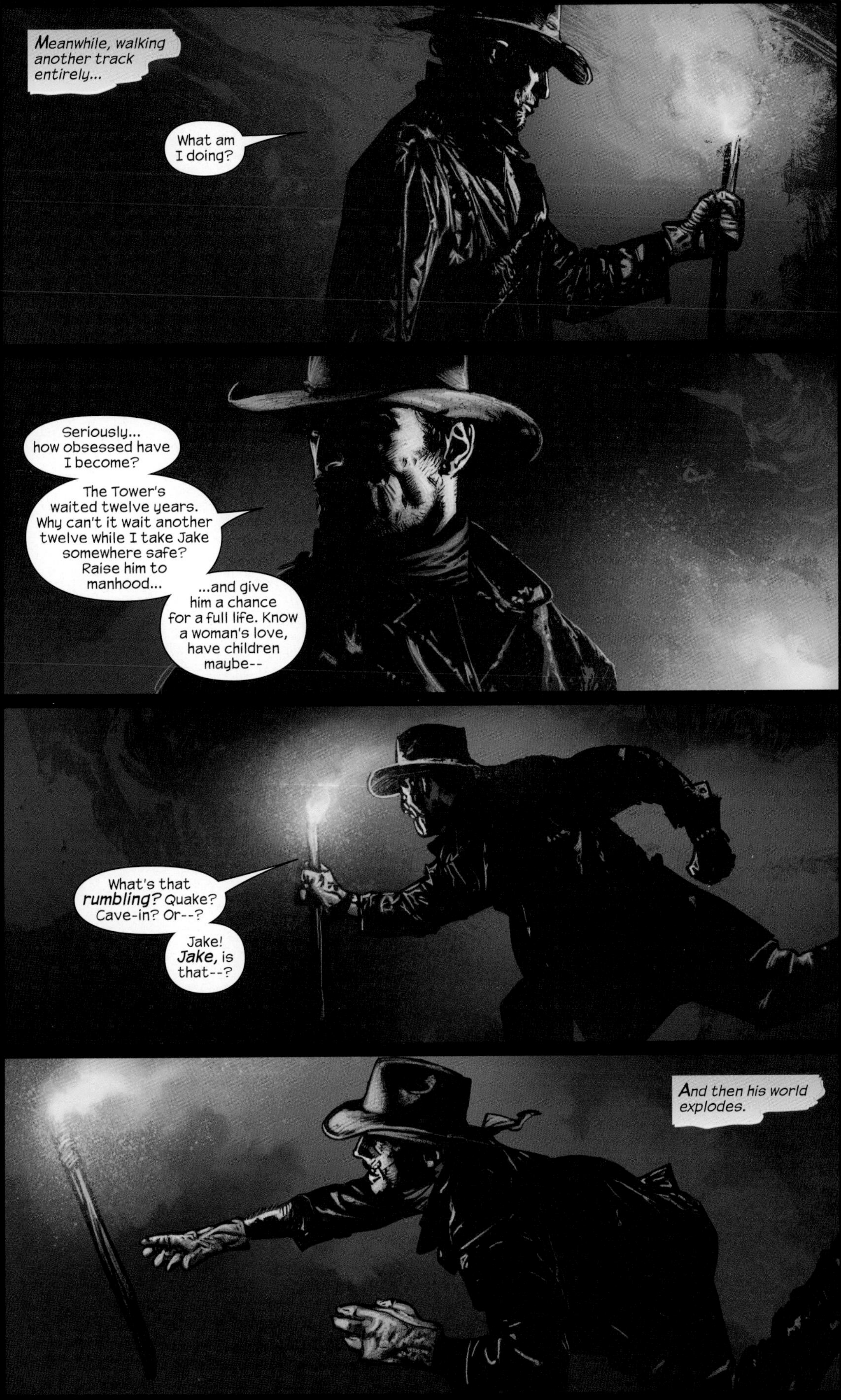
Meanwhile, walking another track entirely...
What am I doing?
Seriously... how obsessed have I become?
The Tower's waited twelve years. Why can't it wait another twelve while I take Jake somewhere safe? Raise him to manhood...
...and give him a chance for a full life. Know a woman's love, have children maybe--
What's that *rumbling?* Quake? Cave-in? Or--?
Jake! *Jake,* is that--?
And then his world explodes.

STEPHEN KING

THE DARK TOWER
~ THE GUNSLINGER ~

THE MAN IN BLACK

CHAPTER TWO

Roland remains on his belly until after the cave stops shaking. Rocks tumble down all around him, but miss hitting him direct, so *that's* something.

He don't know what caused the explosion that set everything to falling. Don't much care, neither.

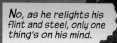

No, as he relights his flint and steel, only one thing's on his mind.

Jake!

Jake, can you *hear* me?

Jake!

R-Roland?

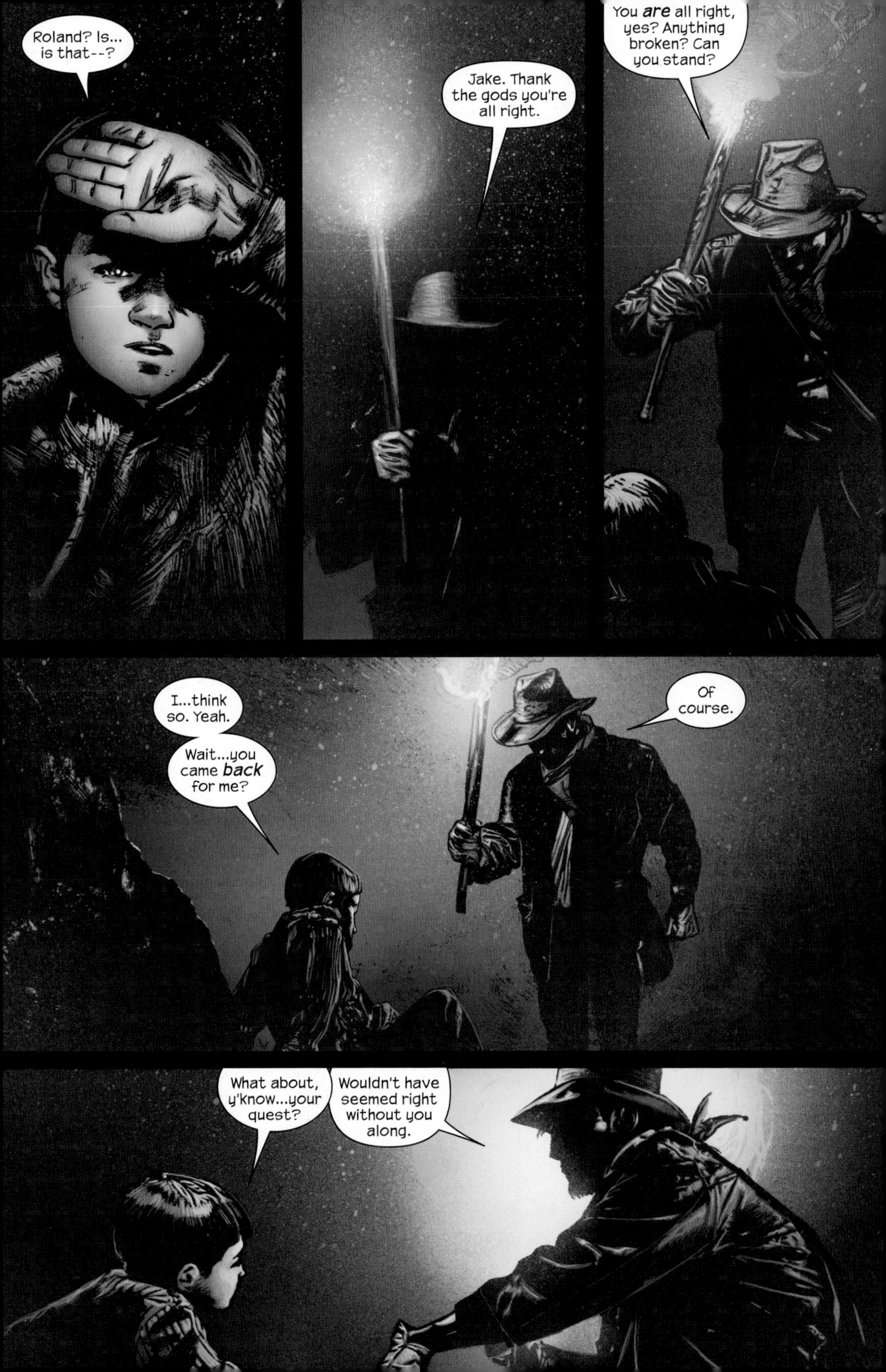
Roland? Is... is that--?
Jake. Thank the gods you're all right.
You *are* all right, yes? Anything broken? Can you stand?
I...think so. Yeah.
Wait...you came *back* for me?
Of course.
What about, y'know...your quest?
Wouldn't have seemed right without you along.

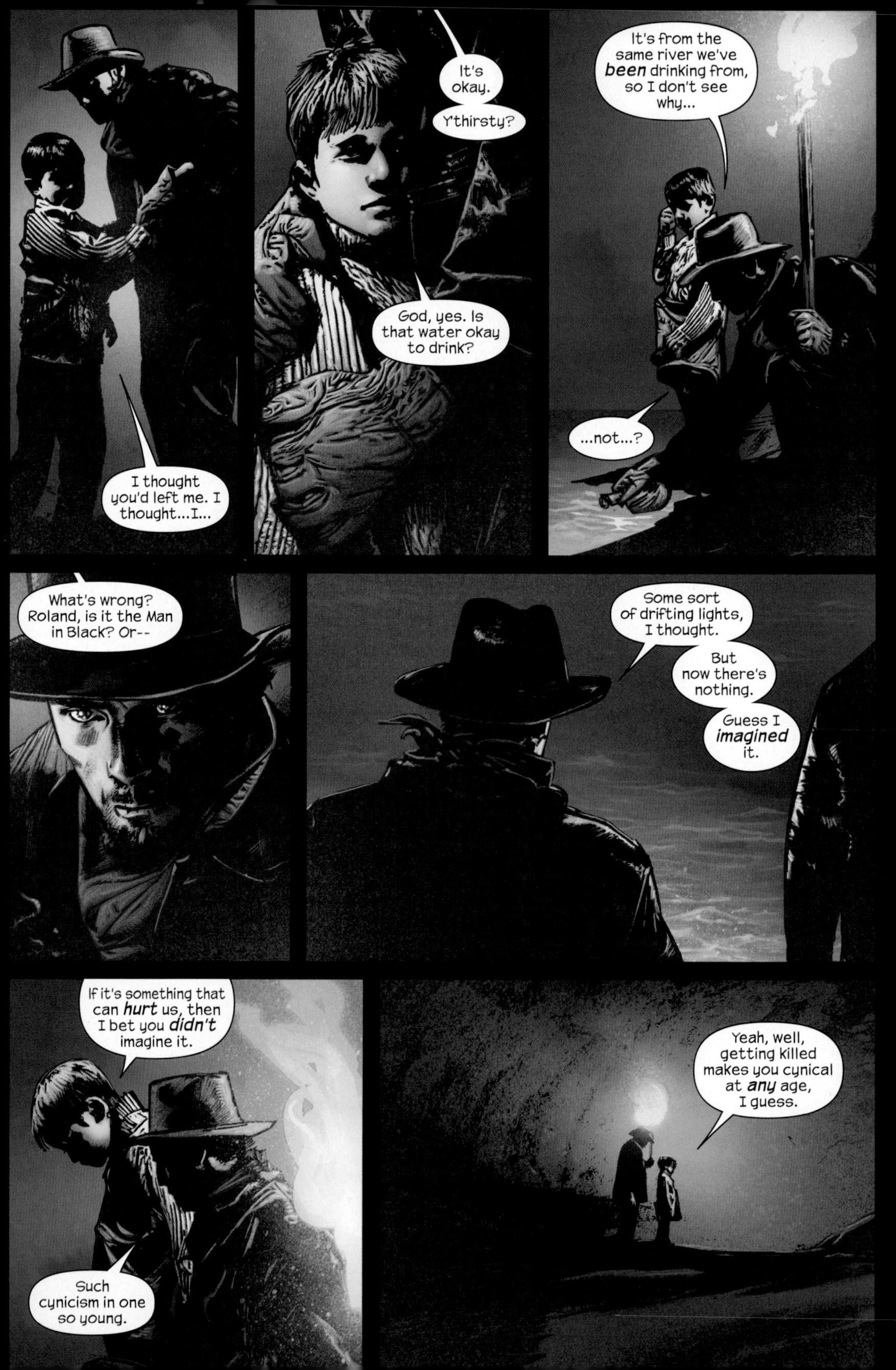
I thought you'd left me. I thought...I...
It's okay.
Y'thirsty?
God, yes. Is that water okay to drink?
It's from the same river we've *been* drinking from, so I don't see why...
...not...?
What's wrong? Roland, is it the Man in Black? Or--
Some sort of drifting lights, I thought.
But now there's nothing.
Guess I *imagined* it.
If it's something that can *hurt* us, then I bet you *didn't* imagine it.
Such cynicism in one so young.
Yeah, well, getting killed makes you cynical at *any* age, I guess.

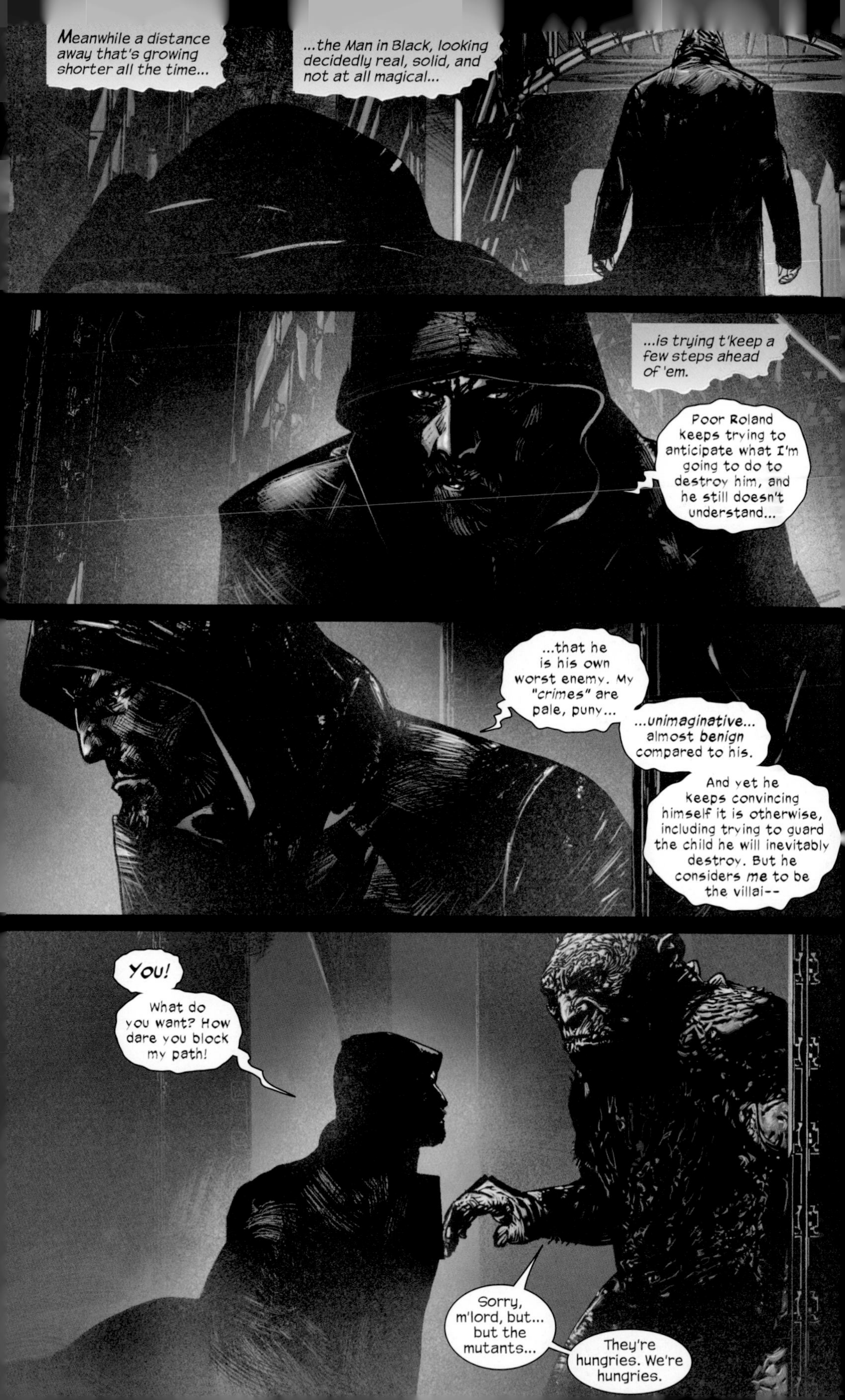

Meanwhile a distance away that's growing shorter all the time...
...the Man in Black, looking decidedly real, solid, and not at all magical...
...is trying t'keep a few steps ahead of 'em.
Poor Roland keeps trying to anticipate what I'm going to do to destroy him, and he still doesn't understand...
...that he is his own worst enemy. My "crimes" are pale, puny...
...unimaginative... almost benign compared to his.
And yet he keeps convincing himself it is otherwise, including trying to guard the child he will inevitably destroy. But he considers me to be the villai--
YOU!
What do you want? How dare you block my path!
Sorry, m'lord, but... but the mutants...
They're hungries. We're hungries.

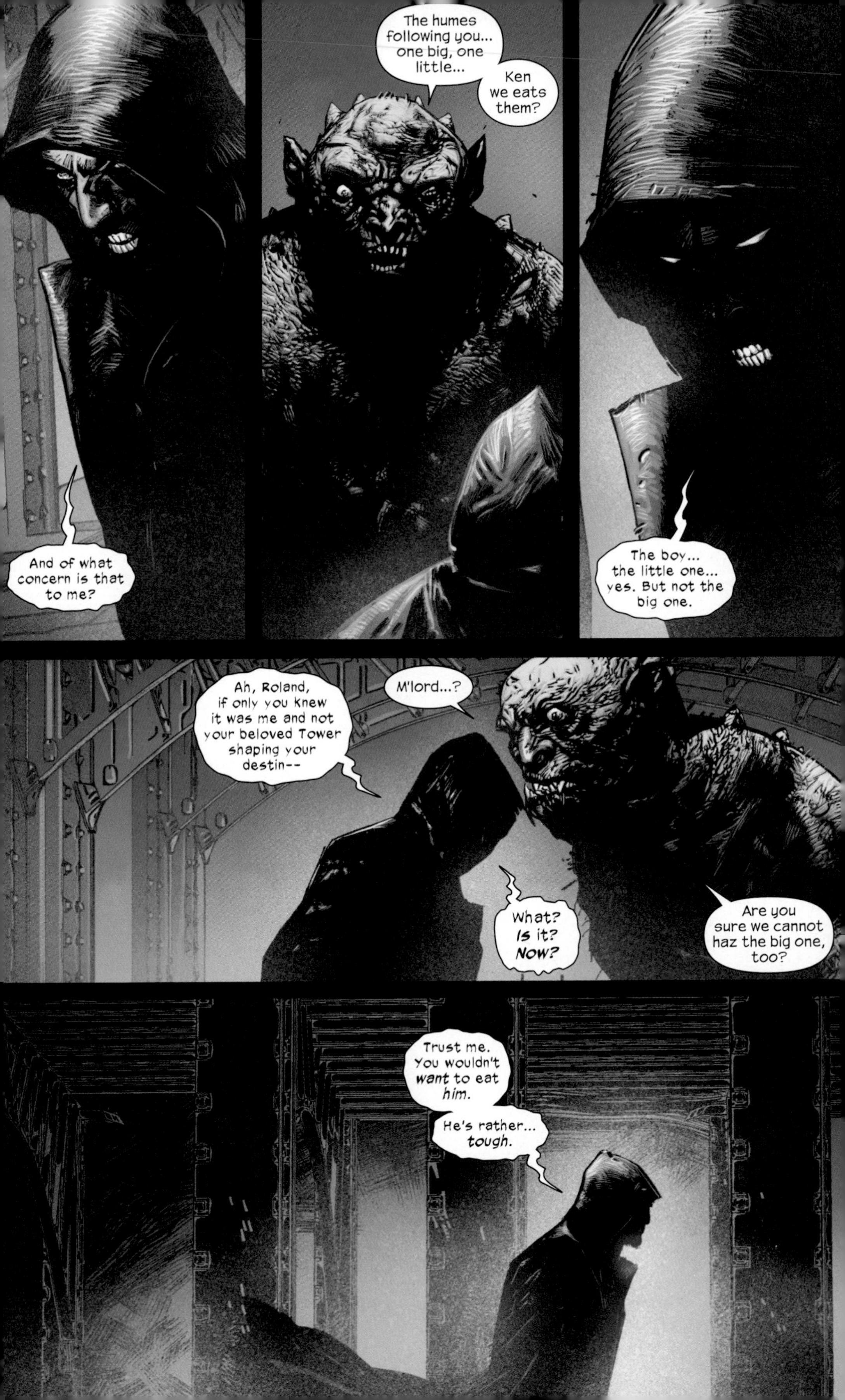
The humes following you... one big, one little...
Ken we eats them?
And of what concern is that to me?
The boy... the little one... yes. But not the big one.
Ah, Roland, if only you knew it was me and not your beloved Tower shaping your destin--
M'lord...?
What? *Is* it? *NOW?*
Are you sure we cannot haz the big one, too?
Trust me. You wouldn't *want* to eat *him*.
He's rather... *tough*.

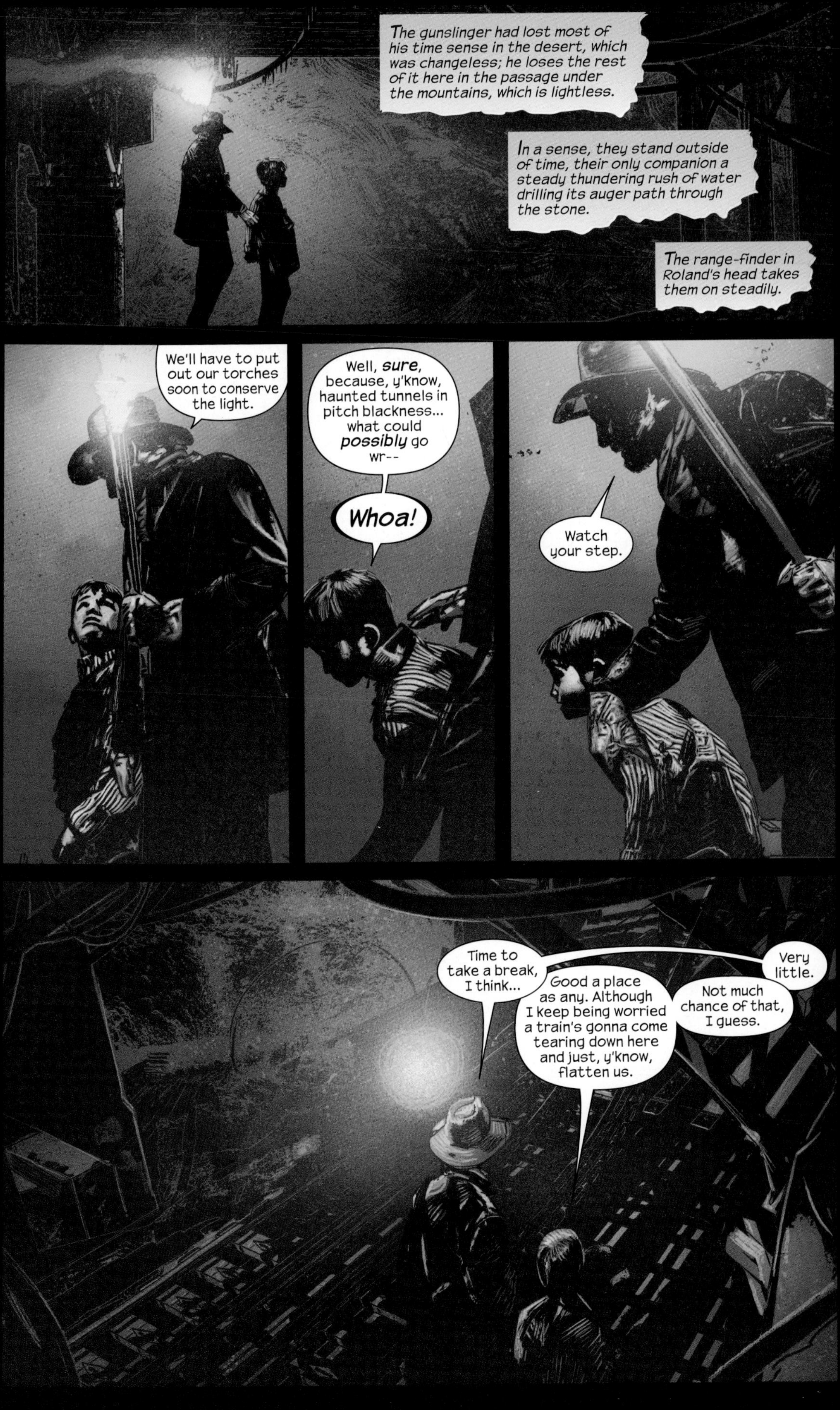

The gunslinger had lost most of his time sense in the desert, which was changeless; he loses the rest of it here in the passage under the mountains, which is lightless.
In a sense, they stand outside of time, their only companion a steady thundering rush of water drilling its auger path through the stone.
The range-finder in Roland's head takes them on steadily.
We'll have to put out our torches soon to conserve the light.
Well, *sure*, because, y'know, haunted tunnels in pitch blackness... what could *possibly* go wr--
Whoa!
Watch your step.
Time to take a break, I think...
Good a place as any. Although I keep being worried a train's gonna come tearing down here and just, y'know, flatten us.
Not much chance of that, I guess.
Very little.

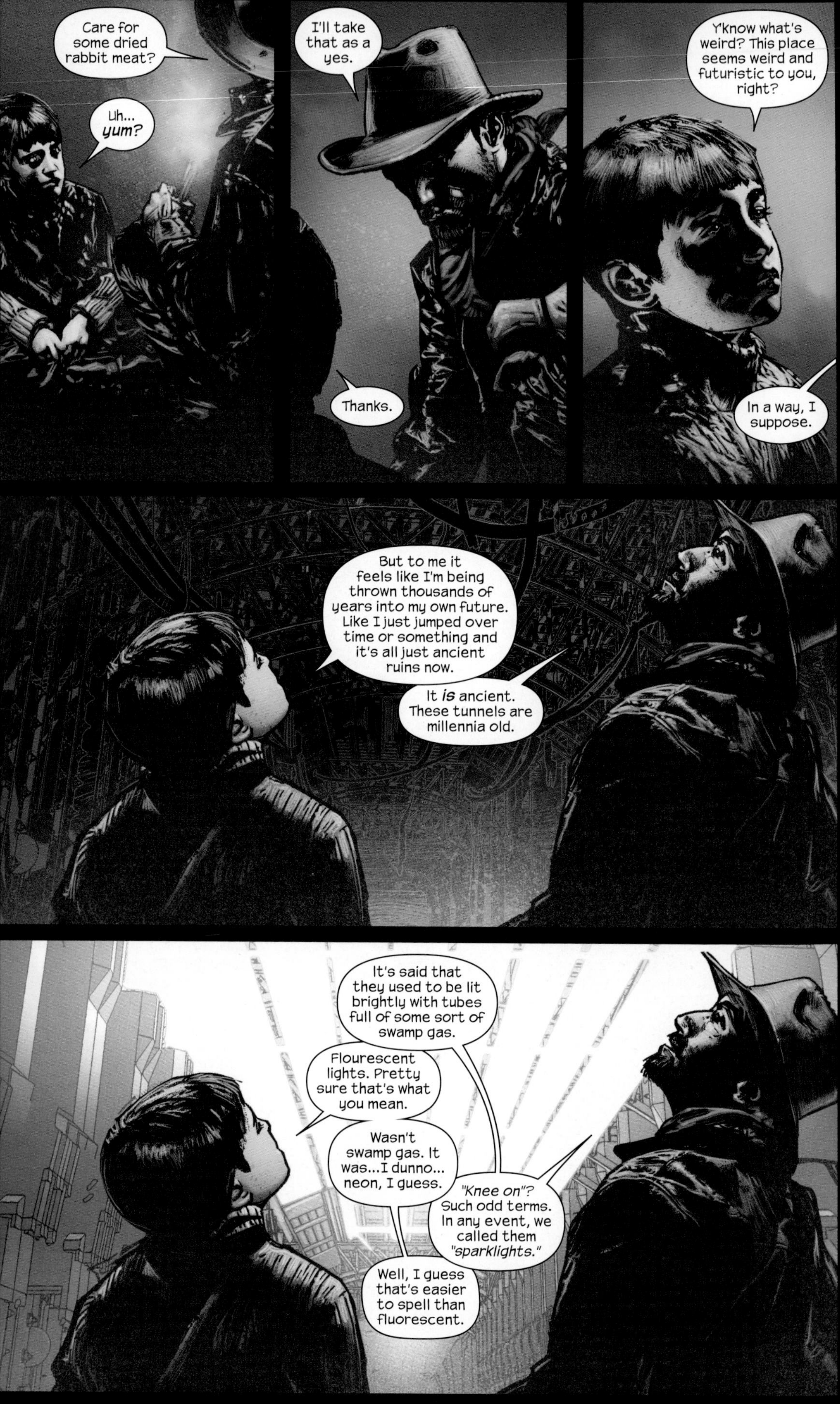
Care for some dried rabbit meat?
Uh... *yum?*
I'll take that as a yes.
Thanks.
Y'know what's weird? This place seems weird and futuristic to you, right?
In a way, I suppose.
But to me it feels like I'm being thrown thousands of years into my own future. Like I just jumped over time or something and it's all just ancient ruins now.
It *is* ancient. These tunnels are millennia old.
It's said that they used to be lit brightly with tubes full of some sort of swamp gas.
Flourescent lights. Pretty sure that's what you mean.
Wasn't swamp gas. It was...I dunno... neon, I guess.
"Knee on"? Such odd terms. In any event, we called them *"sparklights."*
Well, I guess that's easier to spell than fluorescent.

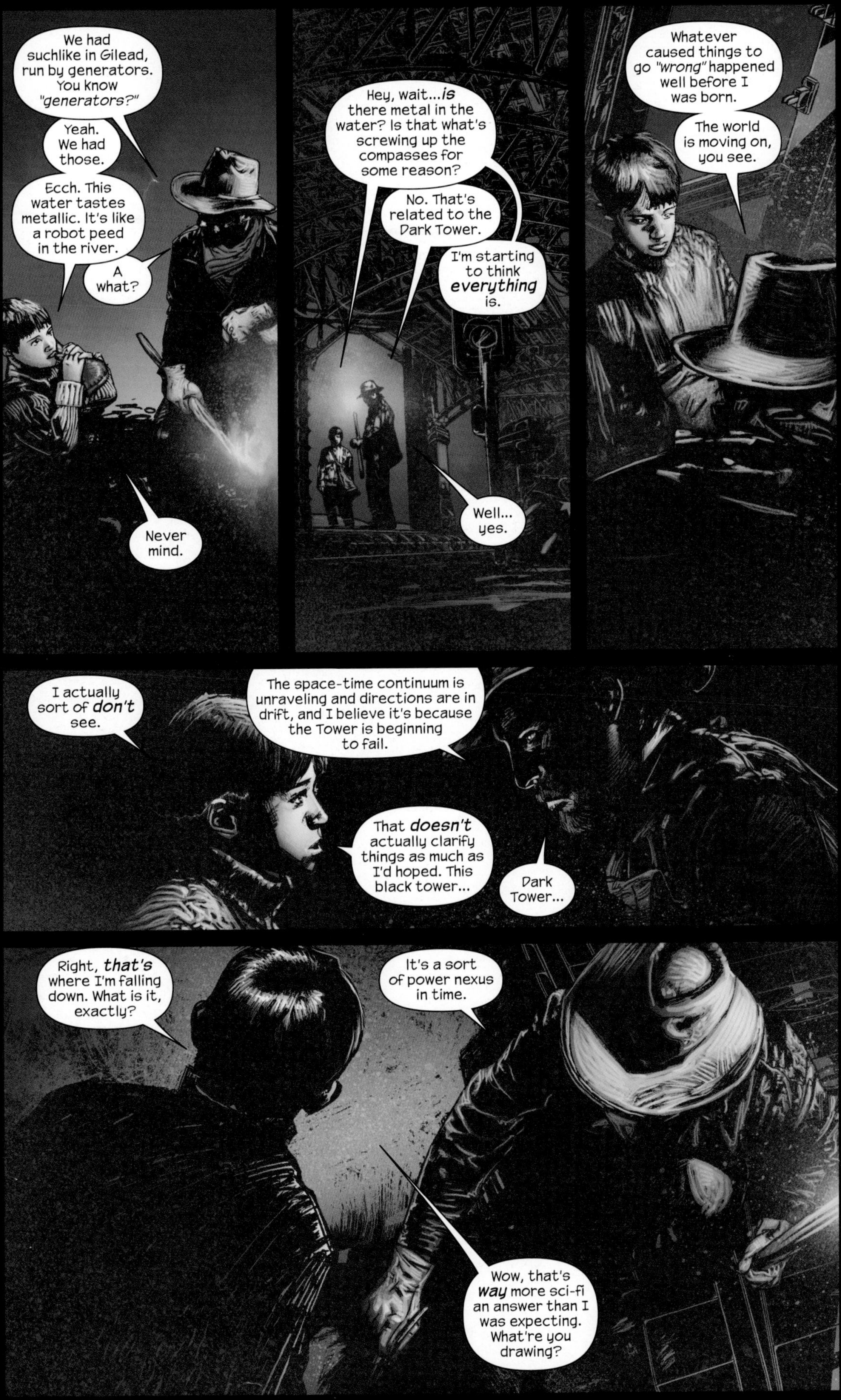
We had suchlike in Gilead, run by generators. You know "generators?"
Yeah. We had those.
Ecch. This water tastes metallic. It's like a robot peed in the river.
A what?
Never mind.
Hey, wait...is there metal in the water? Is that what's screwing up the compasses for some reason?
No. That's related to the Dark Tower.
I'm starting to think everything is.
Well... yes.
Whatever caused things to go "wrong" happened well before I was born.
The world is moving on, you see.
I actually sort of don't see.
The space-time continuum is unraveling and directions are in drift, and I believe it's because the Tower is beginning to fail.
That doesn't actually clarify things as much as I'd hoped. This black tower...
Dark Tower...
Right, that's where I'm falling down. What is it, exactly?
It's a sort of power nexus in time.
Wow, that's way more sci-fi an answer than I was expecting. What're you drawing?

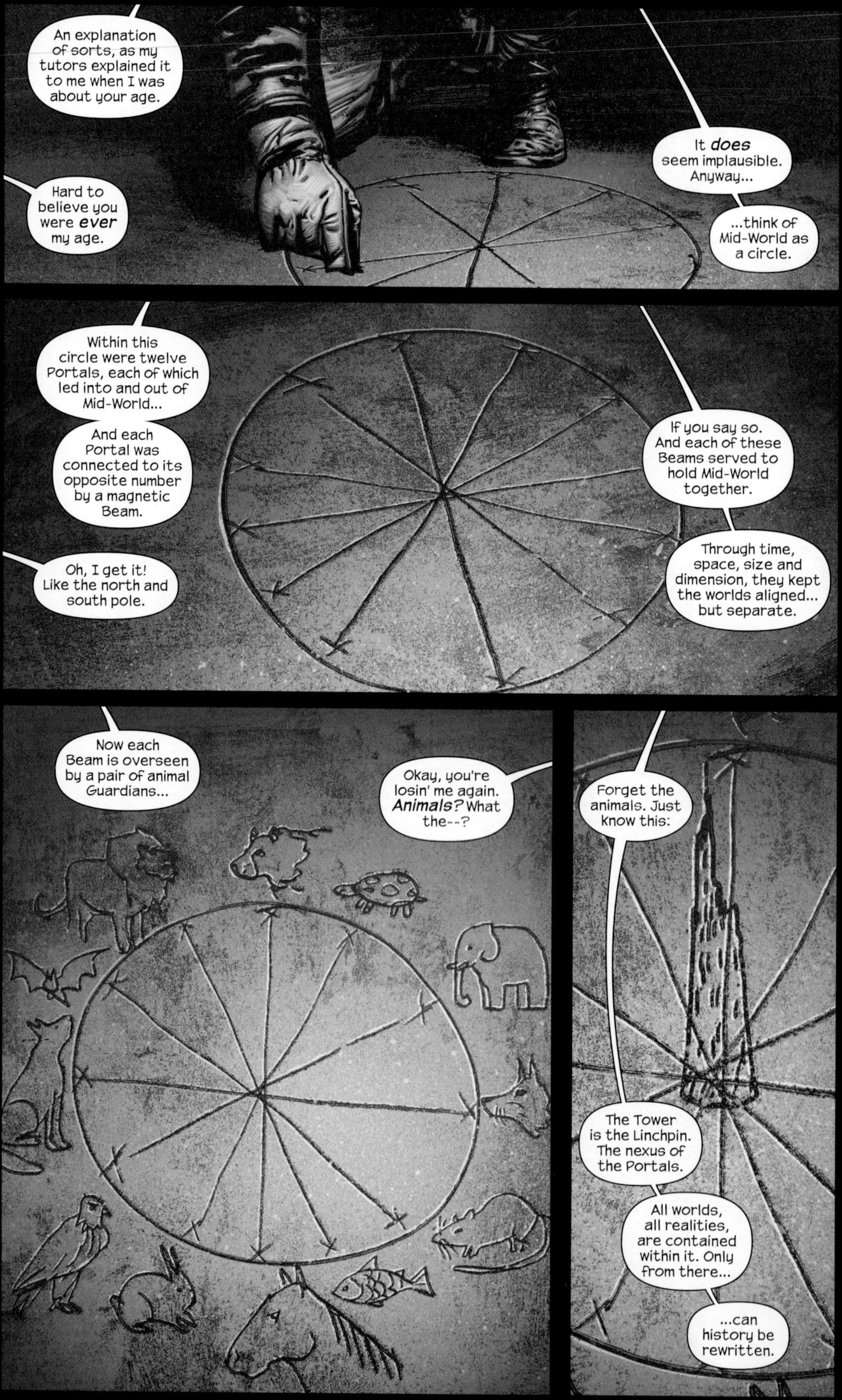
An explanation of sorts, as my tutors explained it to me when I was about your age.
Hard to believe you were *ever* my age.
It *does* seem implausible. Anyway...
...think of Mid-World as a circle.
Within this circle were twelve Portals, each of which led into and out of Mid-World...
And each Portal was connected to its opposite number by a magnetic Beam.
Oh, I get it! Like the north and south pole.
If you say so. And each of these Beams served to hold Mid-World together.
Through time, space, size and dimension, they kept the worlds aligned... but separate.
Now each Beam is overseen by a pair of animal Guardians...
Okay, you're losin' me again. *Animals?* What the--?
Forget the animals. Just know this:
The Tower is the Linchpin. The nexus of the Portals.
All worlds, all realities, are contained within it. Only from there...
...can history be rewritten.

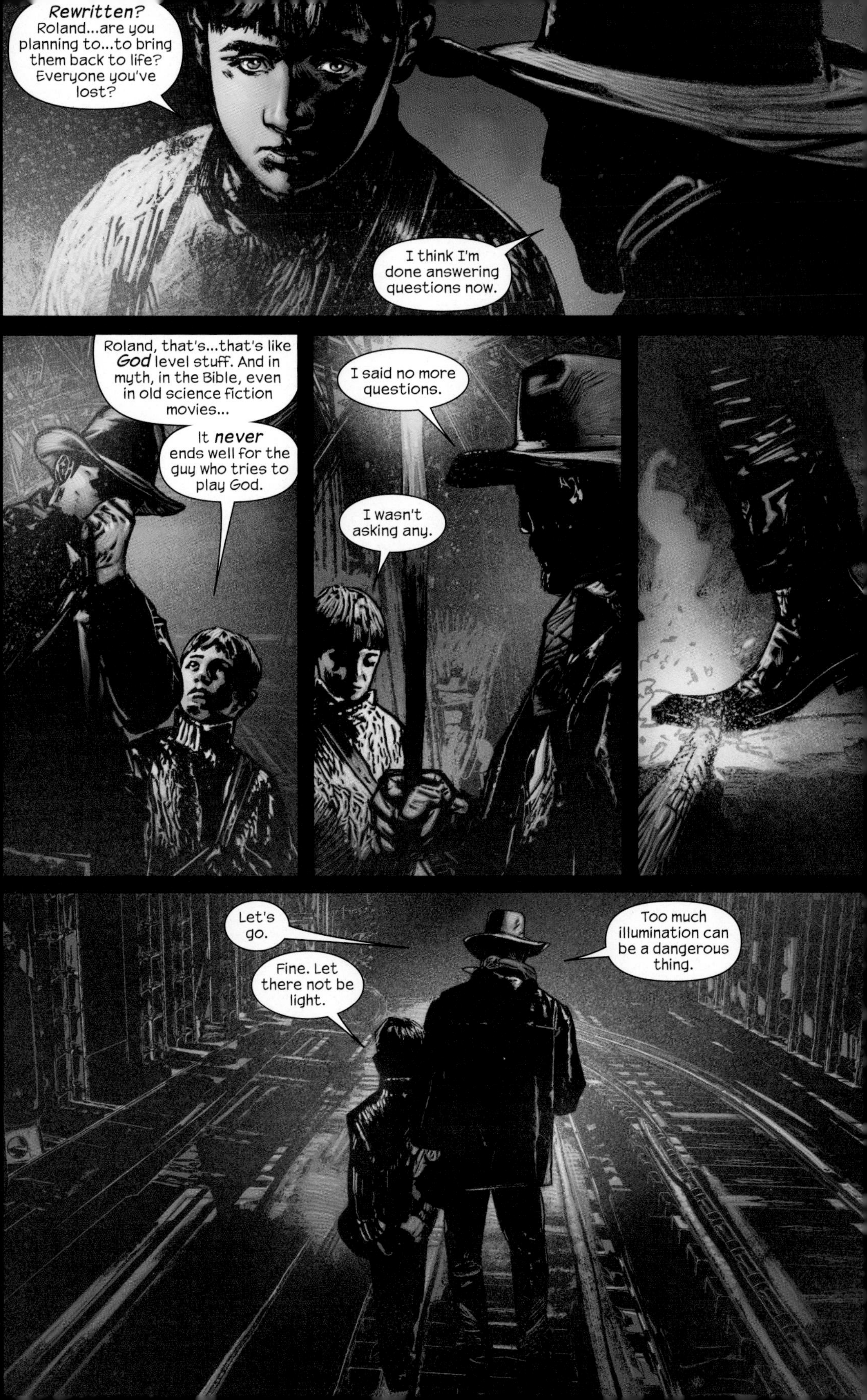
Rewritten? Roland...are you planning to...to bring them back to life? Everyone you've lost?
I think I'm done answering questions now.
Roland, that's...that's like *God* level stuff. And in myth, in the Bible, even in old science fiction movies...
It ***never*** ends well for the guy who tries to play God.
I said no more questions.
I wasn't asking any.
Let's go.
Fine. Let there not be light.
Too much illumination can be a dangerous thing.

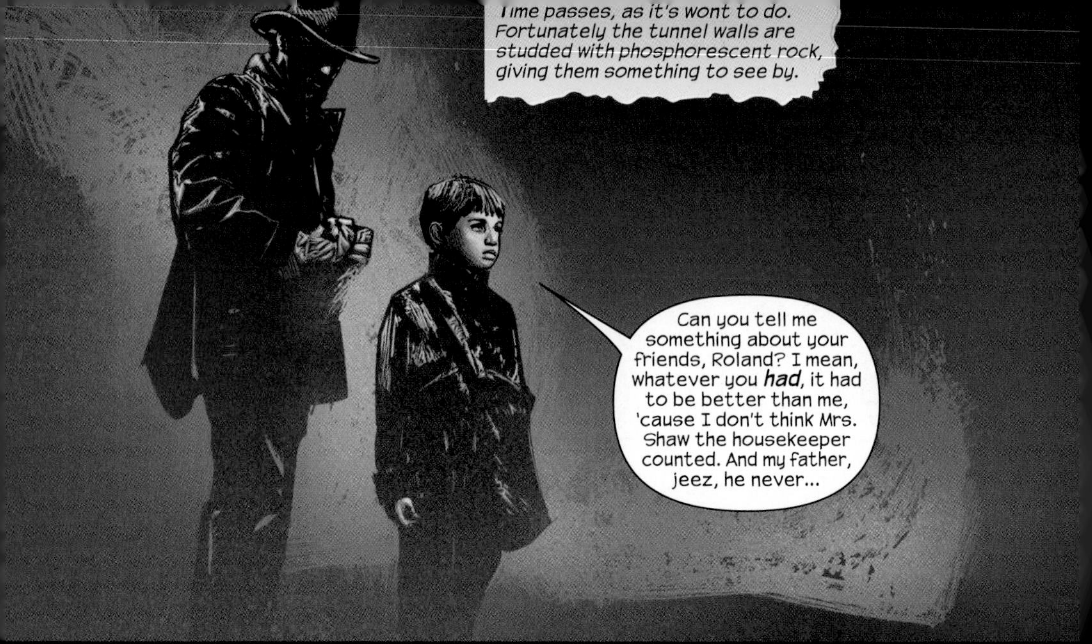
Time passes, as it's wont to do. Fortunately the tunnel walls are studded with phosphorescent rock, giving them something to see by.
Can you tell me something about your friends, Roland? I mean, whatever you *had*, it had to be better than me, 'cause I don't think Mrs. Shaw the housekeeper counted. And my father, jeez, he never...

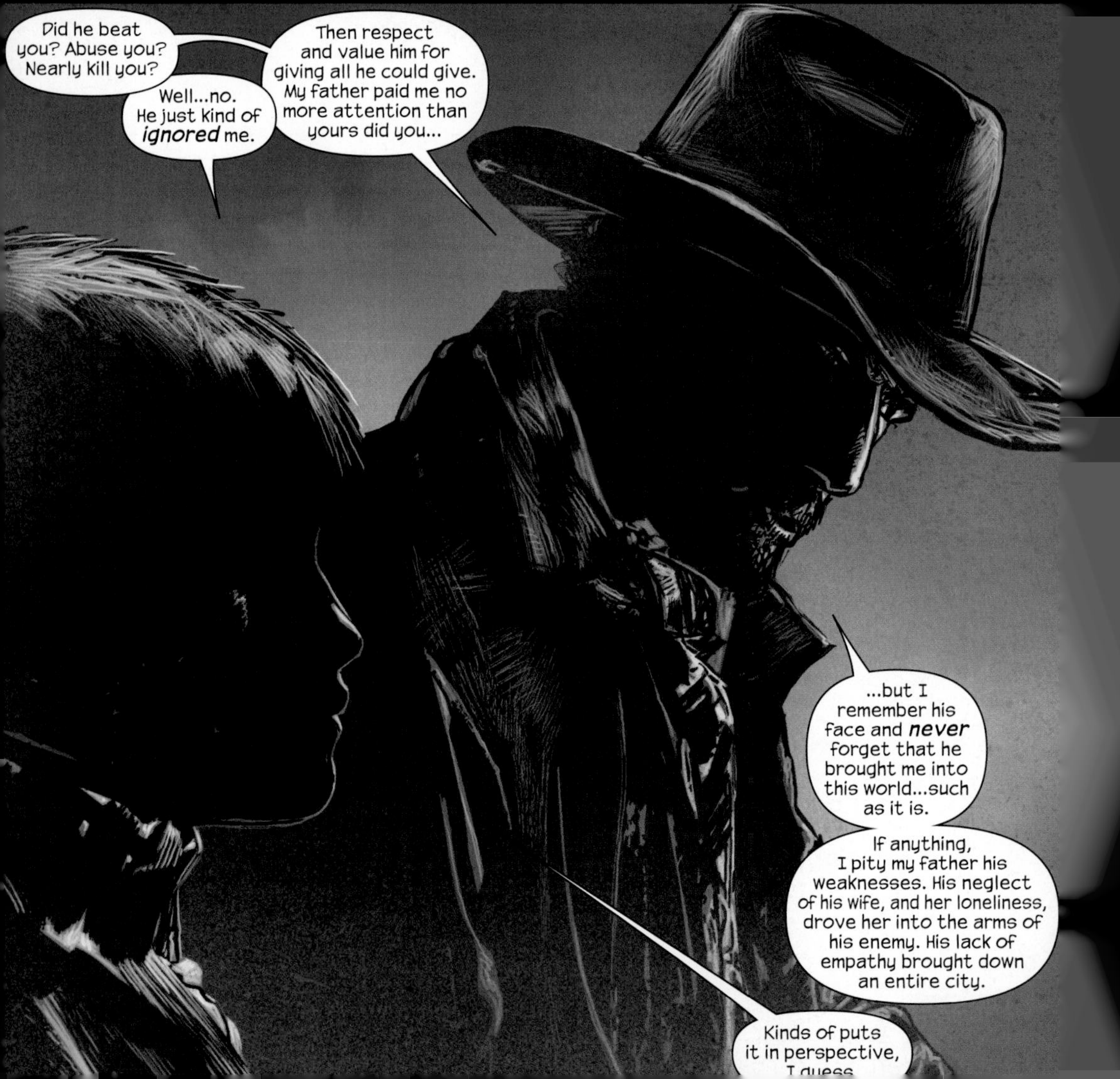
Did he beat you? Abuse you? Nearly kill you?
Well...no. He just kind of *ignored* me.
Then respect and value him for giving all he could give. My father paid me no more attention than yours did you...
...but I remember his face and *never* forget that he brought me into this world...such as it is.
If anything, I pity my father his weaknesses. His neglect of his wife, and her loneliness, drove her into the arms of his enemy. His lack of empathy brought down an entire city.
Kinds of puts it in perspective, I guess.

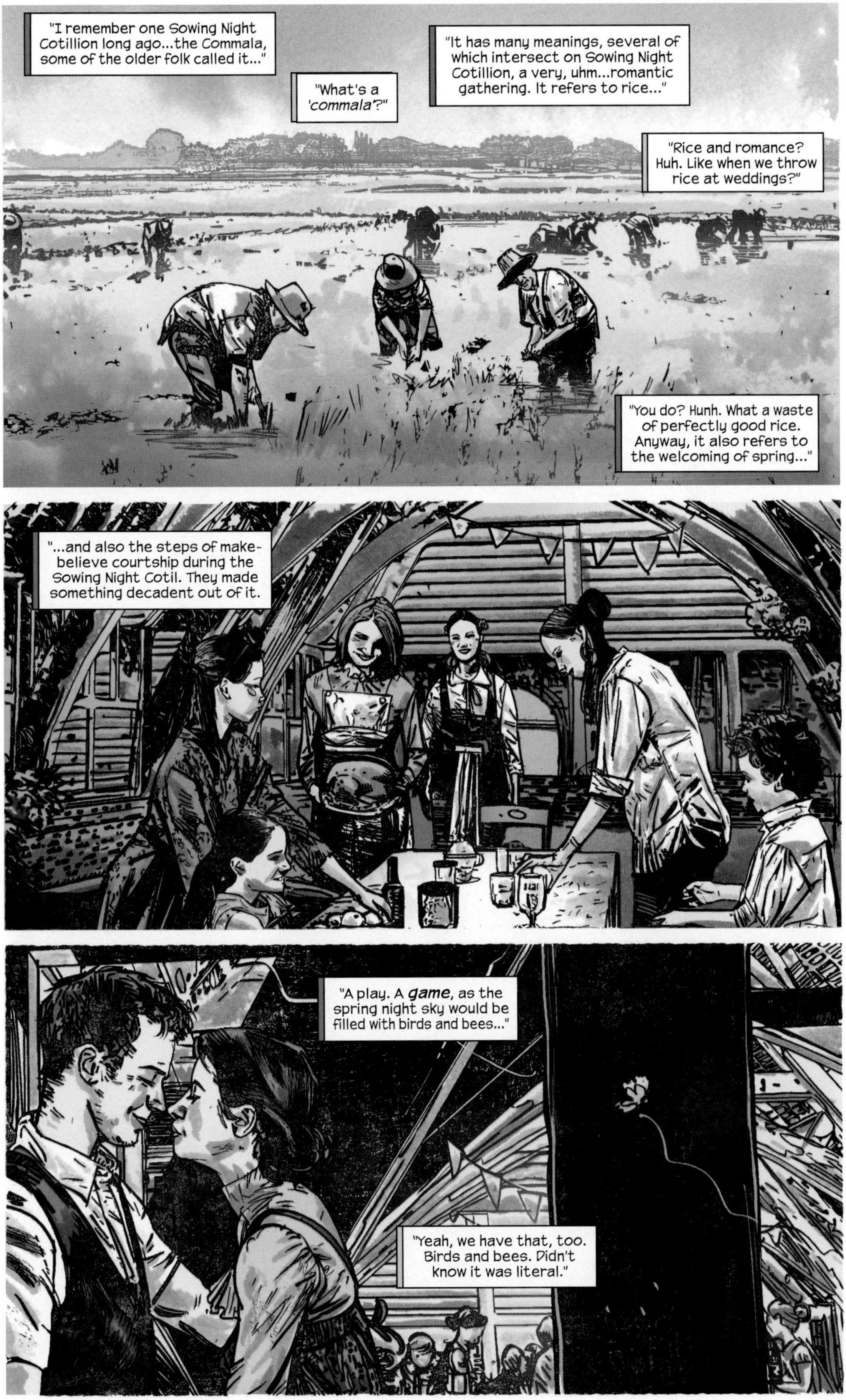
"I remember one Sowing Night Cotillion long ago...the Commala, some of the older folk called it..."
"What's a *'commala'*?"
"It has many meanings, several of which intersect on Sowing Night Cotillion, a very, uhm...romantic gathering. It refers to rice..."
"Rice and romance? Huh. Like when we throw rice at weddings?"
"You do? Hunh. What a waste of perfectly good rice. Anyway, it also refers to the welcoming of spring..."
"...and also the steps of make-believe courtship during the Sowing Night Cotil. They made something decadent out of it.
"A play. A **game**, as the spring night sky would be filled with birds and bees..."
"Yeah, we have that, too. Birds and bees. Didn't know it was literal."

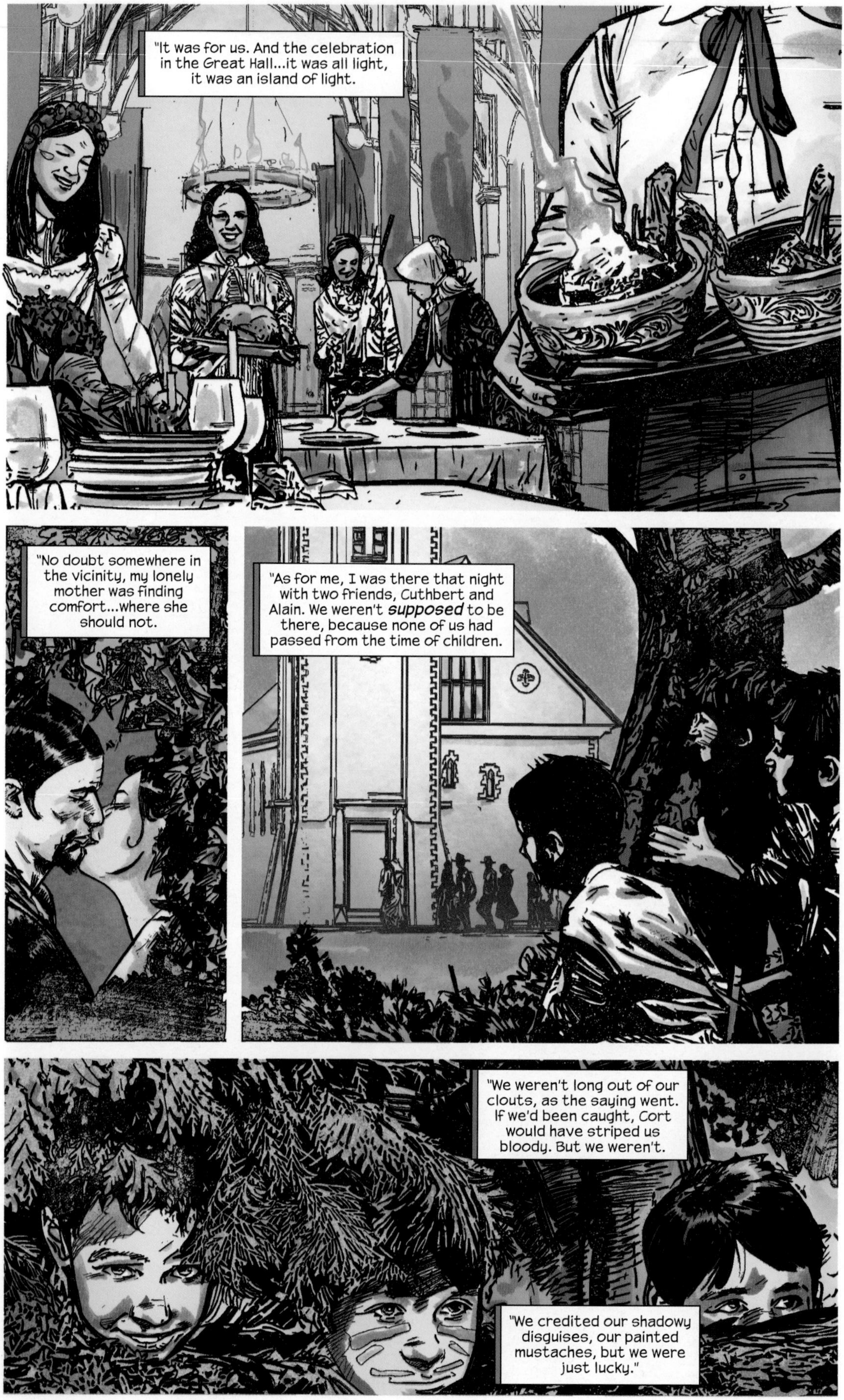
"It was for us. And the celebration in the Great Hall...it was all light, it was an island of light.
"No doubt somewhere in the vicinity, my lonely mother was finding comfort...where she should not.
"As for me, I was there that night with two friends, Cuthbert and Alain. We weren't ***supposed*** to be there, because none of us had passed from the time of children.
"We weren't long out of our clouts, as the saying went. If we'd been caught, Cort would have striped us bloody. But we weren't.
"We credited our shadowy disguises, our painted mustaches, but we were just lucky."

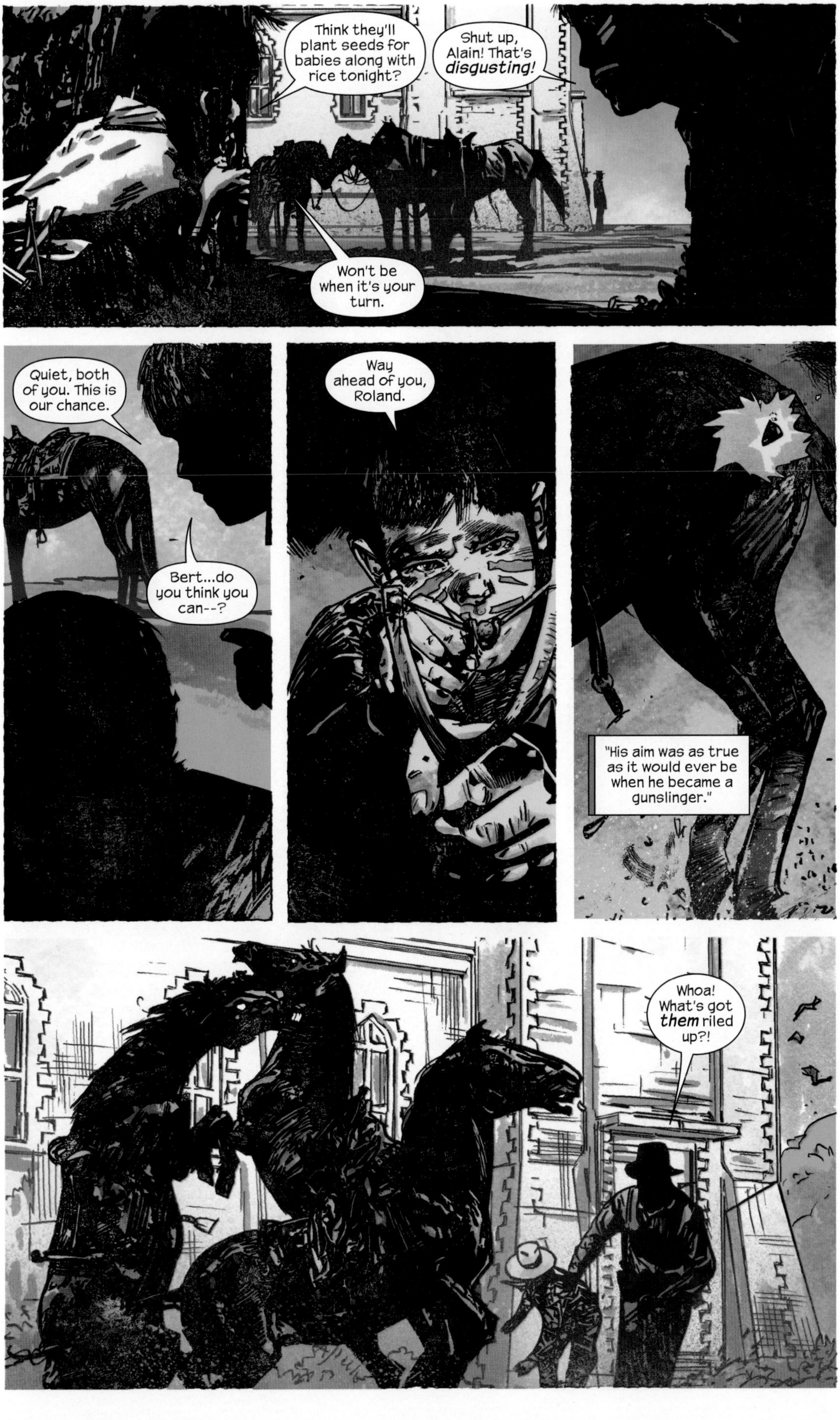
Think they'll plant seeds for babies along with rice tonight?
Shut up, Alain! That's *disgusting!*
Won't be when it's your turn.
Quiet, both of you. This is our chance.
Bert...do you think you can--?
Way ahead of you, Roland.
"His aim was as true as it would ever be when he became a gunslinger."
Whoa! What's got *them* riled up?!

"It was all the distraction we required. Nine years old and yet the shadows were already our allies.

"We sprinted like the thieves in the night that we were...

"...consumed with the joy of our own cleverness.

"Convinced, perhaps, that being witness to adult activities...

"...made us adults by extension.

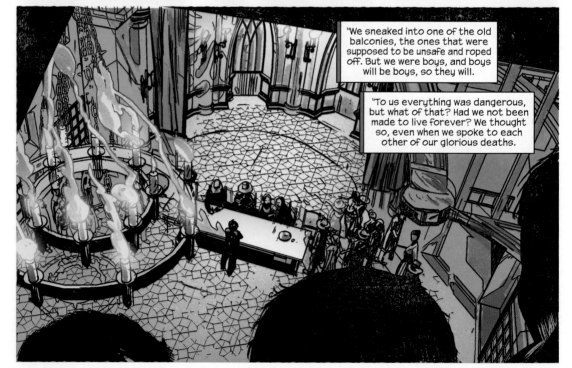

"We sneaked into one of the old balconies, the ones that were supposed to be unsafe and roped off. But we were boys, and boys will be boys, so they will.

"To us everything was dangerous, but what of that? Had we not been made to live forever? We thought so, even when we spoke to each other of our glorious deaths.

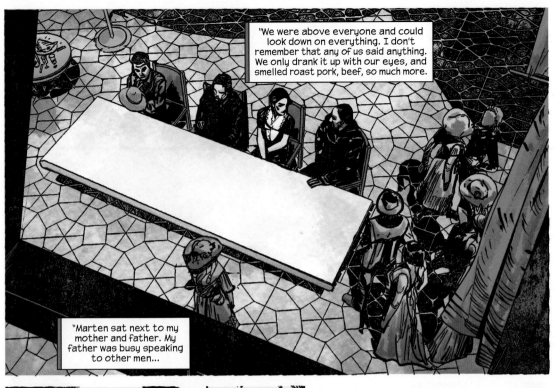

"We were above everyone and could look down on everything. I don't remember that any of us said anything. We only drank it up with our eyes, and smelled roast pork, beef, so much more.

"Marten sat next to my mother and father. My father was busy speaking to other men...

"And at one point, Gabrielle... my mother...

"...danced with Marten, the gunslingers' counselor.

"The others cleared the floor for them, and she and Marten danced.

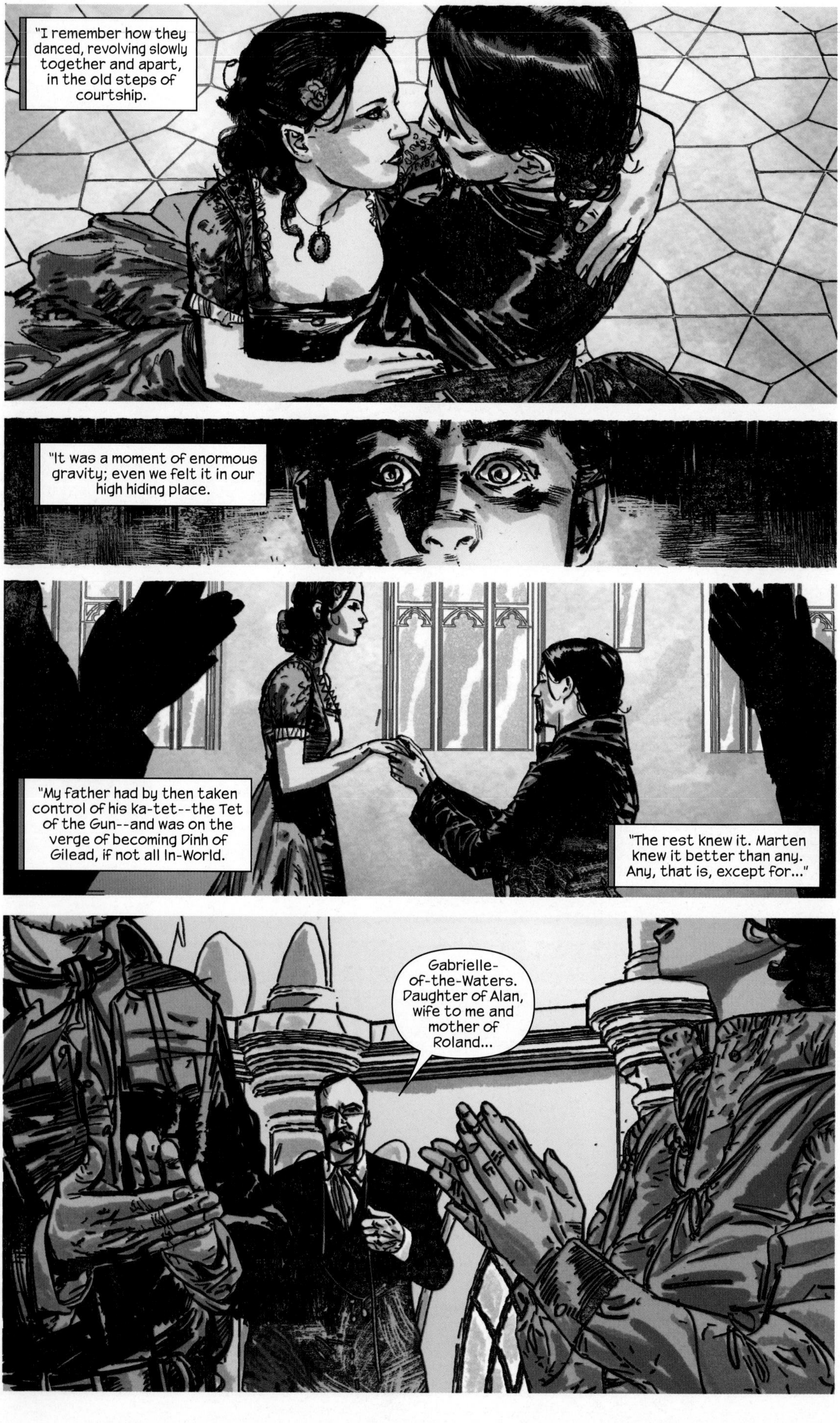
"I remember how they danced, revolving slowly together and apart, in the old steps of courtship.
"It was a moment of enormous gravity; even we felt it in our high hiding place.
"My father had by then taken control of his ka-tet--the Tet of the Gun--and was on the verge of becoming Dinh of Gilead, if not all In-World.
"The rest knew it. Marten knew it better than any. Any, that is, except for..."
Gabrielle-of-the-Waters. Daughter of Alan, wife to me and mother of Roland...

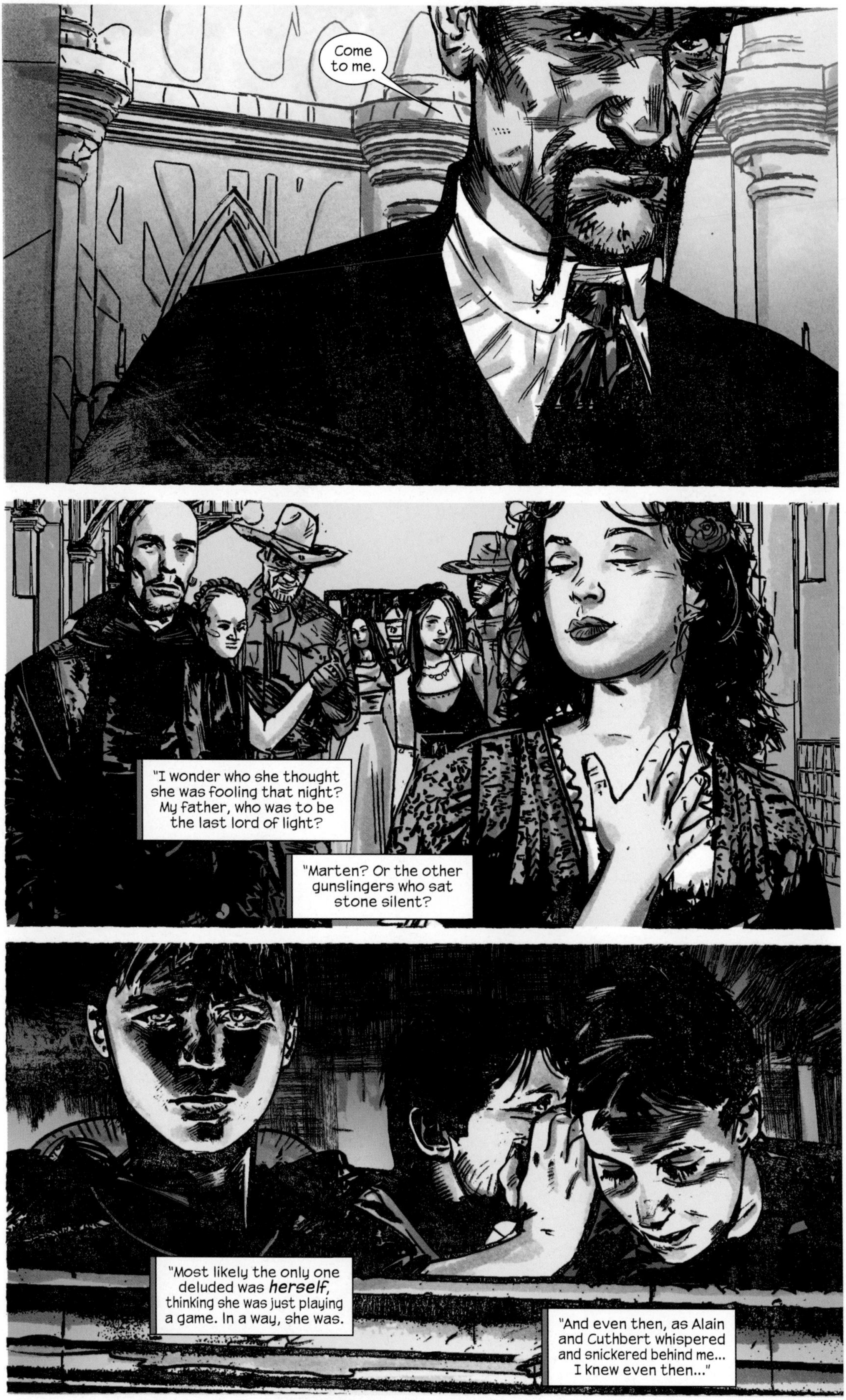
Come to me.
"I wonder who she thought she was fooling that night? My father, who was to be the last lord of light?
"Marten? Or the other gunslingers who sat stone silent?
"Most likely the only one deluded was *herself*, thinking she was just playing a game. In a way, she was.
"And even then, as Alain and Cuthbert whispered and snickered behind me... I knew even then..."

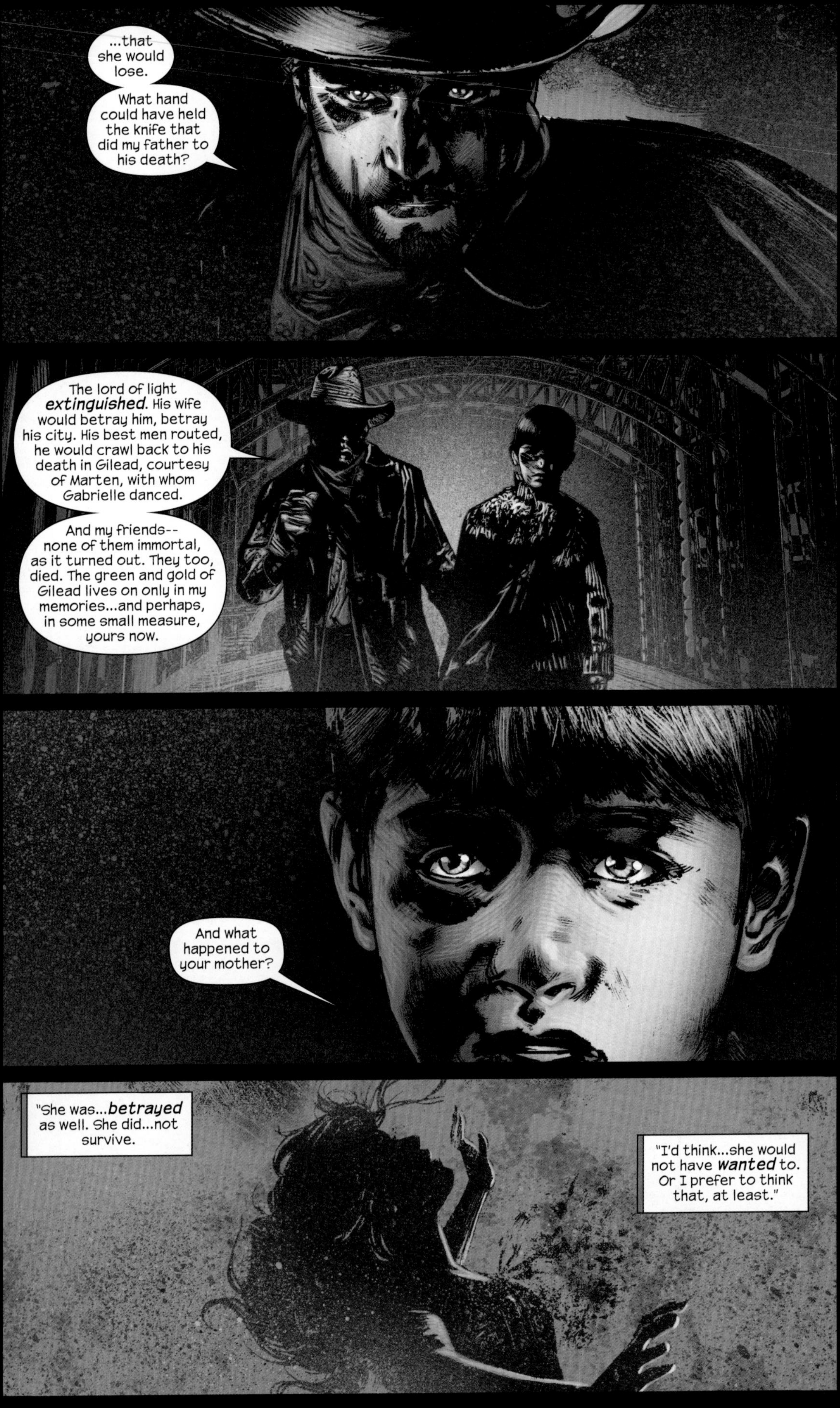
...that she would lose.
What hand could have held the knife that did my father to his death?
The lord of light *extinguished*. His wife would betray him, betray his city. His best men routed, he would crawl back to his death in Gilead, courtesy of Marten, with whom Gabrielle danced.
And my friends-- none of them immortal, as it turned out. They too, died. The green and gold of Gilead lives on only in my memories...and perhaps, in some small measure, yours now.
And what happened to your mother?
"She was...*betrayed* as well. She did...not survive.
"I'd think...she would not have *wanted* to. Or I prefer to think that, at least."

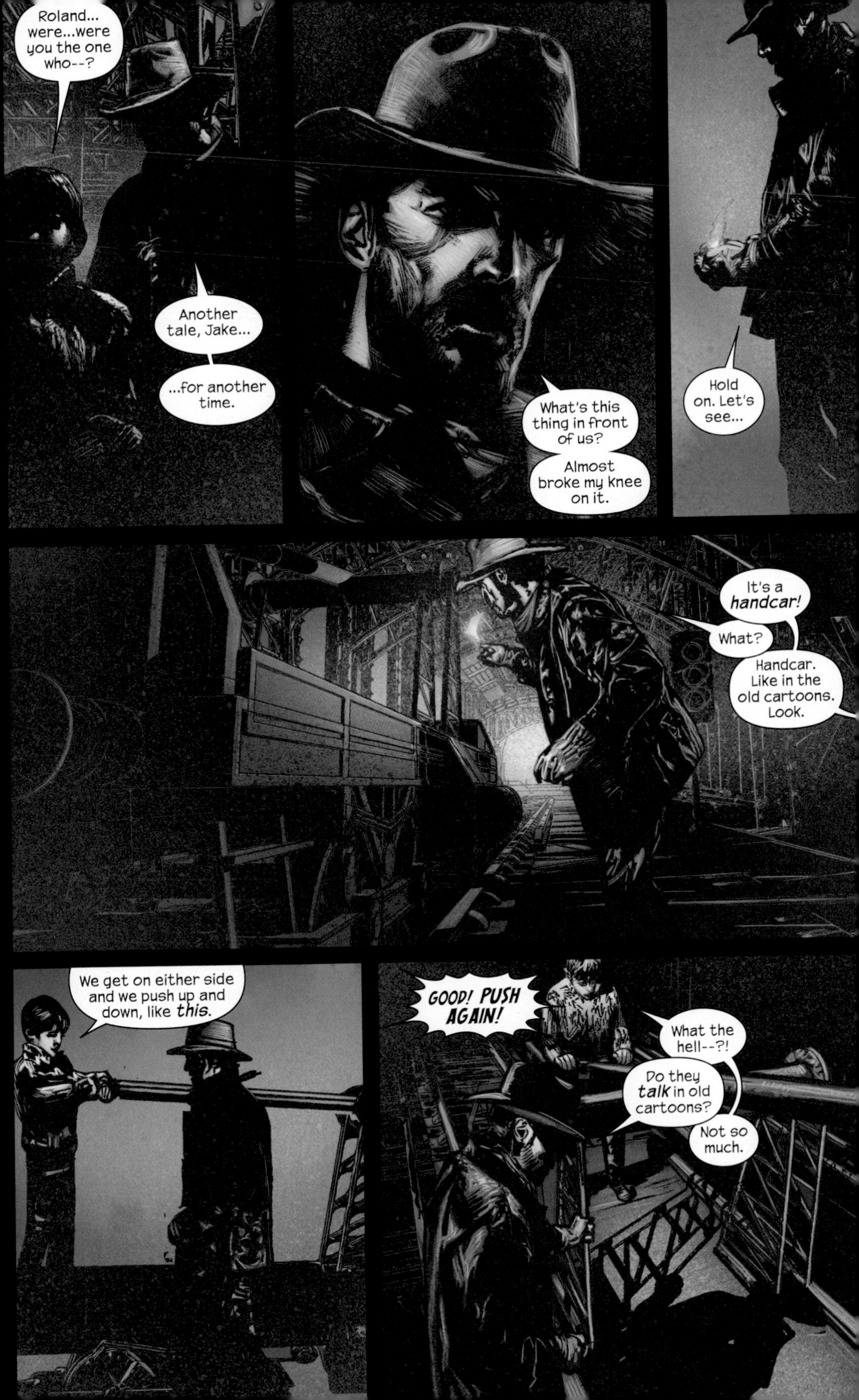
Roland... were...were you the one who--?
Another tale, Jake...
...for another time.
What's this thing in front of us?
Almost broke my knee on it.
Hold on. Let's see...
It's a handcar!
What?
Handcar. Like in the old cartoons. Look.
We get on either side and we push up and down, like this.
GOOD! PUSH AGAIN!
What the hell--?!
Do they talk in old cartoons?
Not so much.

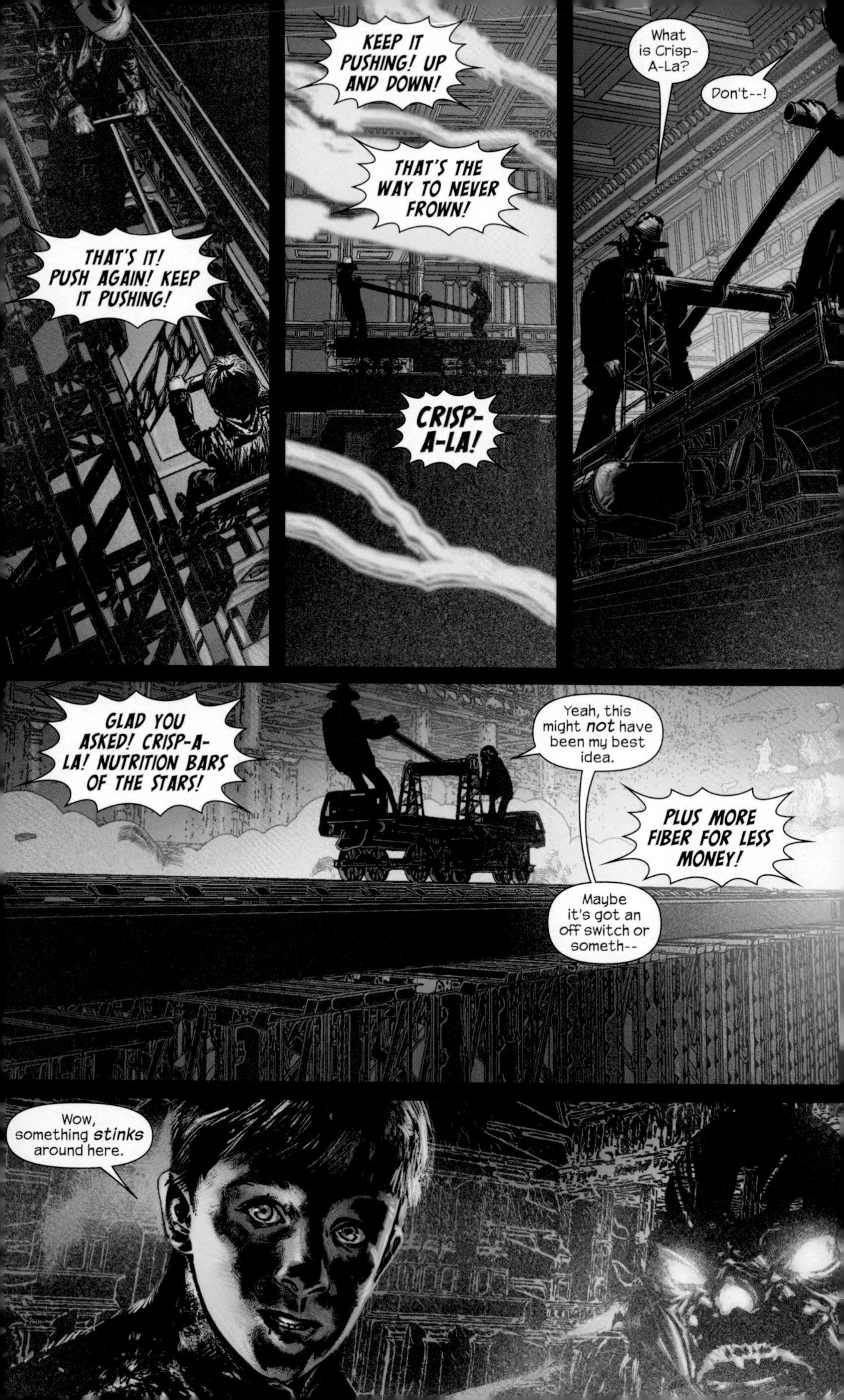

THAT'S IT! PUSH AGAIN! KEEP IT PUSHING!
KEEP IT PUSHING! UP AND DOWN!
THAT'S THE WAY TO NEVER FROWN!
CRISP-A-LA!
What is Crisp-A-La?
Don't--!
GLAD YOU ASKED! CRISP-A-LA! NUTRITION BARS OF THE STARS!
Yeah, this might not have been my best idea.
PLUS MORE FIBER FOR LESS MONEY!
Maybe it's got an off switch or someth--
Wow, something stinks around here.

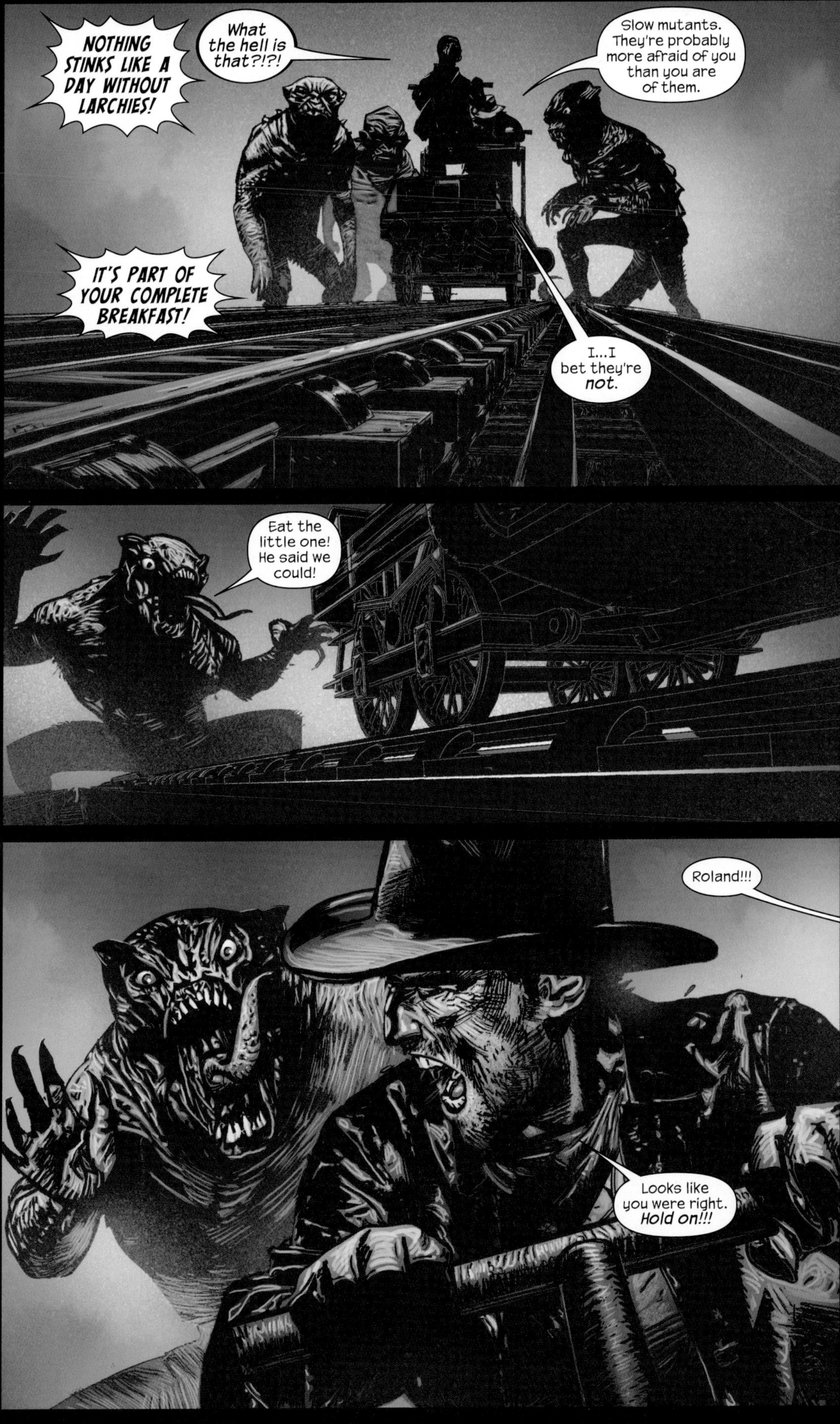
NOTHING STINKS LIKE A DAY WITHOUT LARCHIES!
What the hell is that?!?!
Slow mutants. They're probably more afraid of you than you are of them.
IT'S PART OF YOUR COMPLETE BREAKFAST!
I...I bet they're *not*.
Eat the little one! He said we could!
Roland!!!
Looks like you were right. ***Hold on!!!***

STEPHEN KING

THE DARK TOWER
~THE GUNSLINGER~

THE MAN IN BLACK

CHAPTER THREE

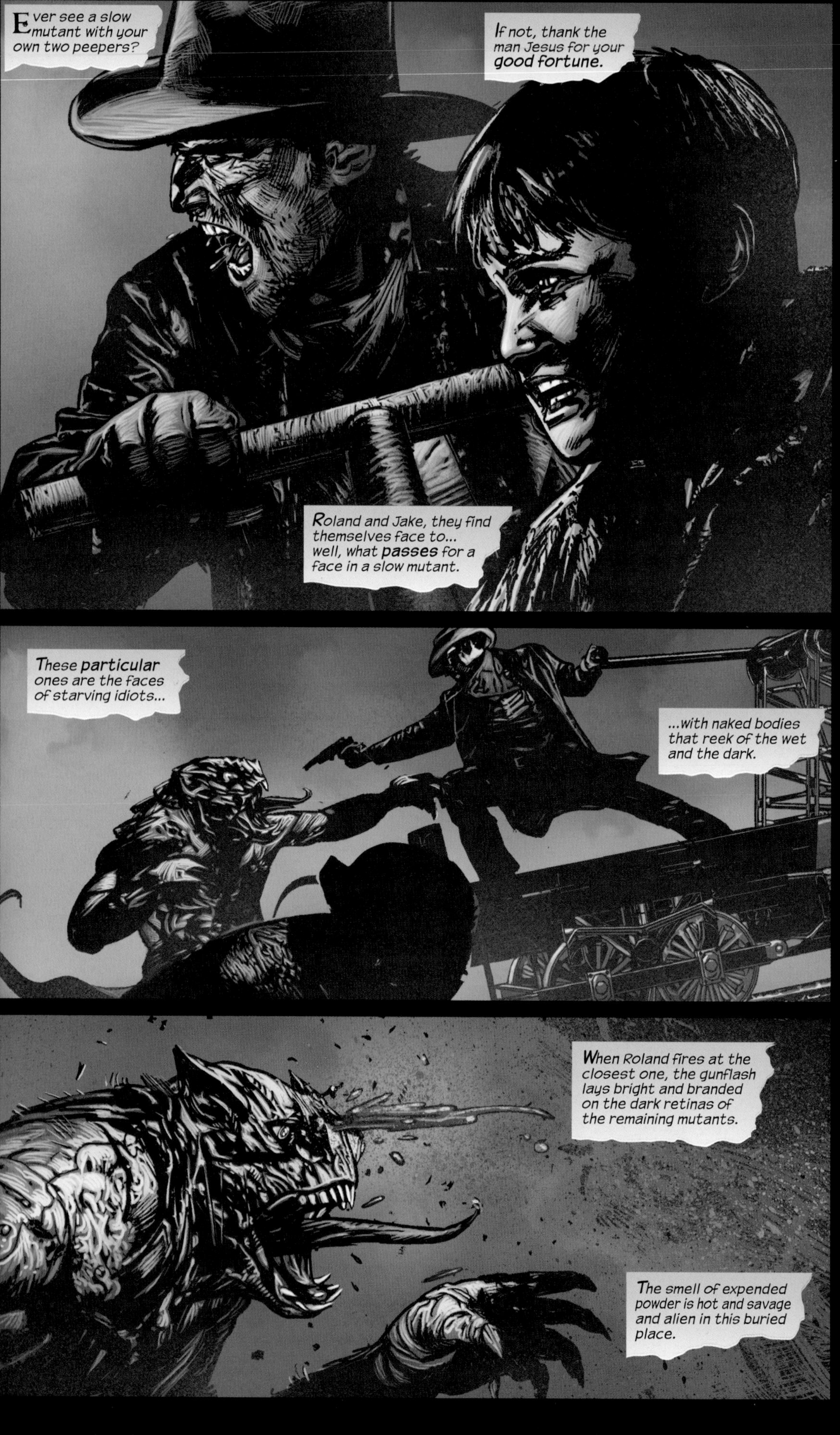

Ever see a slow mutant with your own two peepers?
If not, thank the man Jesus for your good fortune.
Roland and Jake, they find themselves face to... well, what passes for a face in a slow mutant.
These particular ones are the faces of starving idiots...
...with naked bodies that reek of the wet and the dark.
When Roland fires at the closest one, the gunflash lays bright and branded on the dark retinas of the remaining mutants.
The smell of expended powder is hot and savage and alien in this buried place.

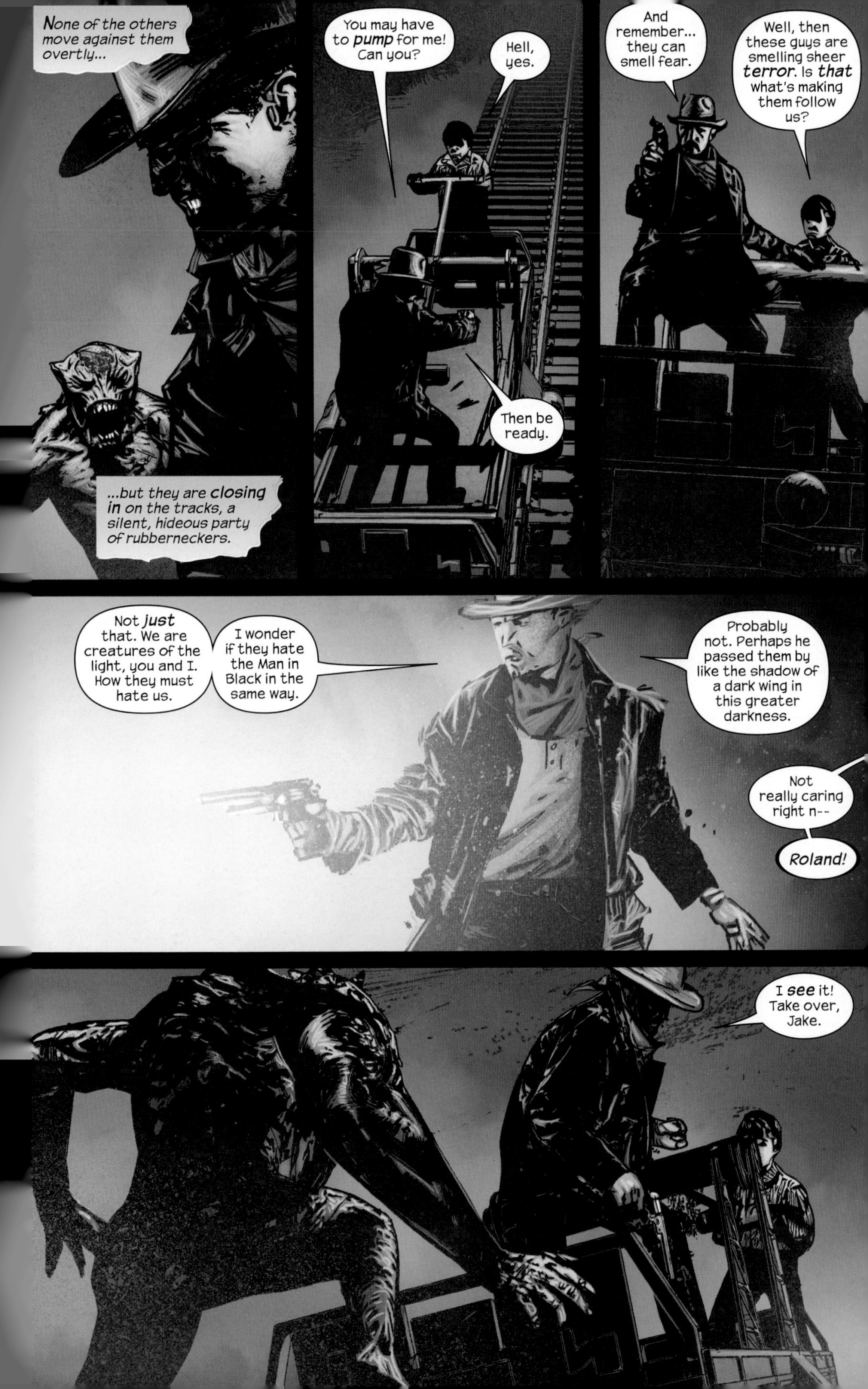
None of the others move against them overtly...
...but they are closing in on the tracks, a silent, hideous party of rubberneckers.
You may have to pump for me! Can you?
Hell, yes.
Then be ready.
And remember... they can smell fear.
Well, then these guys are smelling sheer terror. Is that what's making them follow us?
Not just that. We are creatures of the light, you and I. How they must hate us.
I wonder if they hate the Man in Black in the same way.
Probably not. Perhaps he passed them by like the shadow of a dark wing in this greater darkness.
Not really caring right n--
Roland!
I see it! Take over, Jake.

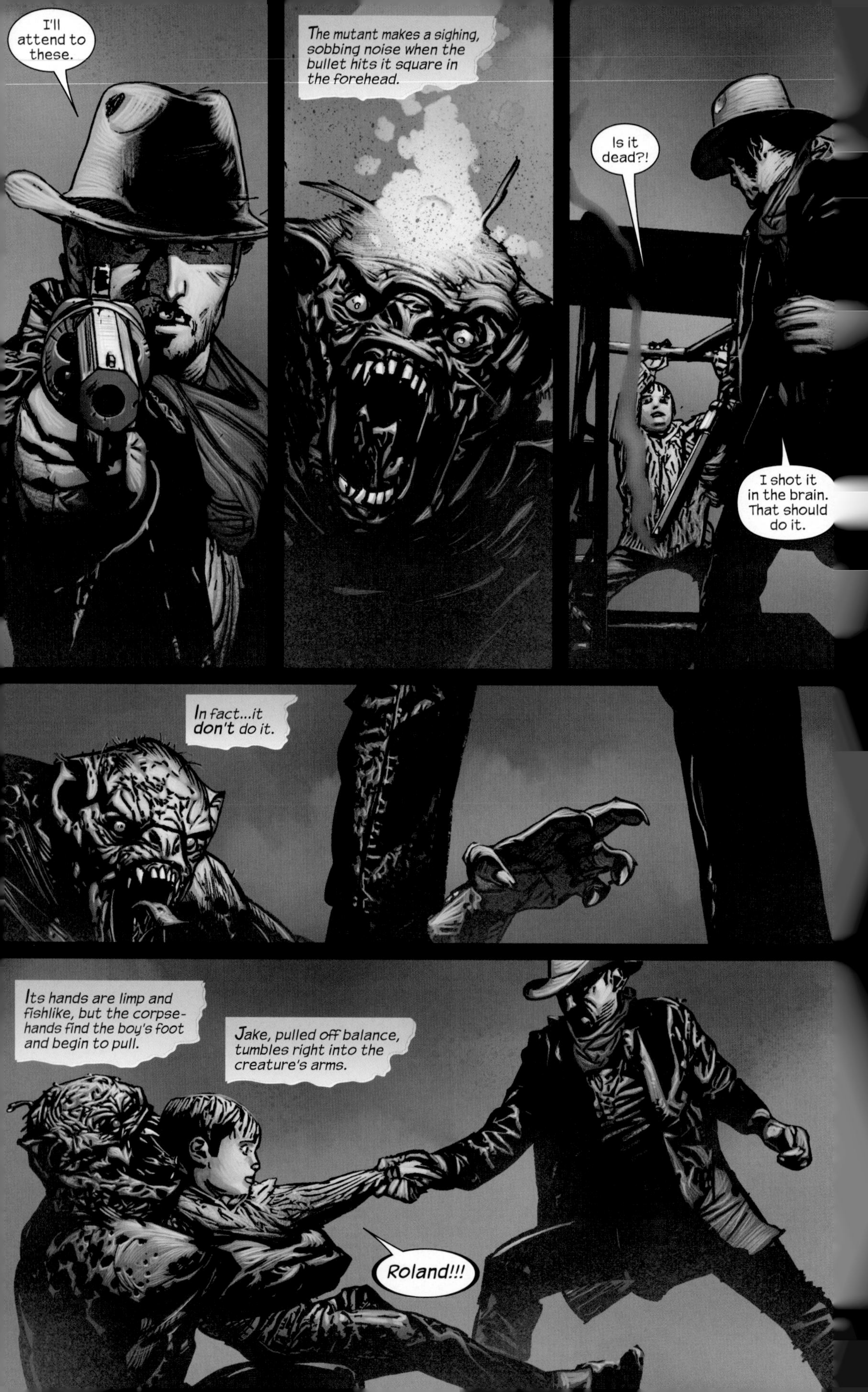

I'll attend to these.
The mutant makes a sighing, sobbing noise when the bullet hits it square in the forehead.
Is it dead?!
I shot it in the brain. That should do it.
In fact...it don't do it.
Its hands are limp and fishlike, but the corpse-hands find the boy's foot and begin to pull.
Jake, pulled off balance, tumbles right into the creature's arms.
Roland!!!

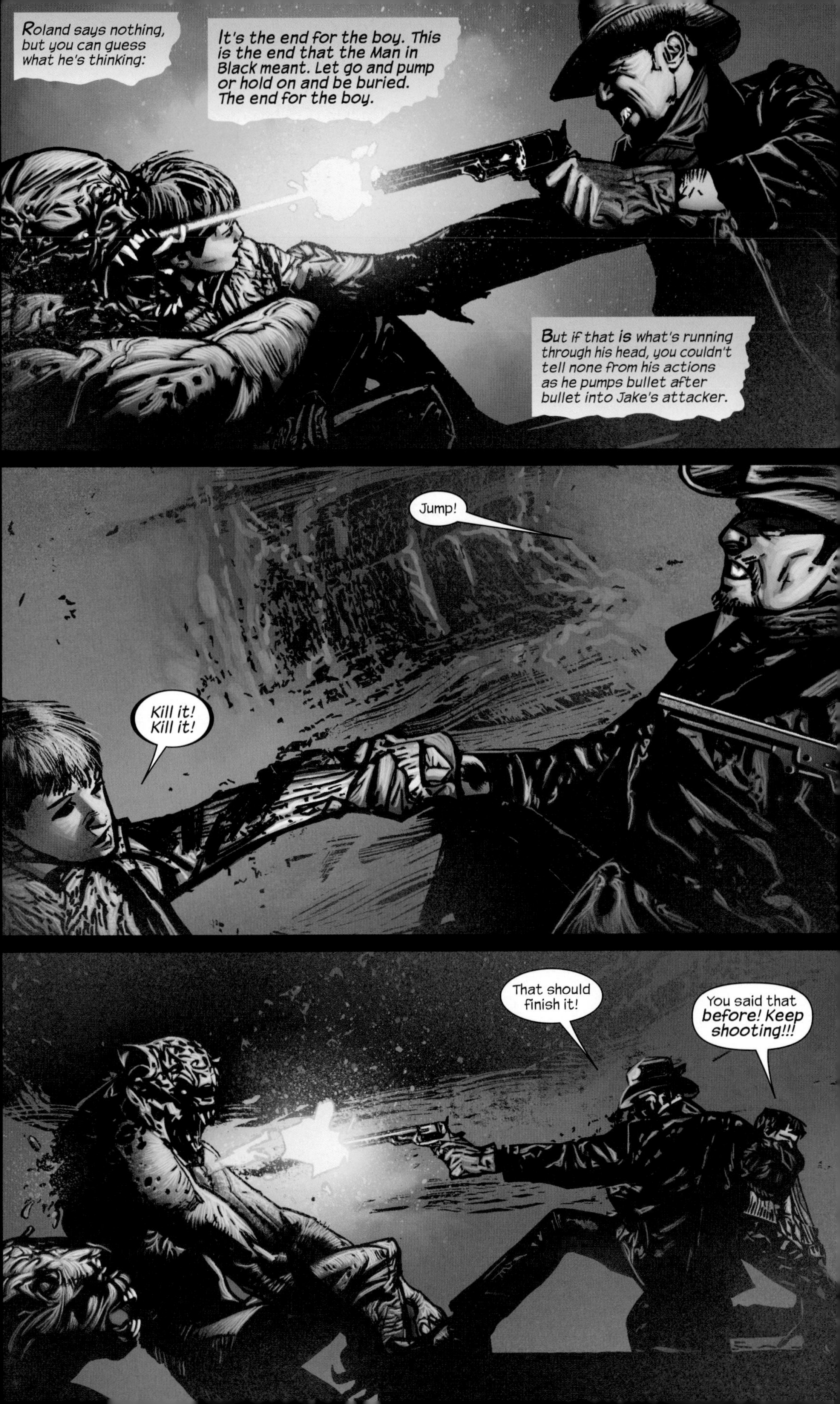
Roland says nothing, but you can guess what he's thinking:
It's the end for the boy. This is the end that the Man in Black meant. Let go and pump or hold on and be buried. The end for the boy.
But if that is what's running through his head, you couldn't tell none from his actions as he pumps bullet after bullet into Jake's attacker.
Jump!
Kill it! Kill it!
That should finish it!
You said that before! Keep shooting!!!

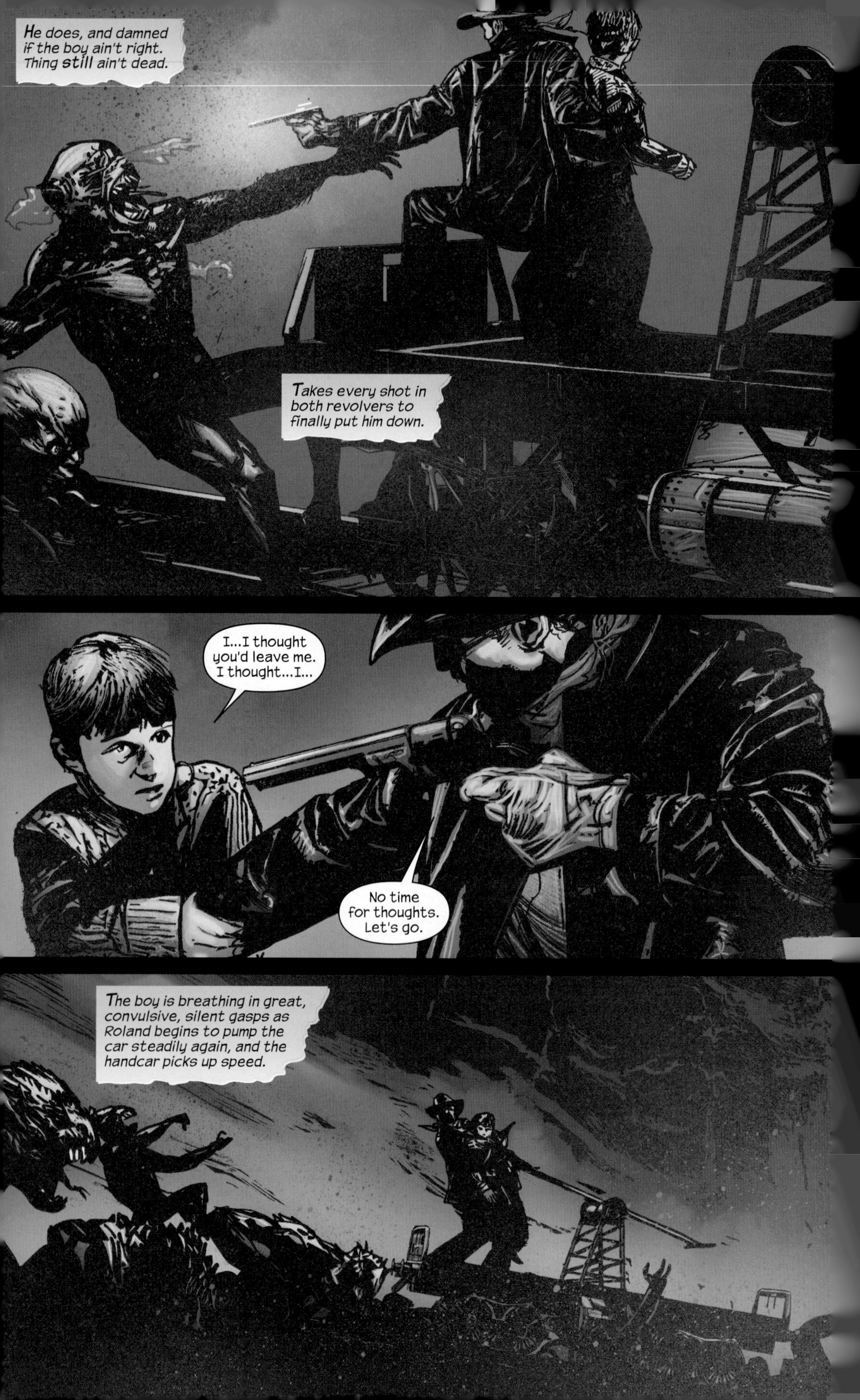
He does, and damned if the boy ain't right. Thing still ain't dead.
Takes every shot in both revolvers to finally put him down.
I...I thought you'd leave me. I thought...I...
No time for thoughts. Let's go.
The boy is breathing in great, convulsive, silent gasps as Roland begins to pump the car steadily again, and the handcar picks up speed.

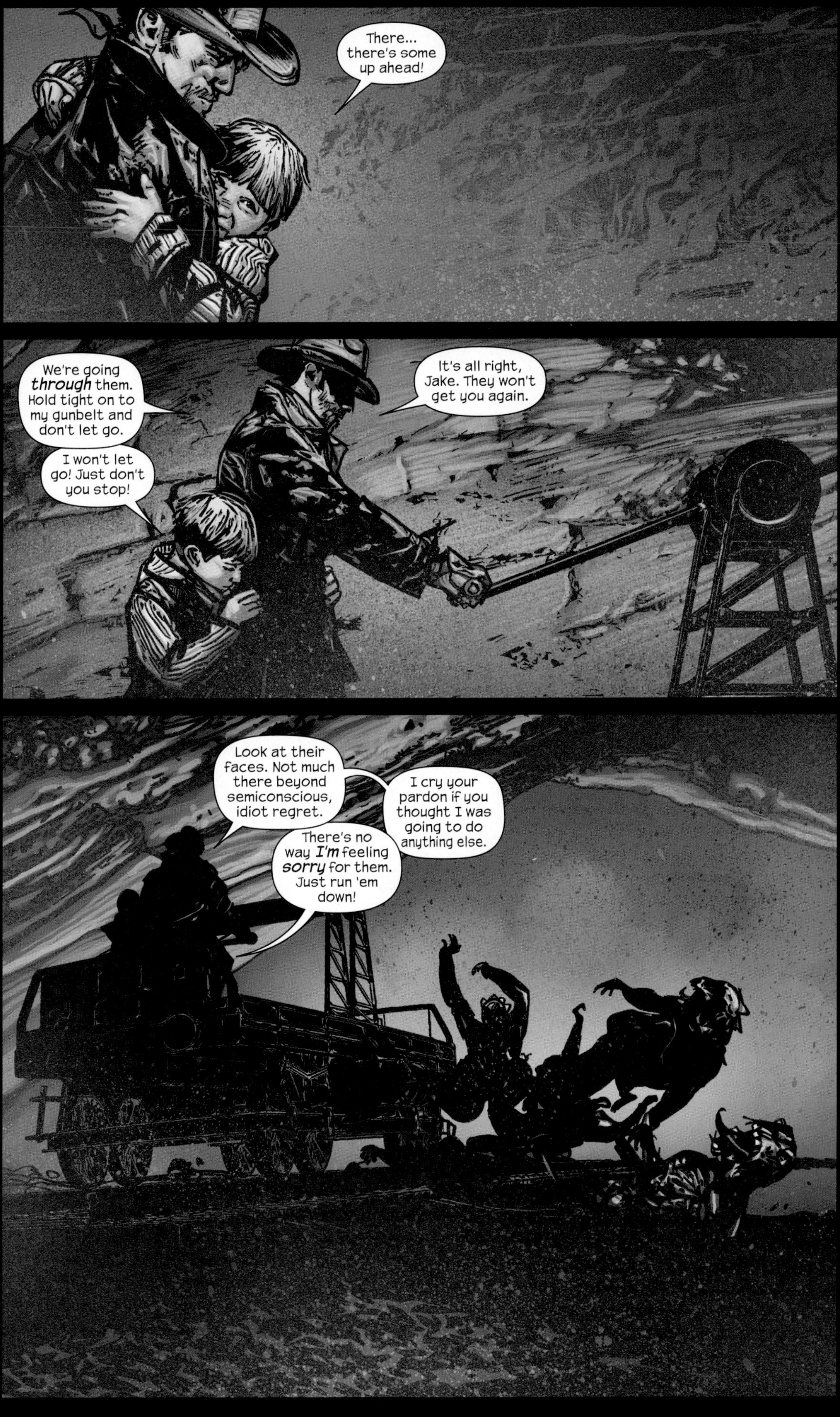
There... there's some up ahead!
We're going *through* them. Hold tight on to my gunbelt and don't let go.
I won't let go! Just don't you stop!
It's all right, Jake. They won't get you again.
Look at their faces. Not much there beyond semiconscious, idiot regret.
There's no way *I'm* feeling *sorry* for them. Just run 'em down!
I cry your pardon if you thought I was going to do anything else.

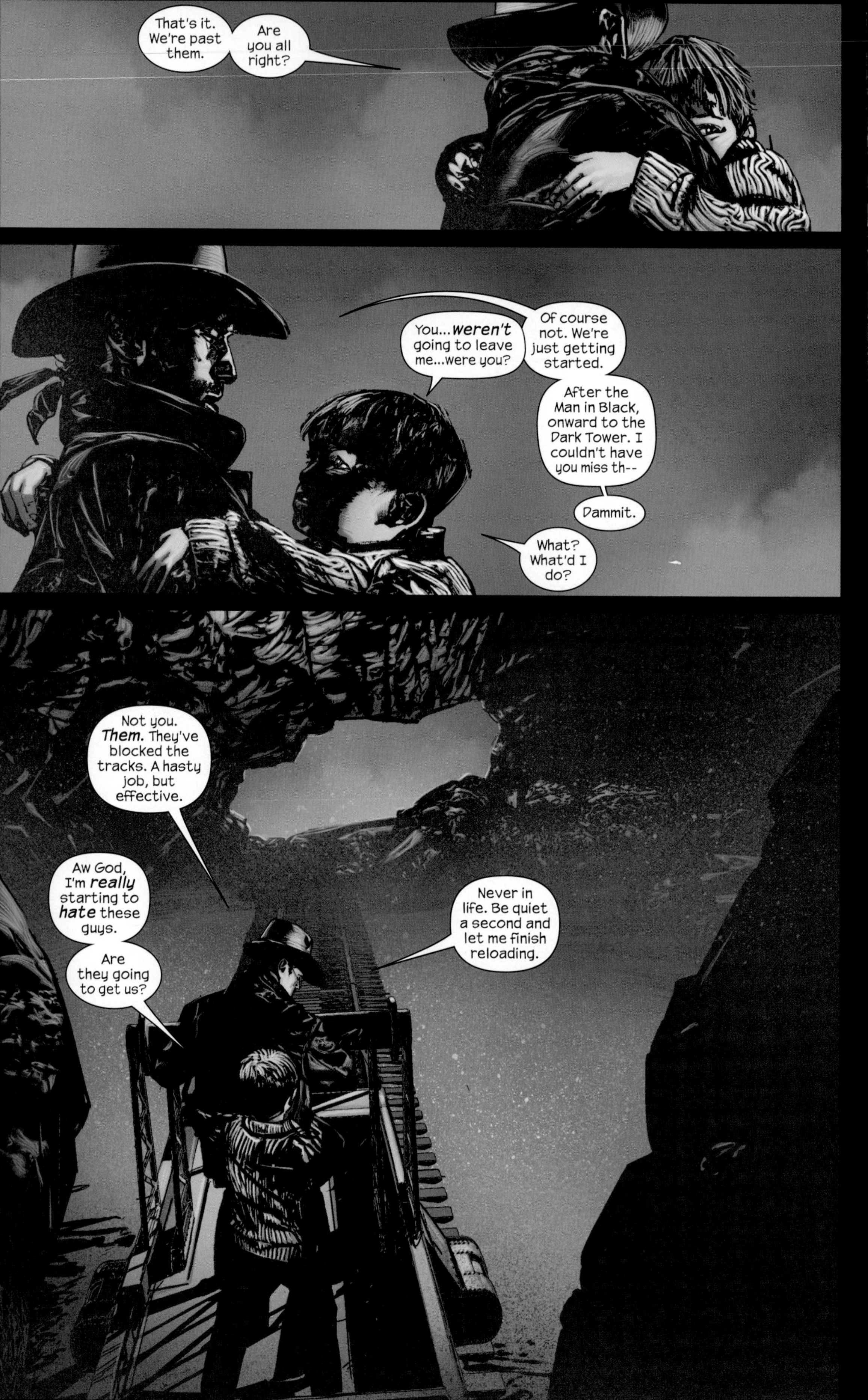
That's it. We're past them.
Are you all right?
You... *weren't* going to leave me...were you?
Of course not. We're just getting started.
After the Man in Black, onward to the Dark Tower. I couldn't have you miss th--
Dammit.
What? What'd I do?
Not you. *Them.* They've blocked the tracks. A hasty job, but effective.
Aw God, I'm *really* starting to *hate* these guys.
Are they going to get us?
Never in life. Be quiet a second and let me finish reloading.

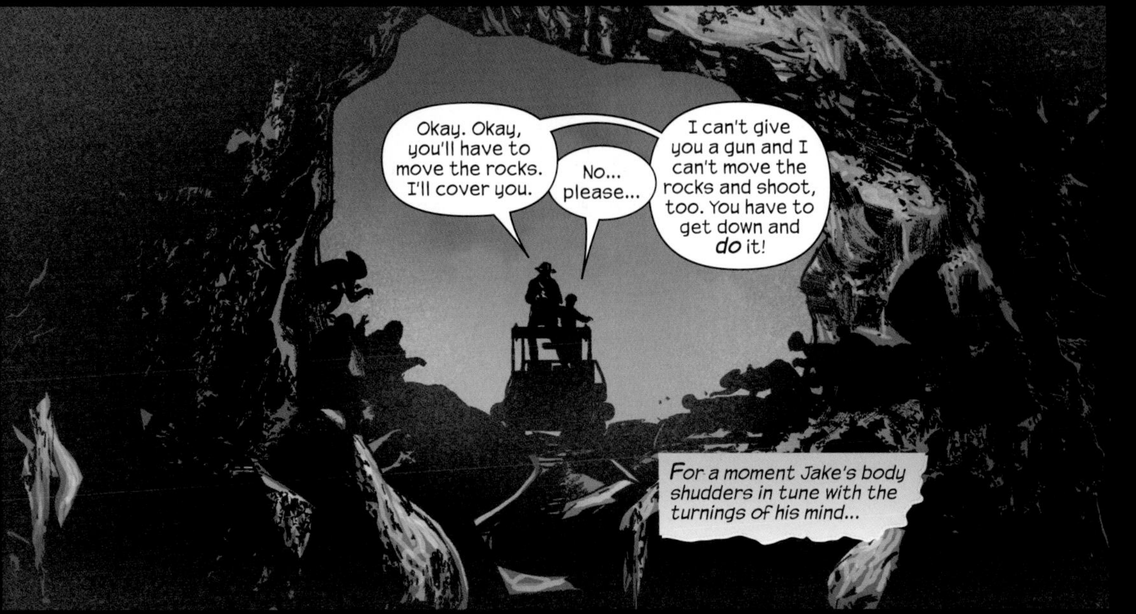
Okay. Okay, you'll have to move the rocks. I'll cover you.
No... please...
I can't give you a gun and I can't move the rocks and shoot, too. You have to get down and *do* it!
For a moment Jake's body shudders in tune with the turnings of his mind...

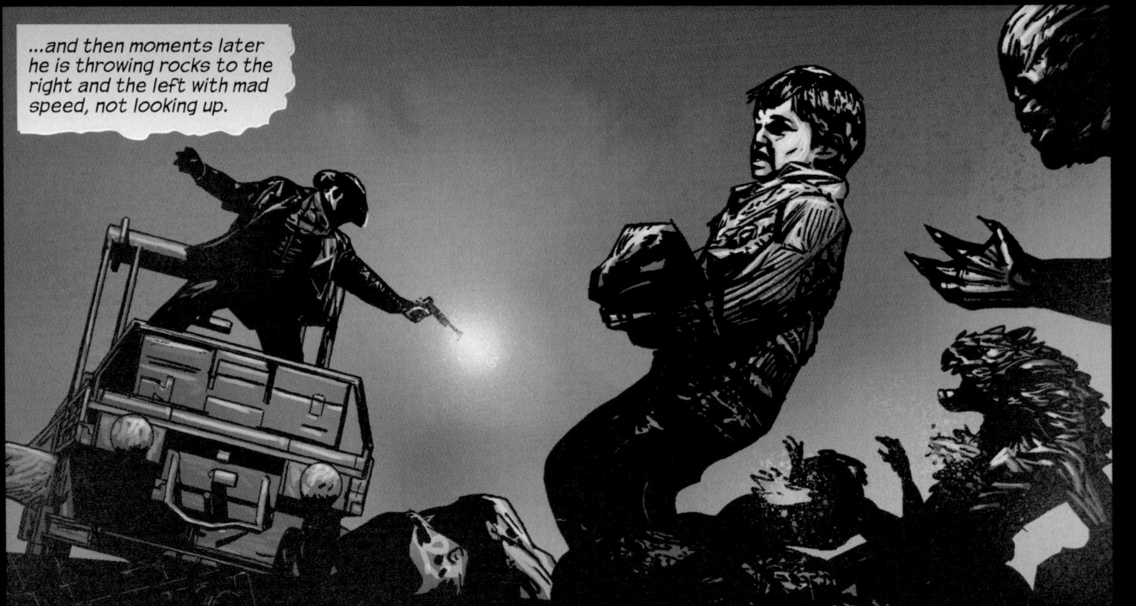
...and then moments later he is throwing rocks to the right and the left with mad speed, not looking up.

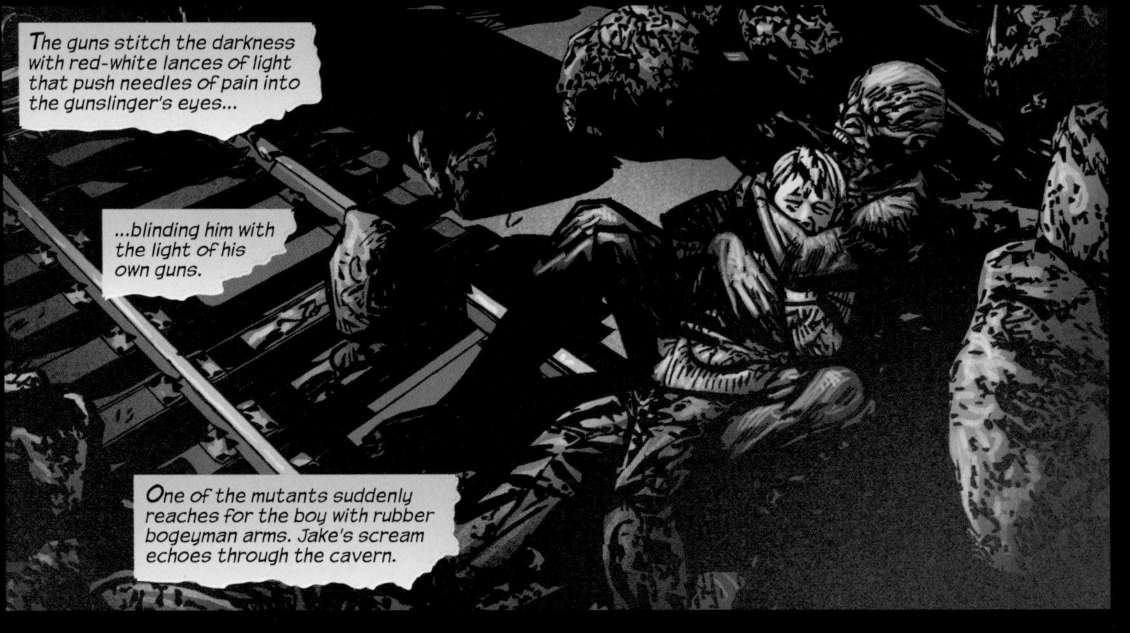
The guns stitch the darkness with red-white lances of light that push needles of pain into the gunslinger's eyes...
...blinding him with the light of his own guns.
One of the mutants suddenly reaches for the boy with rubber bogeyman arms. Jake's scream echoes through the cavern.

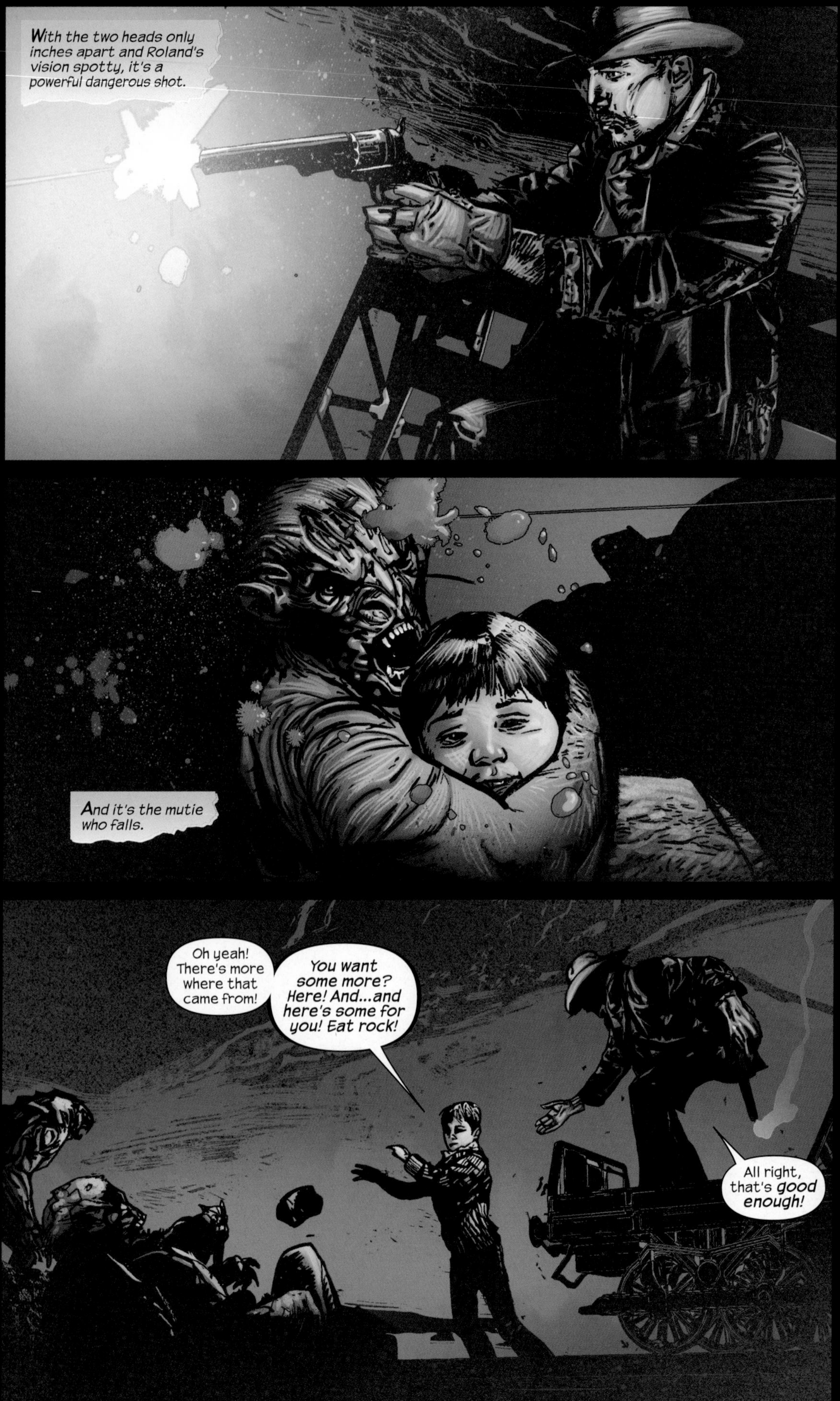
With the two heads only inches apart and Roland's vision spotty, it's a powerful dangerous shot.
And it's the mutie who falls.
Oh yeah! There's more where that came from!
You want some more? Here! And...and here's some for you! Eat rock!
All right, that's good enough!

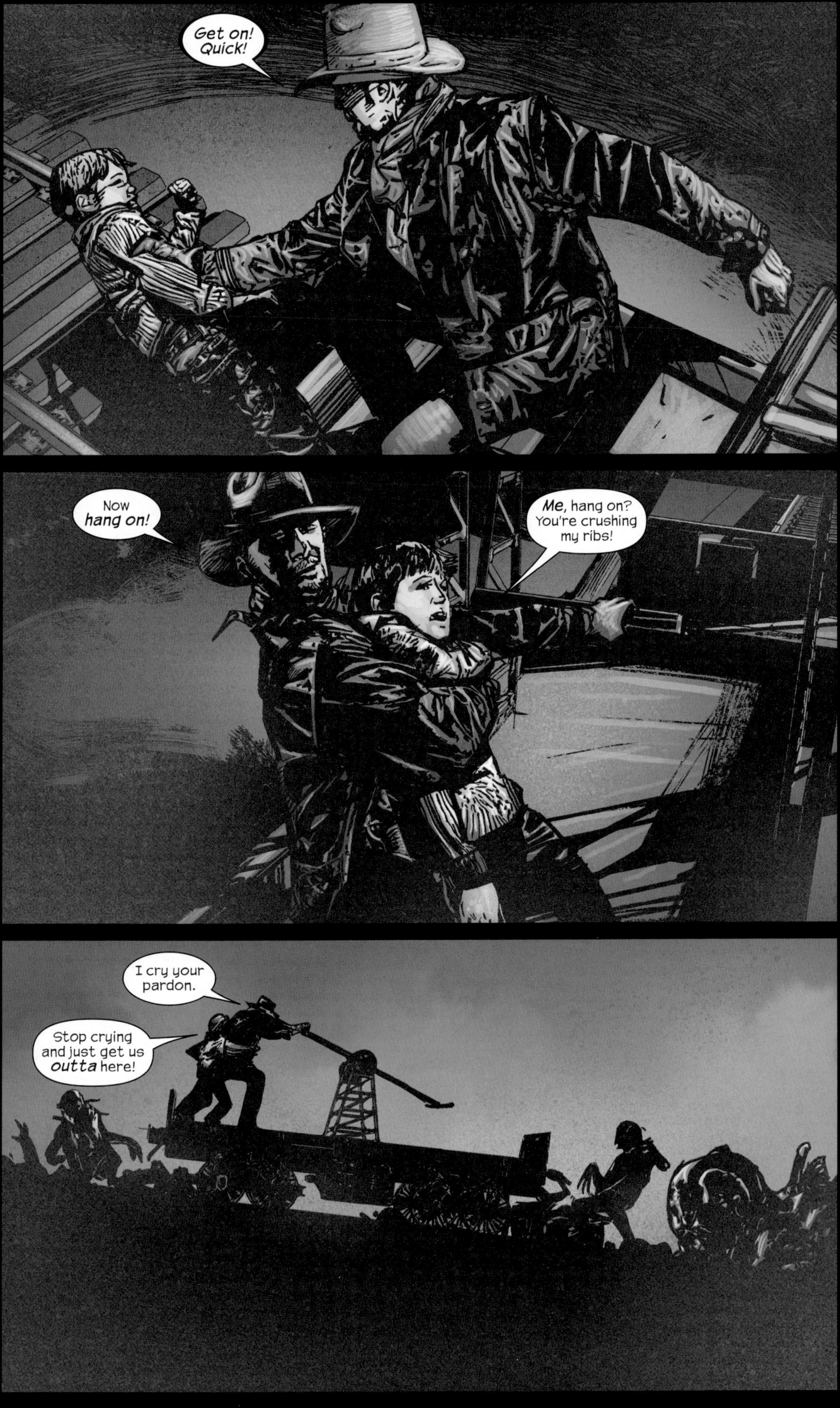
Get on! Quick!
Now *hang on!*
Me, hang on? You're crushing my ribs!
I cry your pardon.
Stop crying and just get us *outta* here!

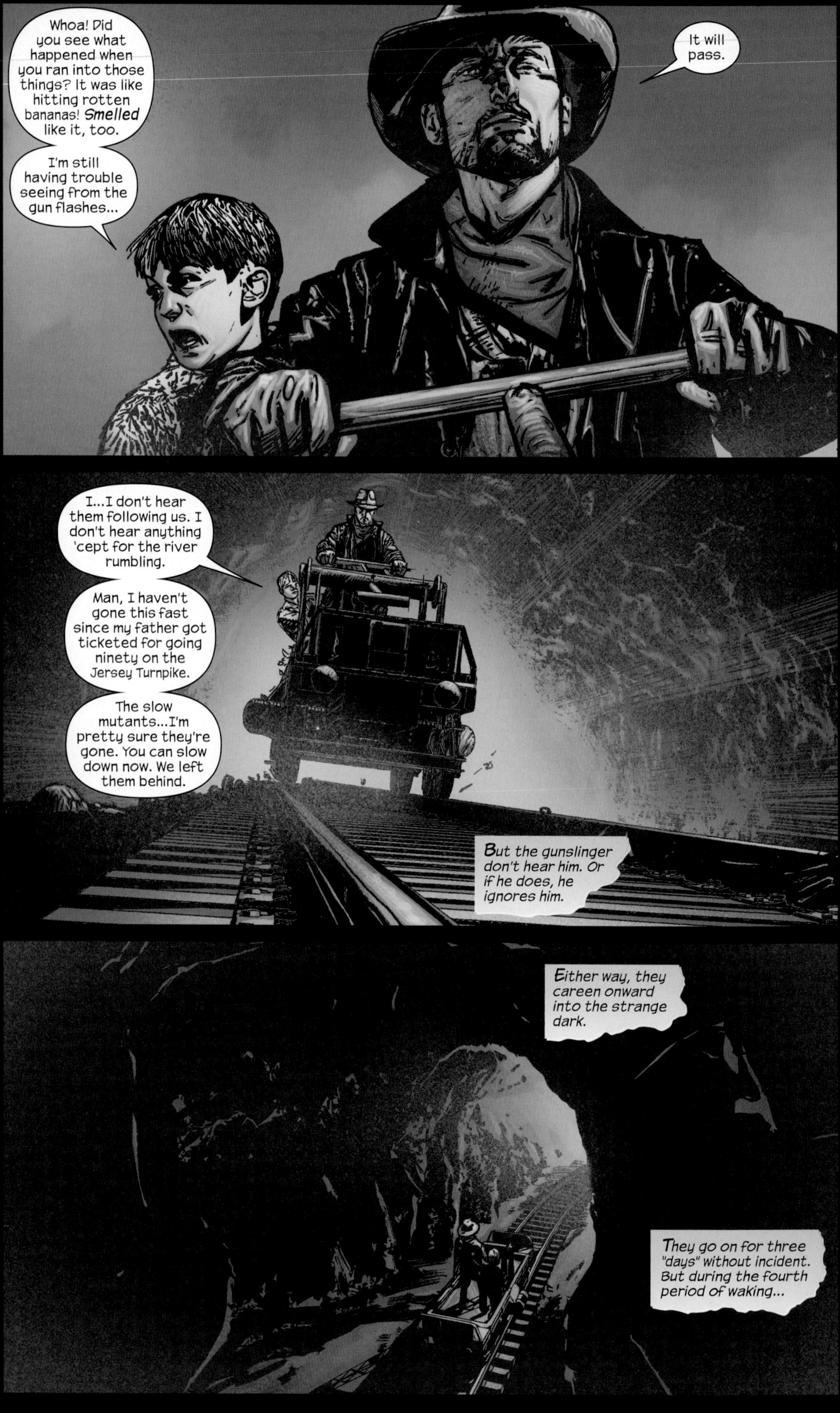
Whoa! Did you see what happened when you ran into those things? It was like hitting rotten bananas! *Smelled* like it, too.
It will pass.
I'm still having trouble seeing from the gun flashes...
I...I don't hear them following us. I don't hear anything 'cept for the river rumbling.
Man, I haven't gone this fast since my father got ticketed for going ninety on the Jersey Turnpike.
The slow mutants...I'm pretty sure they're gone. You can slow down now. We left them behind.
But the gunslinger don't hear him. Or if he does, he ignores him.
Either way, they careen onward into the strange dark.
They go on for three "days" without incident. But during the fourth period of waking...

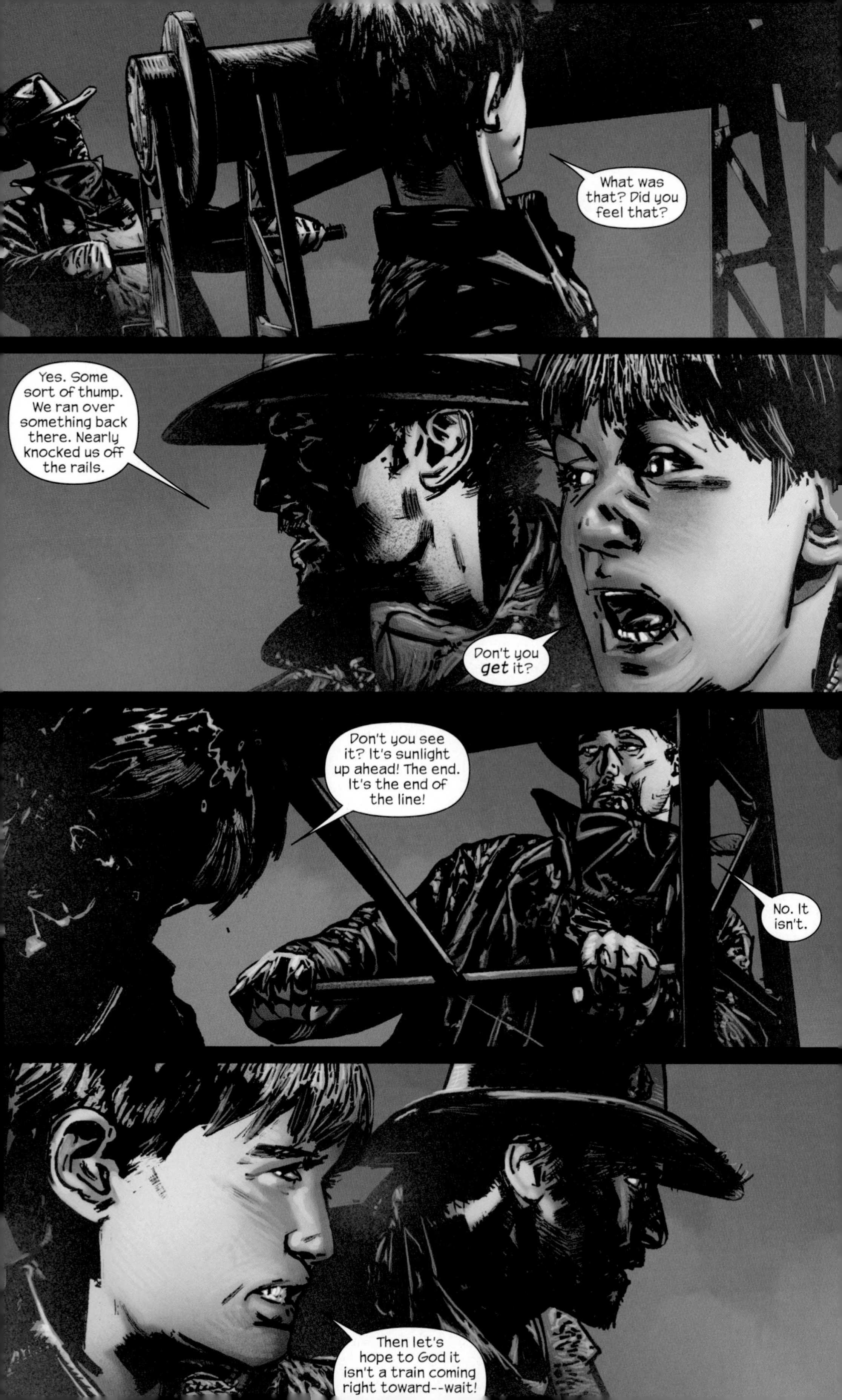

What was that? Did you feel that?
Yes. Some sort of thump. We ran over something back there. Nearly knocked us off the rails.
Don't you *get* it?
Don't you see it? It's sunlight up ahead! The end. It's the end of the line!
No. It isn't.
Then let's hope to God it isn't a train coming right toward--wait!

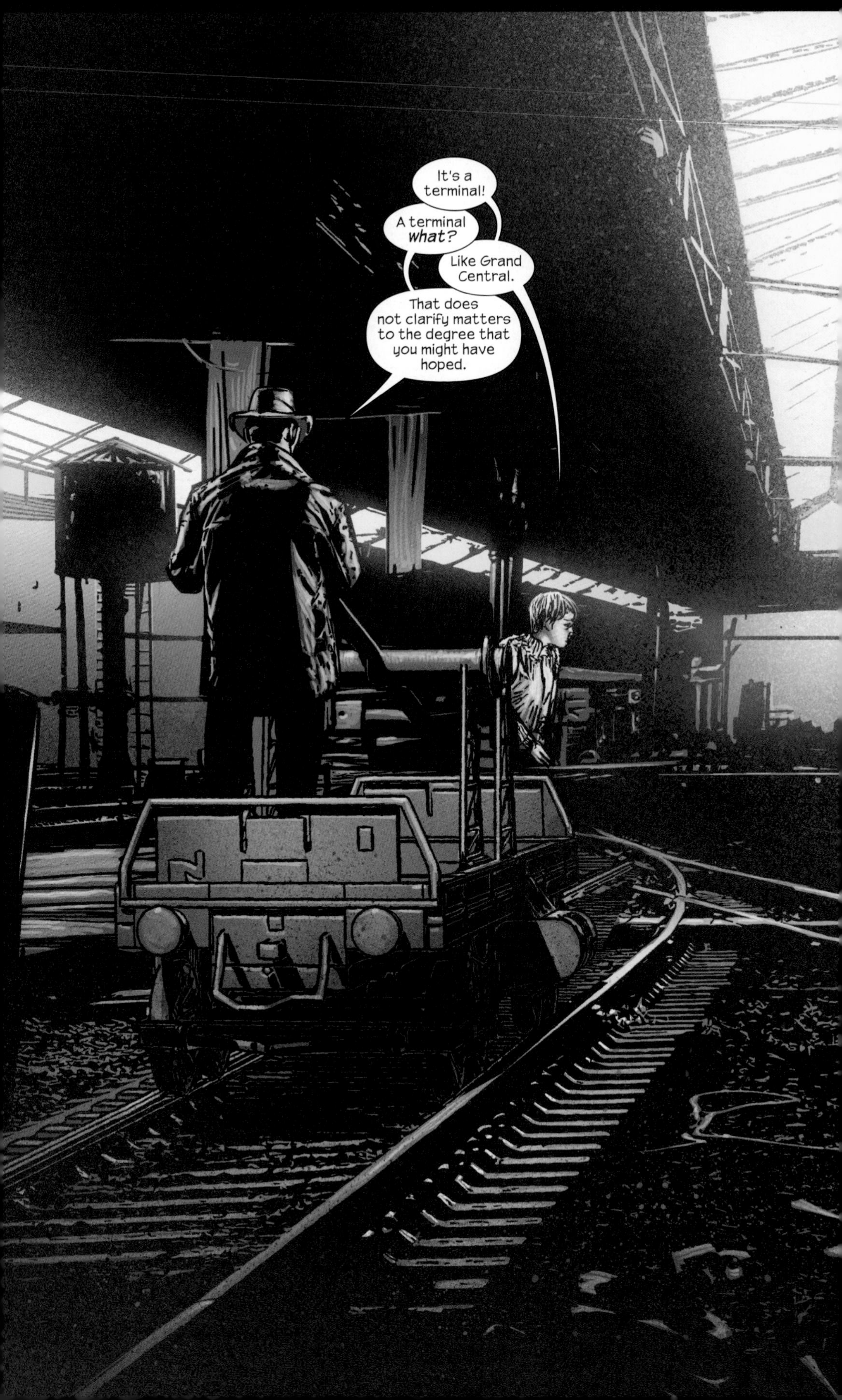
It's a terminal!
A terminal *what?*
Like Grand Central.
That does not clarify matters to the degree that you might have hoped.

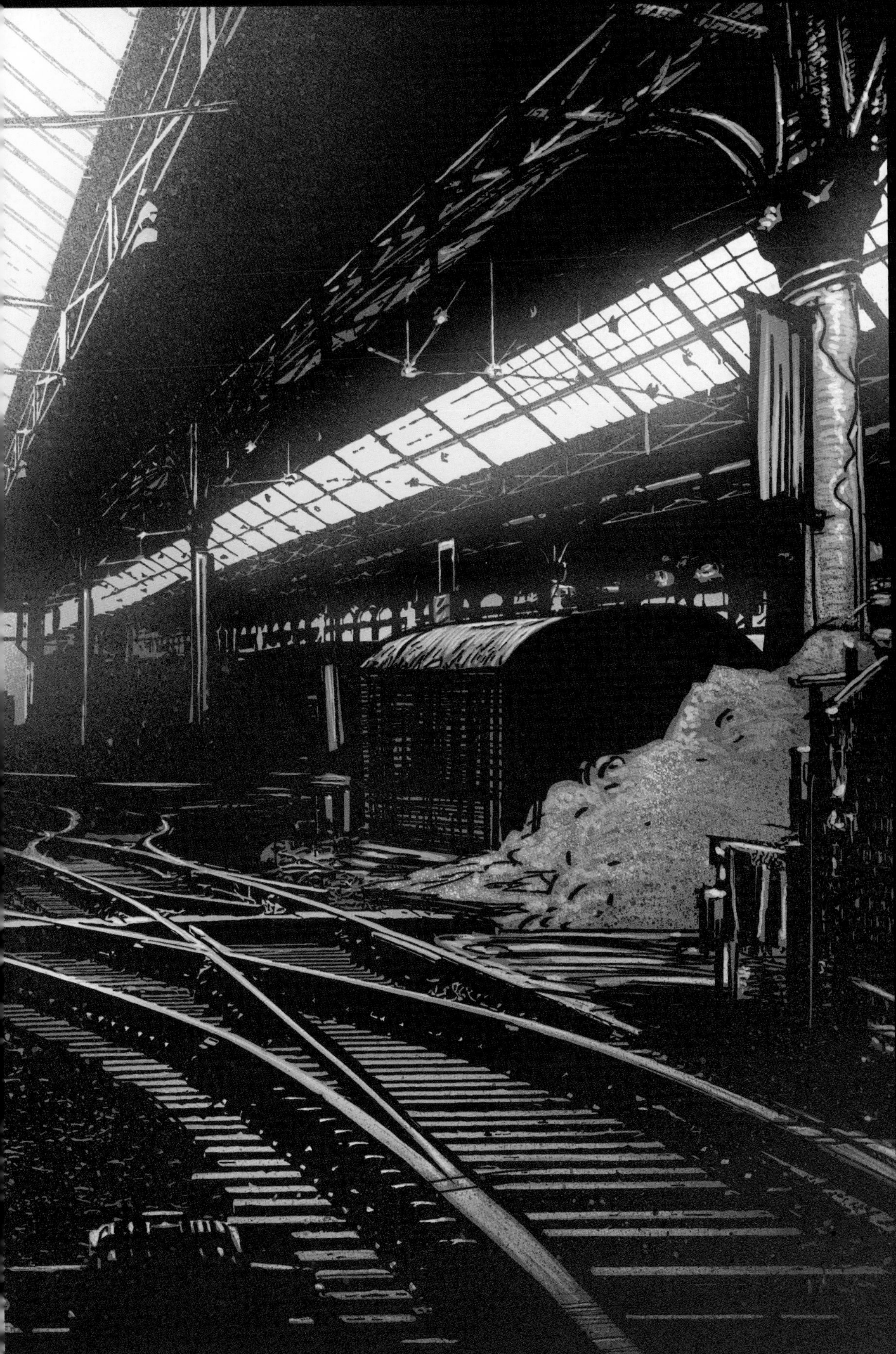

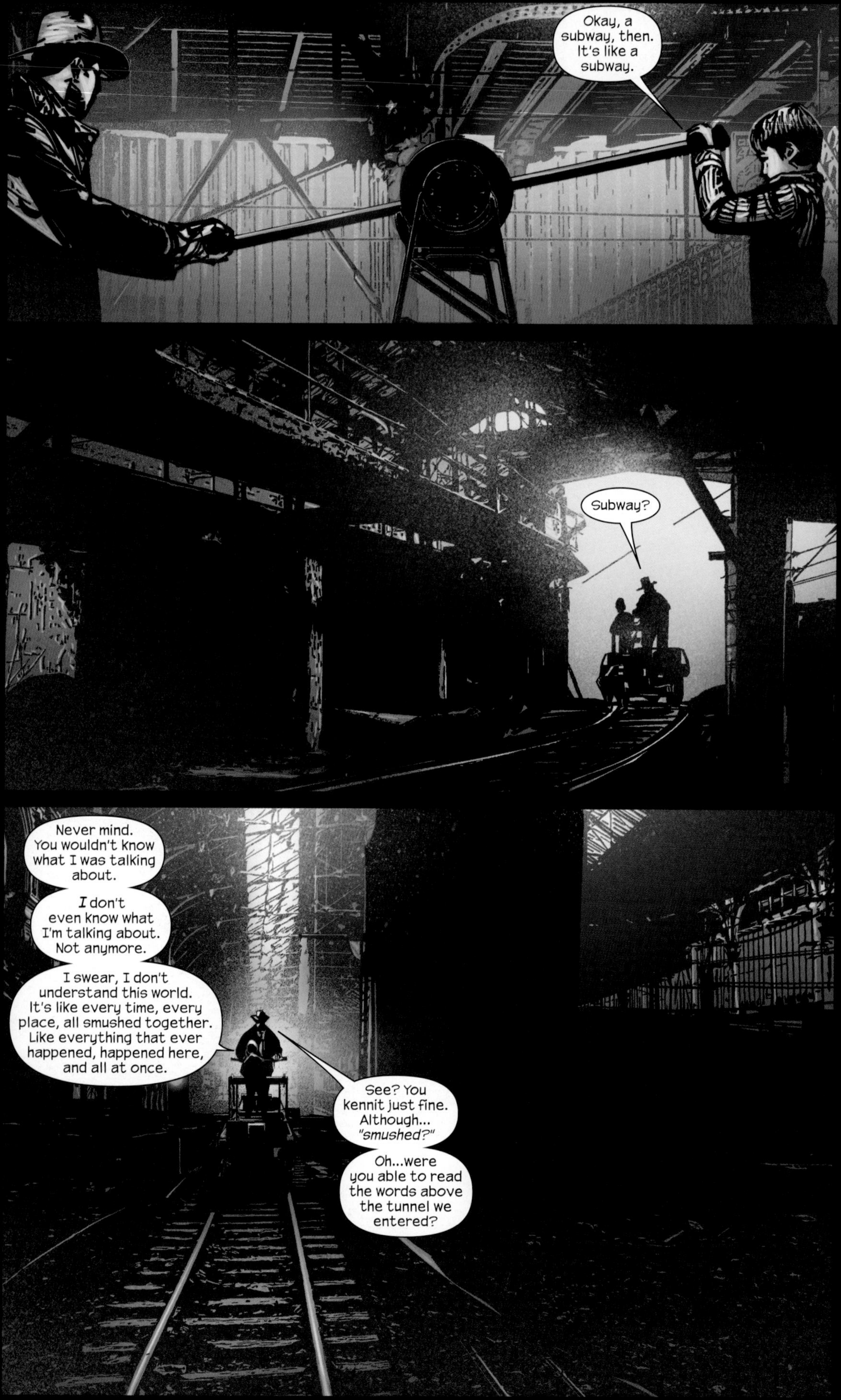
Okay, a subway, then. It's like a subway.
Subway?
Never mind. You wouldn't know what I was talking about.
I don't even know what I'm talking about. Not anymore.
I swear, I don't understand this world. It's like every time, every place, all smushed together. Like everything that ever happened, happened here, and all at once.
See? You kennit just fine. Although... *"smushed?"*
Oh...were you able to read the words above the tunnel we entered?

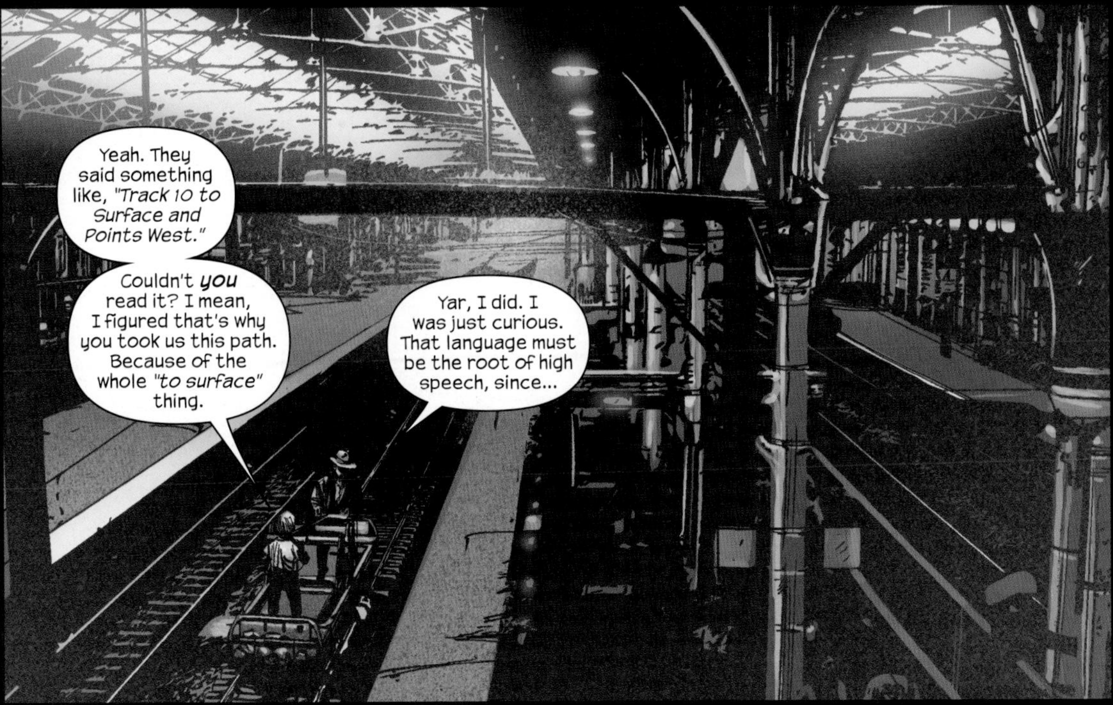
Yeah. They said something like, "Track 10 to Surface and Points West."
Couldn't *you* read it? I mean, I figured that's why you took us this path. Because of the whole "to surface" thing.
Yar, I did. I was just curious. That language must be the root of high speech, since...

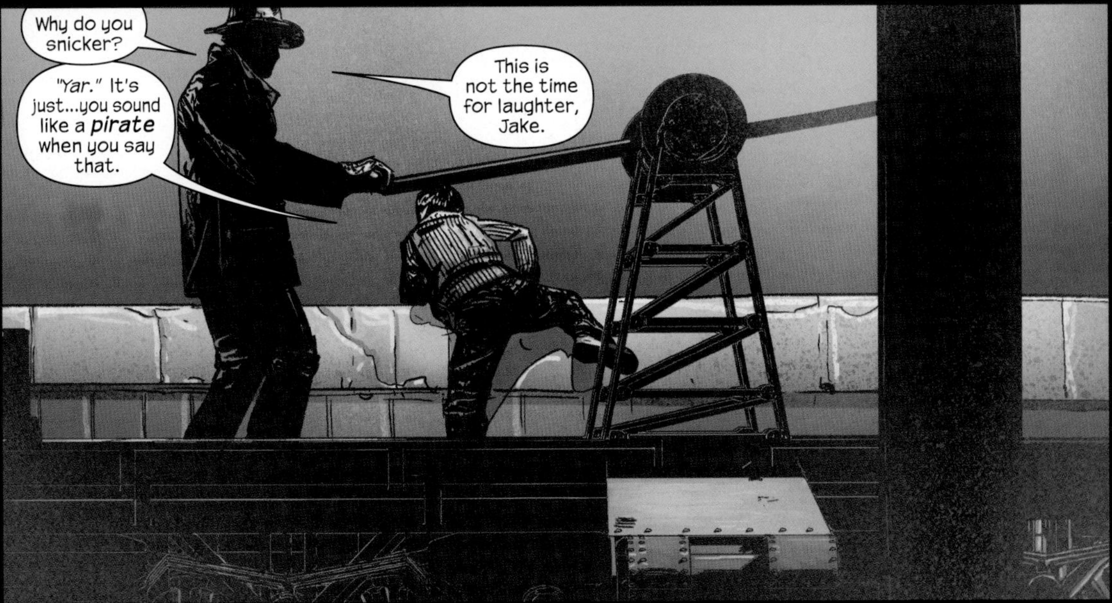
Why do you snicker?
"Yar." It's just...you sound like a *pirate* when you say that.
This is not the time for laughter, Jake.

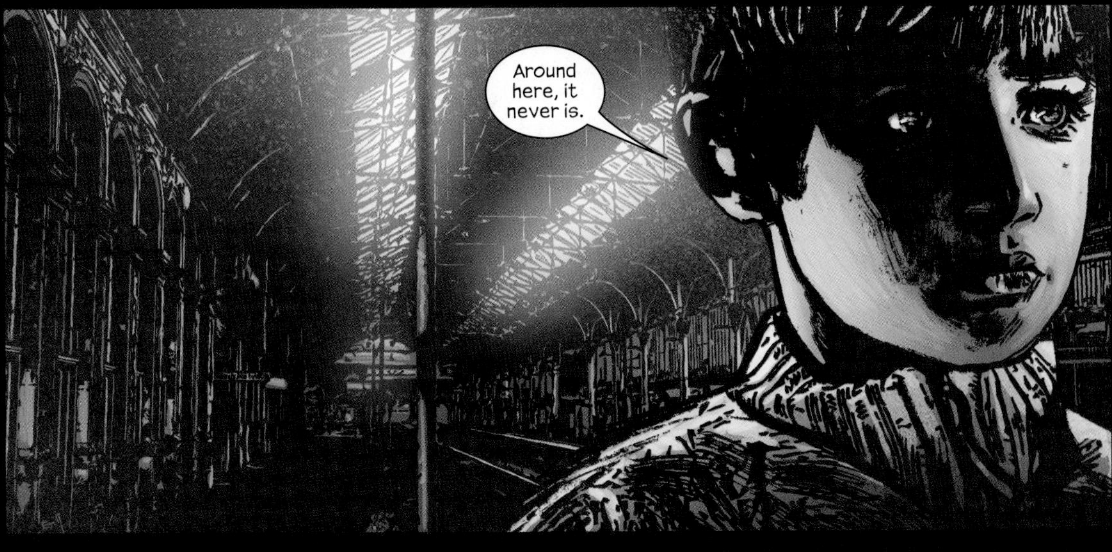
Around here, it never is.

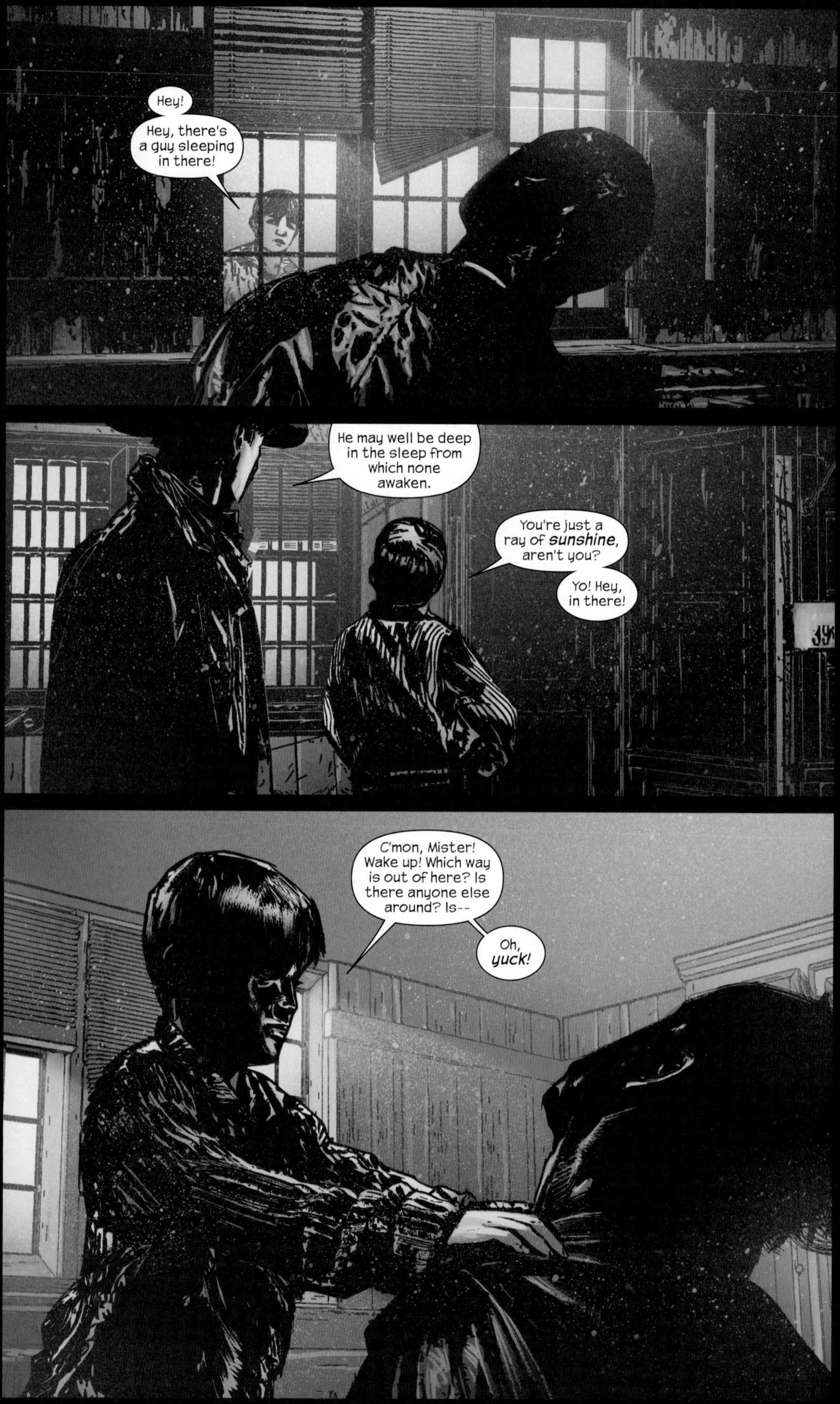
Hey!
Hey, there's a guy sleeping in there!
He may well be deep in the sleep from which none awaken.
You're just a ray of *sunshine*, aren't you?
Yo! Hey, in there!
C'mon, Mister! Wake up! Which way is out of here? Is there anyone else around? Is--
Oh, *yuck!*

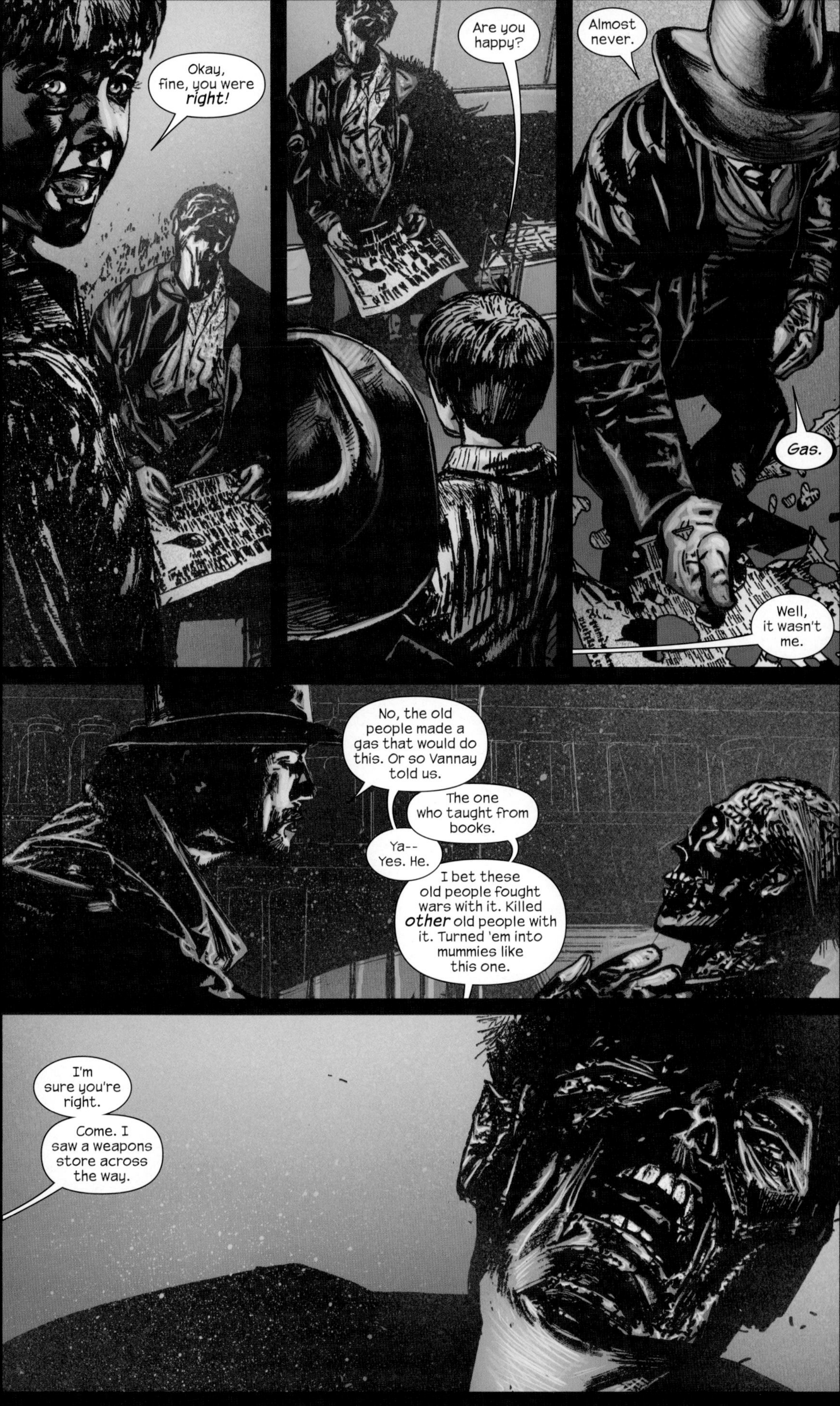
Okay, fine, you were *right!*
Are you happy?
Almost never.
Gas.
Well, it wasn't me.
No, the old people made a gas that would do this. Or so Vannay told us.
The one who taught from books.
Ya-- Yes. He.
I bet these old people fought wars with it. Killed *other* old people with it. Turned 'em into mummies like this one.
I'm sure you're right.
Come. I saw a weapons store across the way.

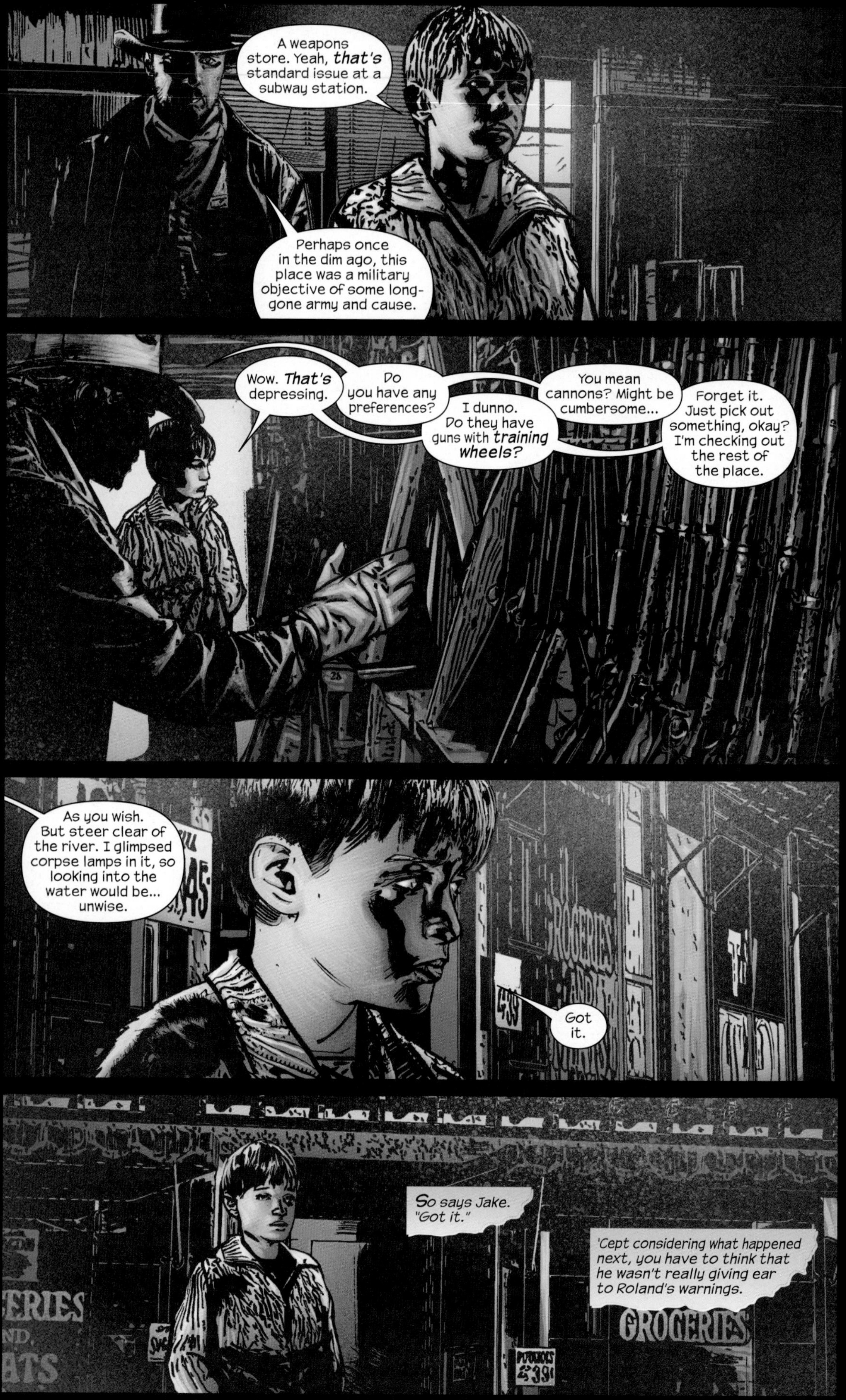
A weapons store. Yeah, *that's* standard issue at a subway station.
Perhaps once in the dim ago, this place was a military objective of some long-gone army and cause.
Wow. *That's* depressing.
Do you have any preferences?
I dunno. Do they have guns with *training wheels?*
You mean cannons? Might be cumbersome...
Forget it. Just pick out something, okay? I'm checking out the rest of the place.
As you wish. But steer clear of the river. I glimpsed corpse lamps in it, so looking into the water would be... unwise.
Got it.
So says Jake. "Got it."
'Cept considering what happened next, you have to think that he wasn't really giving ear to Roland's warnings.
GROCERIES

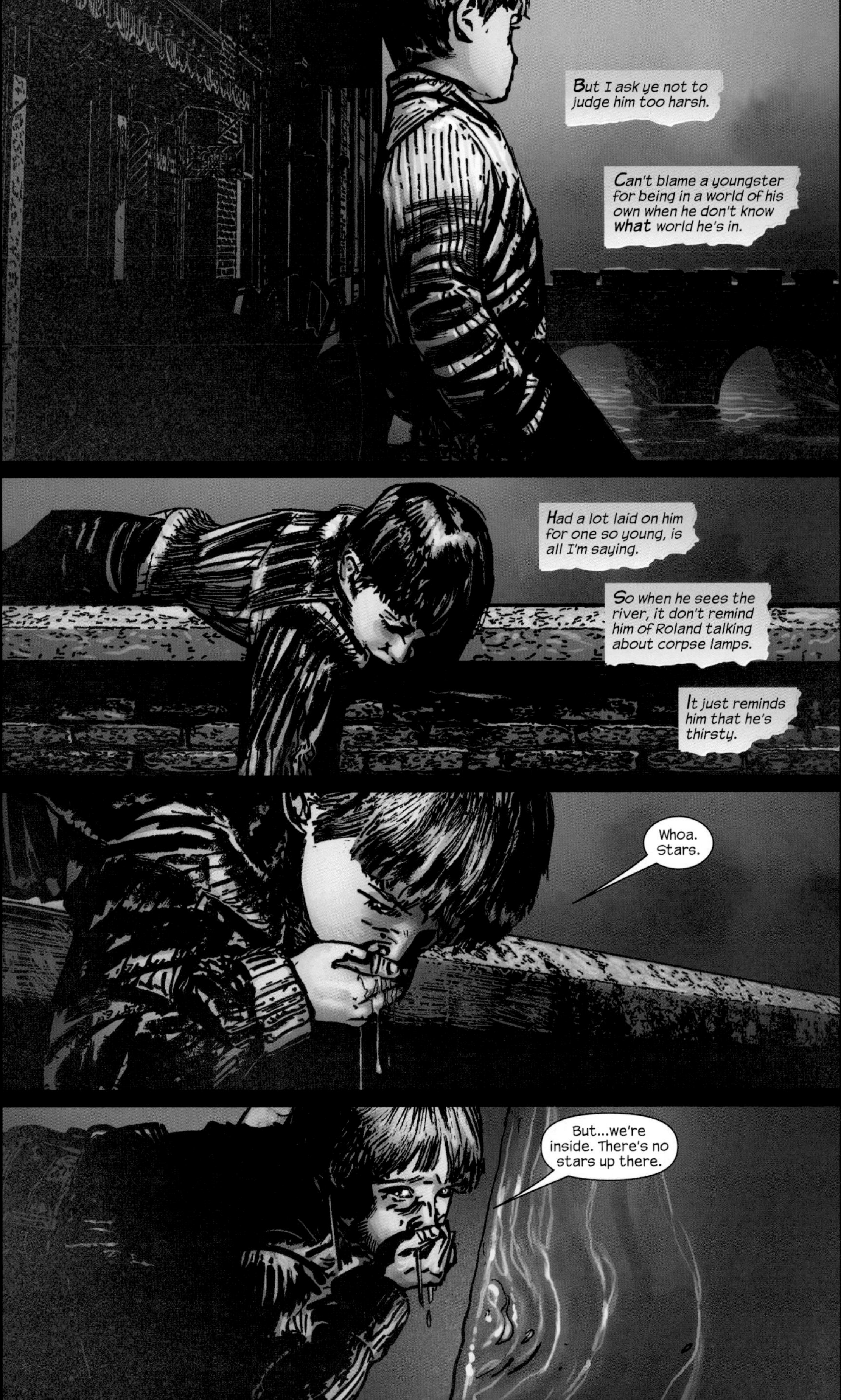
But I ask ye not to judge him too harsh.
Can't blame a youngster for being in a world of his own when he don't know what world he's in.
Had a lot laid on him for one so young, is all I'm saying.
So when he sees the river, it don't remind him of Roland talking about corpse lamps.
It just reminds him that he's thirsty.
Whoa. Stars.
But...we're inside. There's no stars up there.

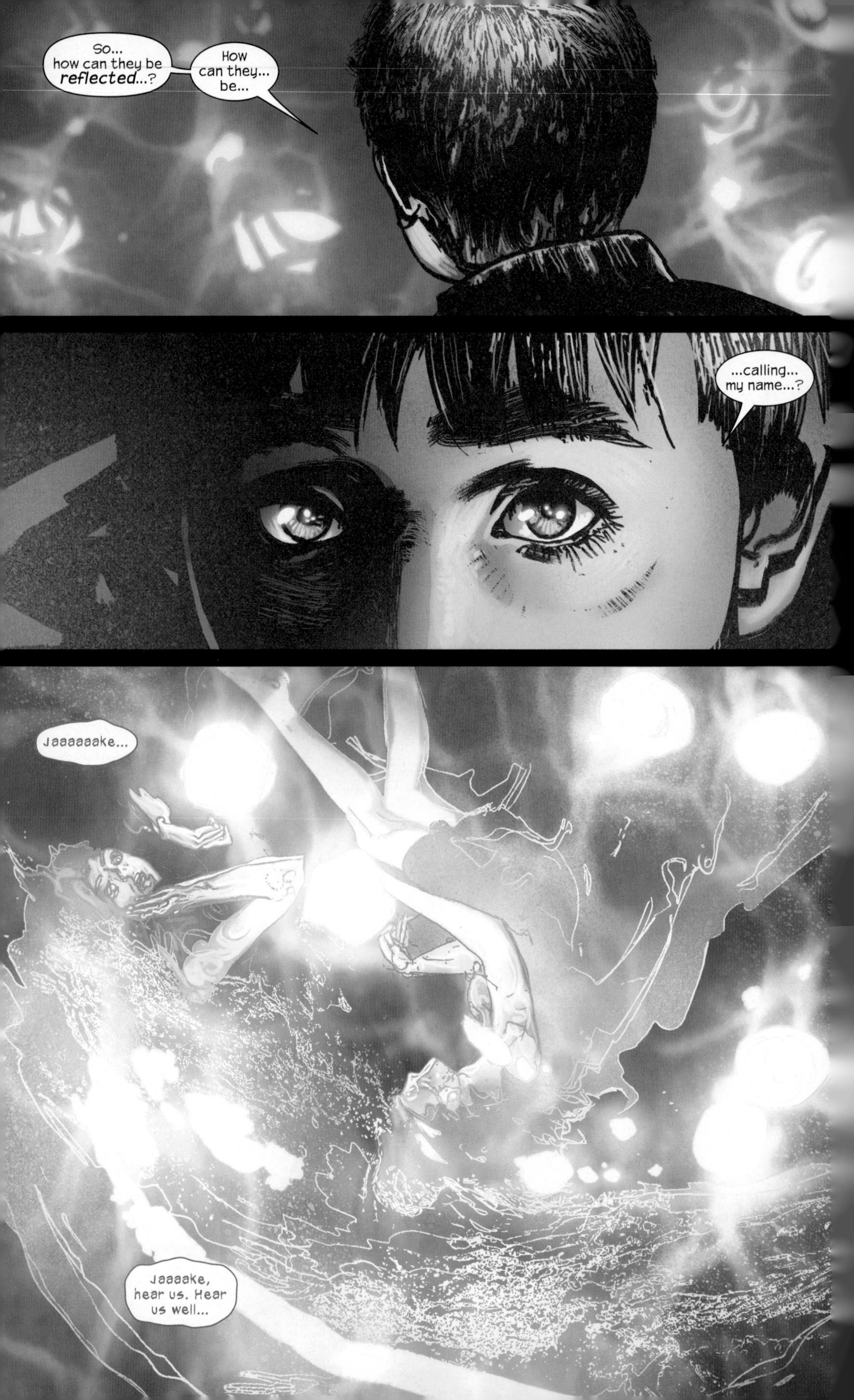
So... how can they be reflected...?
How can they... be...
...calling... my name...?
Jaaaaaake...
Jaaaake, hear us. Hear us well...

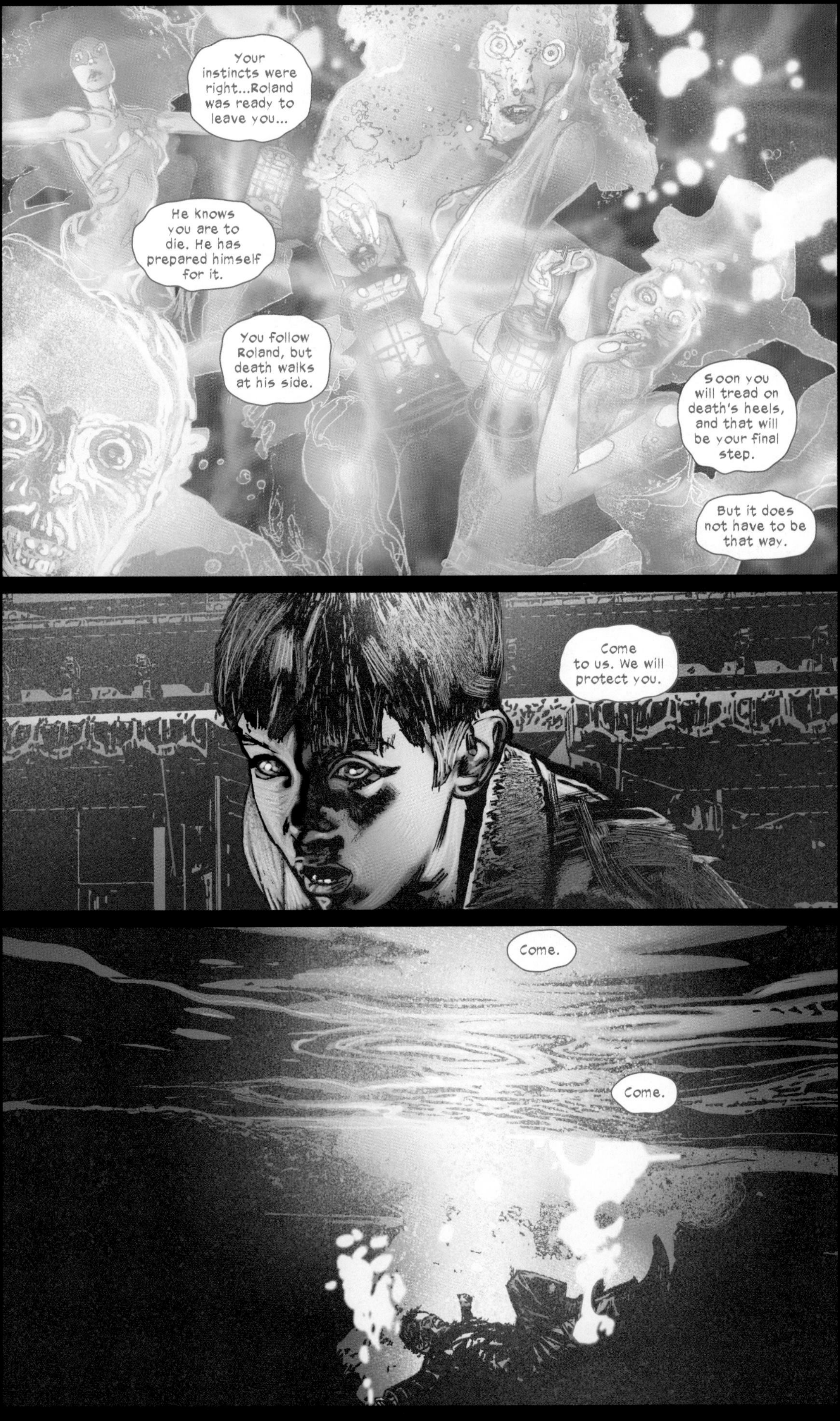
Your instincts were right...Roland was ready to leave you...
He knows you are to die. He has prepared himself for it.
You follow Roland, but death walks at his side.
Soon you will tread on death's heels, and that will be your final step.
But it does not have to be that way.
Come to us. We will protect you.
Come.
Come.

STEPHEN KING

THE DARK TOWER
~ THE GUNSLINGER ~

THE MAN IN BLACK

CHAPTER FOUR

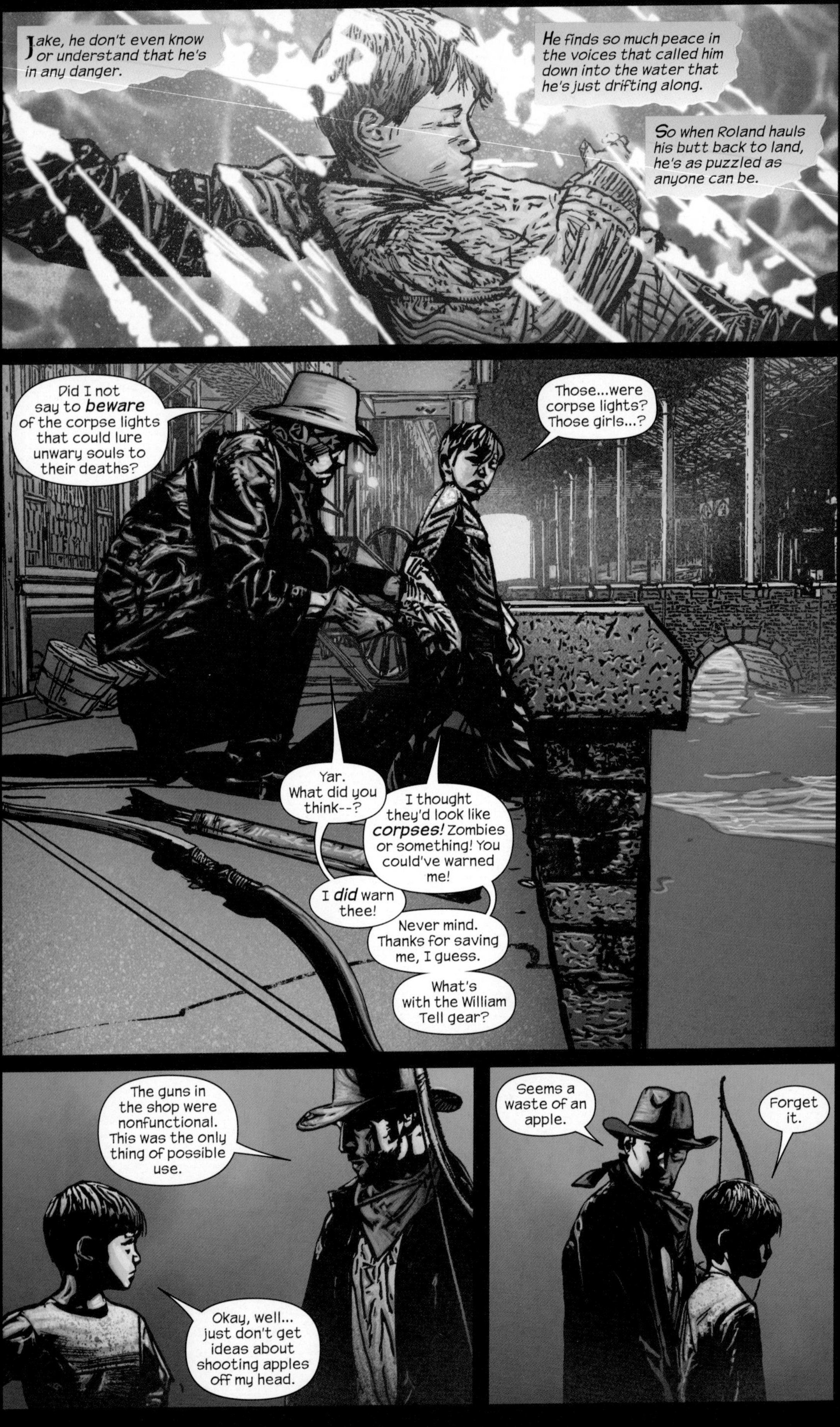
Jake, he don't even know or understand that he's in any danger.
He finds so much peace in the voices that called him down into the water that he's just drifting along.
So when Roland hauls his butt back to land, he's as puzzled as anyone can be.
Did I not say to beware of the corpse lights that could lure unwary souls to their deaths?
Those...were corpse lights? Those girls...?
Yar. What did you think--?
I thought they'd look like corpses! Zombies or something! You could've warned me!
I did warn thee!
Never mind. Thanks for saving me, I guess.
What's with the William Tell gear?
The guns in the shop were nonfunctional. This was the only thing of possible use.
Okay, well... just don't get ideas about shooting apples off my head.
Seems a waste of an apple.
Forget it.

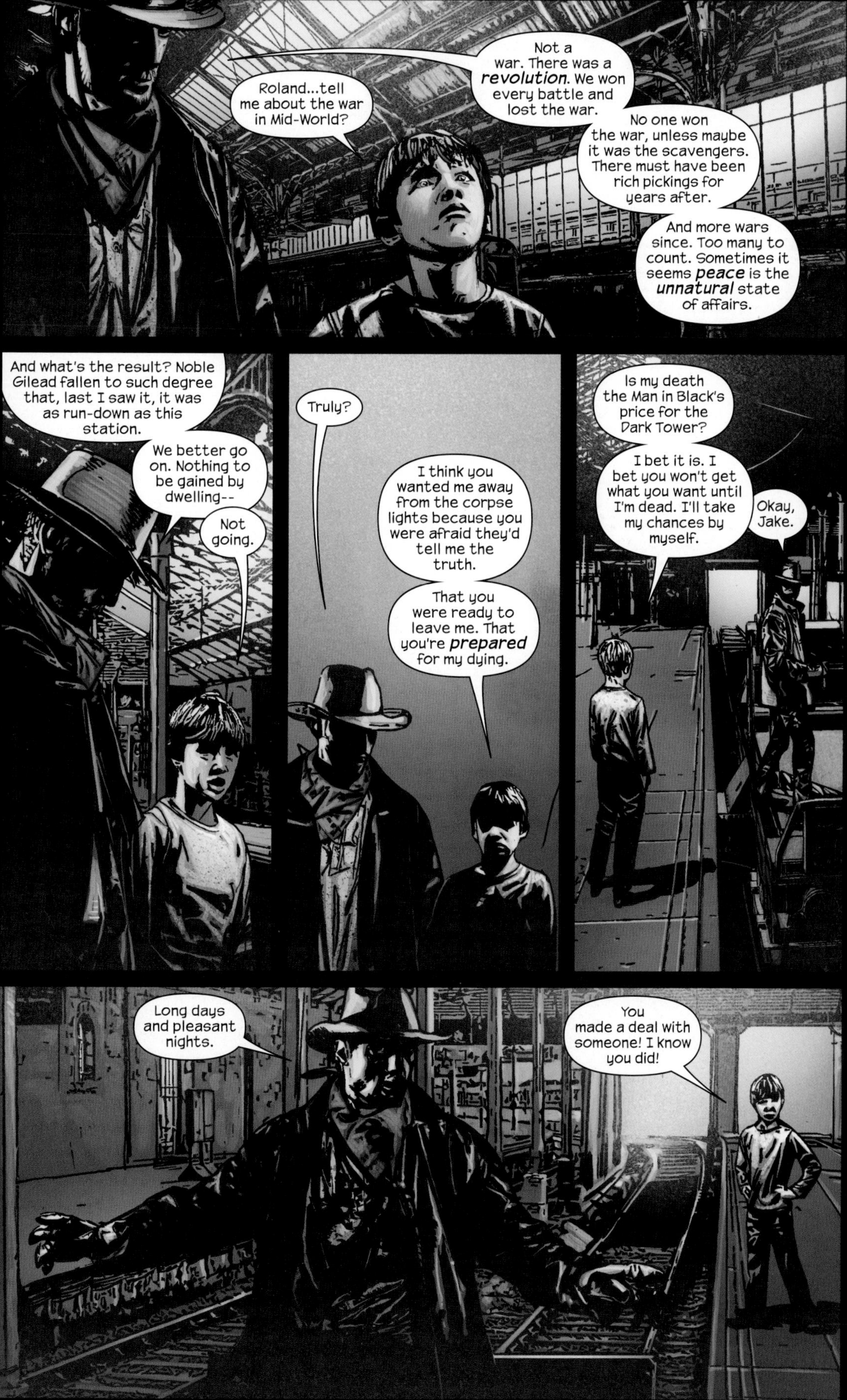
Roland...tell me about the war in Mid-World?
Not a war. There was a revolution. We won every battle and lost the war.
No one won the war, unless maybe it was the scavengers. There must have been rich pickings for years after.
And more wars since. Too many to count. Sometimes it seems peace is the unnatural state of affairs.
And what's the result? Noble Gilead fallen to such degree that, last I saw it, it was as run-down as this station.
We better go on. Nothing to be gained by dwelling--
Not going.
Truly?
I think you wanted me away from the corpse lights because you were afraid they'd tell me the truth.
That you were ready to leave me. That you're prepared for my dying.
Is my death the Man in Black's price for the Dark Tower?
I bet it is. I bet you won't get what you want until I'm dead. I'll take my chances by myself.
Okay, Jake.
Long days and pleasant nights.
You made a deal with someone! I know you did!

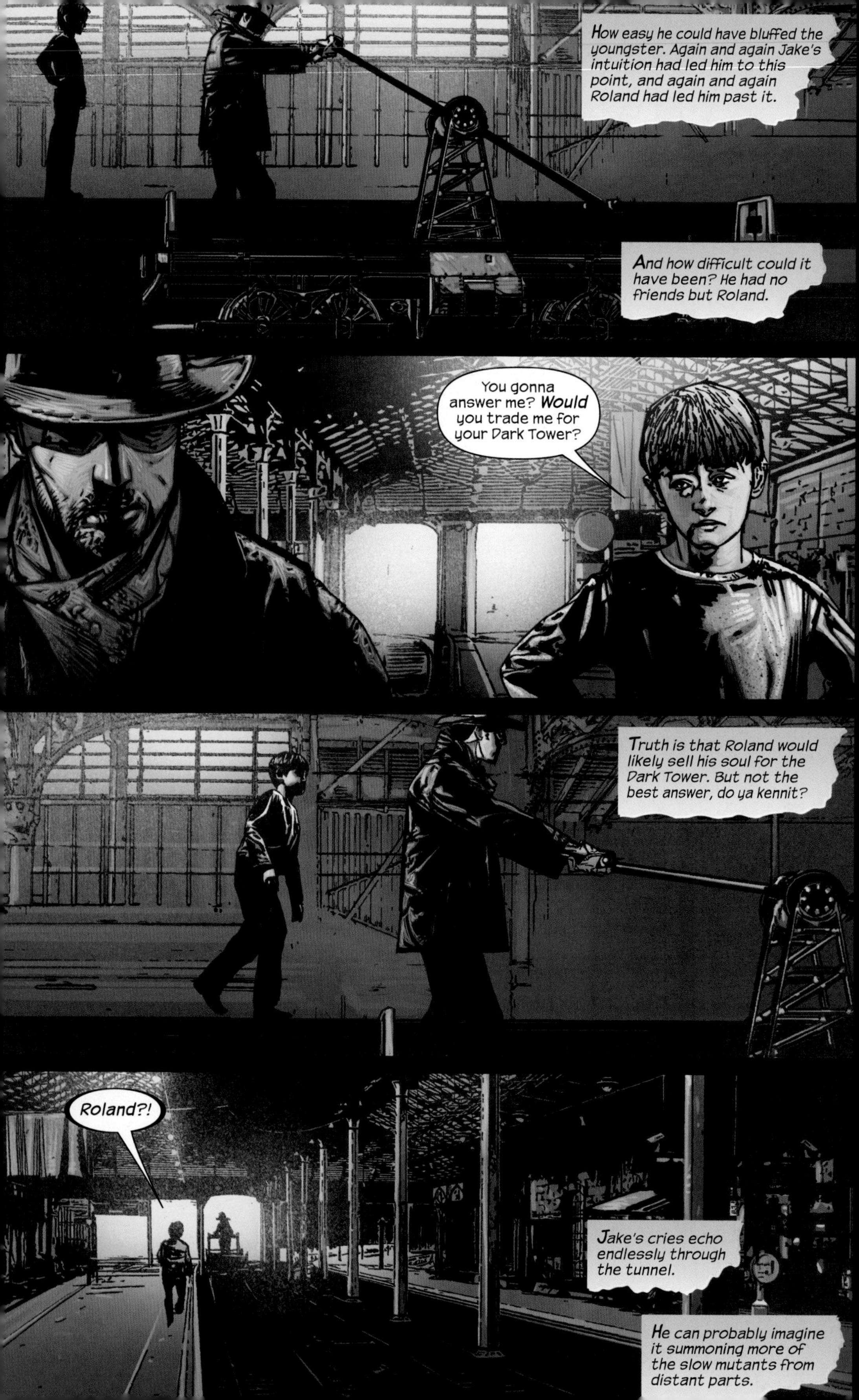
How easy he could have bluffed the youngster. Again and again Jake's intuition had led him to this point, and again and again Roland had led him past it.
And how difficult could it have been? He had no friends but Roland.
You gonna answer me? Would you trade me for your Dark Tower?
Truth is that Roland would likely sell his soul for the Dark Tower. But not the best answer, do ya kennit?
Roland?!
Jake's cries echo endlessly through the tunnel.
He can probably imagine it summoning more of the slow mutants from distant parts.

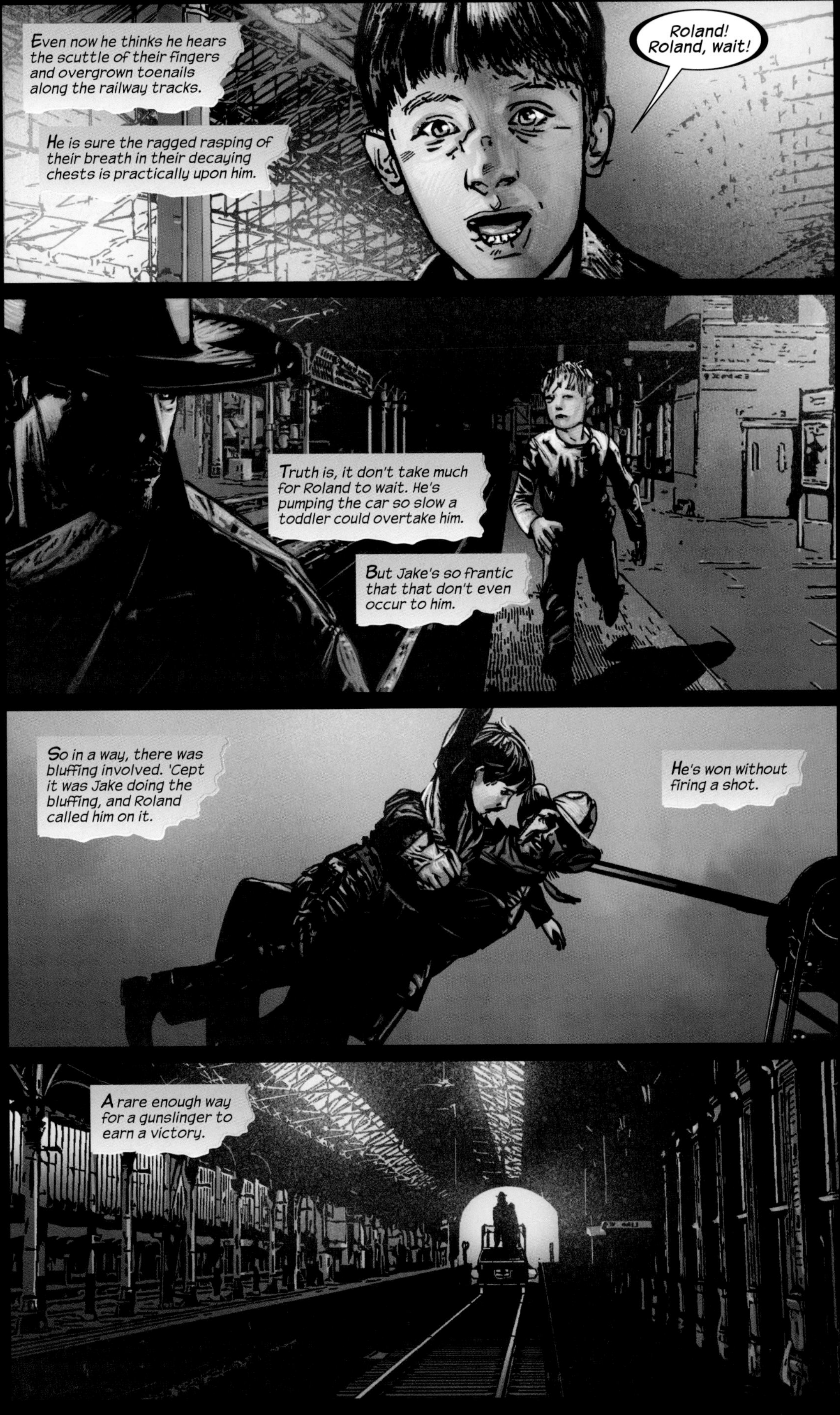
Even now he thinks he hears the scuttle of their fingers and overgrown toenails along the railway tracks.
He is sure the ragged rasping of their breath in their decaying chests is practically upon him.
Roland! Roland, wait!
Truth is, it don't take much for Roland to wait. He's pumping the car so slow a toddler could overtake him.
But Jake's so frantic that that don't even occur to him.
So in a way, there was bluffing involved. 'Cept it was Jake doing the bluffing, and Roland called him on it.
He's won without firing a shot.
A rare enough way for a gunslinger to earn a victory.

The sound of the river has become very loud, filling their heads with its thunder.

Why are you having *me* pump? What're you doing?

Trying to get an idea of what lies ahead.

The bow isn't worth much no matter how much I restring it, but I can probably get it to fly about sixty yards.

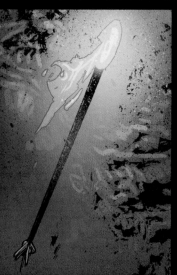

It went out, Roland.

Aye, it did. Means there's water, or at least moisture, up ahead.

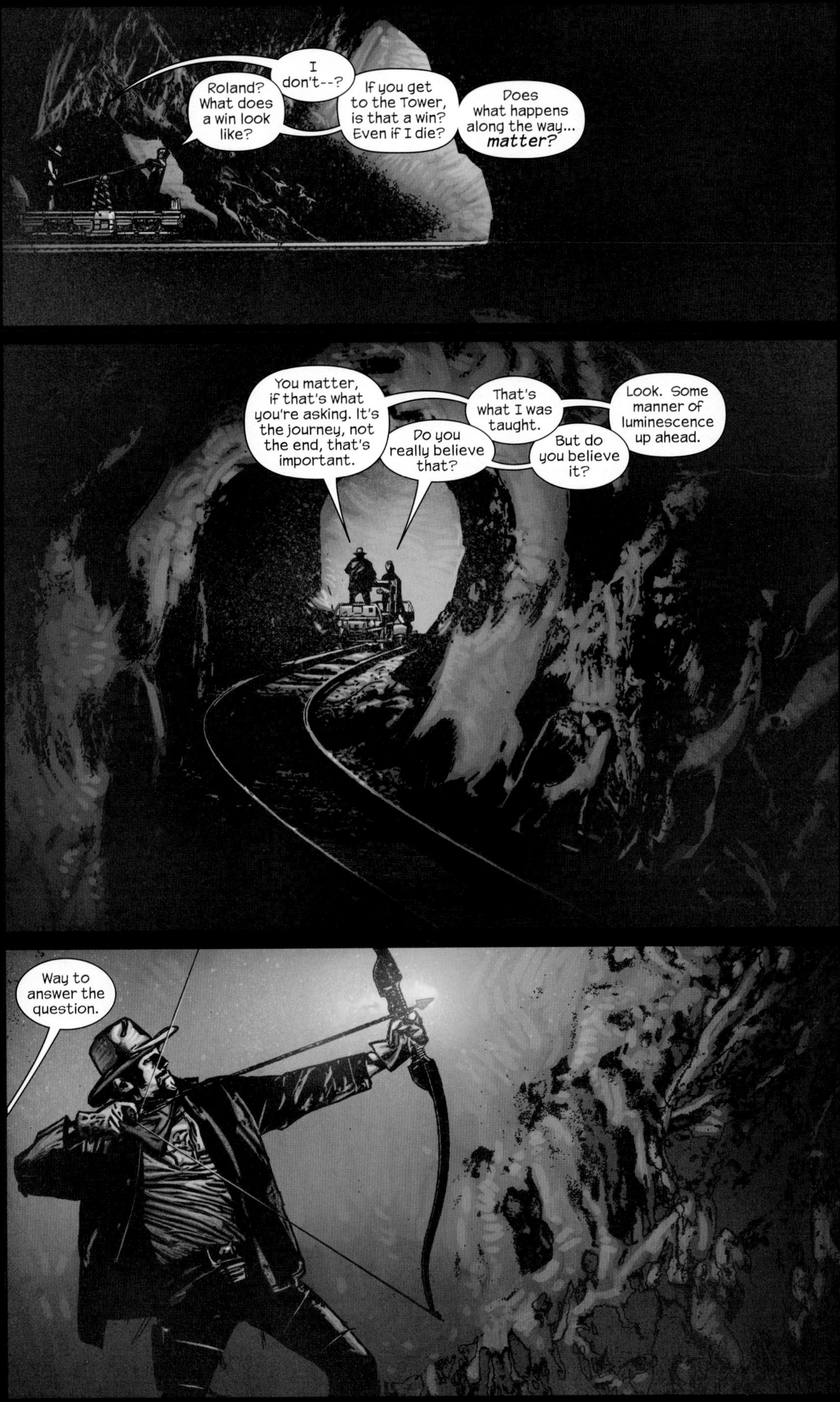
Roland? What does a win look like?
I don't--?
If you get to the Tower, is that a win? Even if I die?
Does what happens along the way... *matter?*
You matter, if that's what you're asking. It's the journey, not the end, that's important.
Do you really believe that?
That's what I was taught.
But do you believe it?
Look. Some manner of luminescence up ahead.
Way to answer the question.

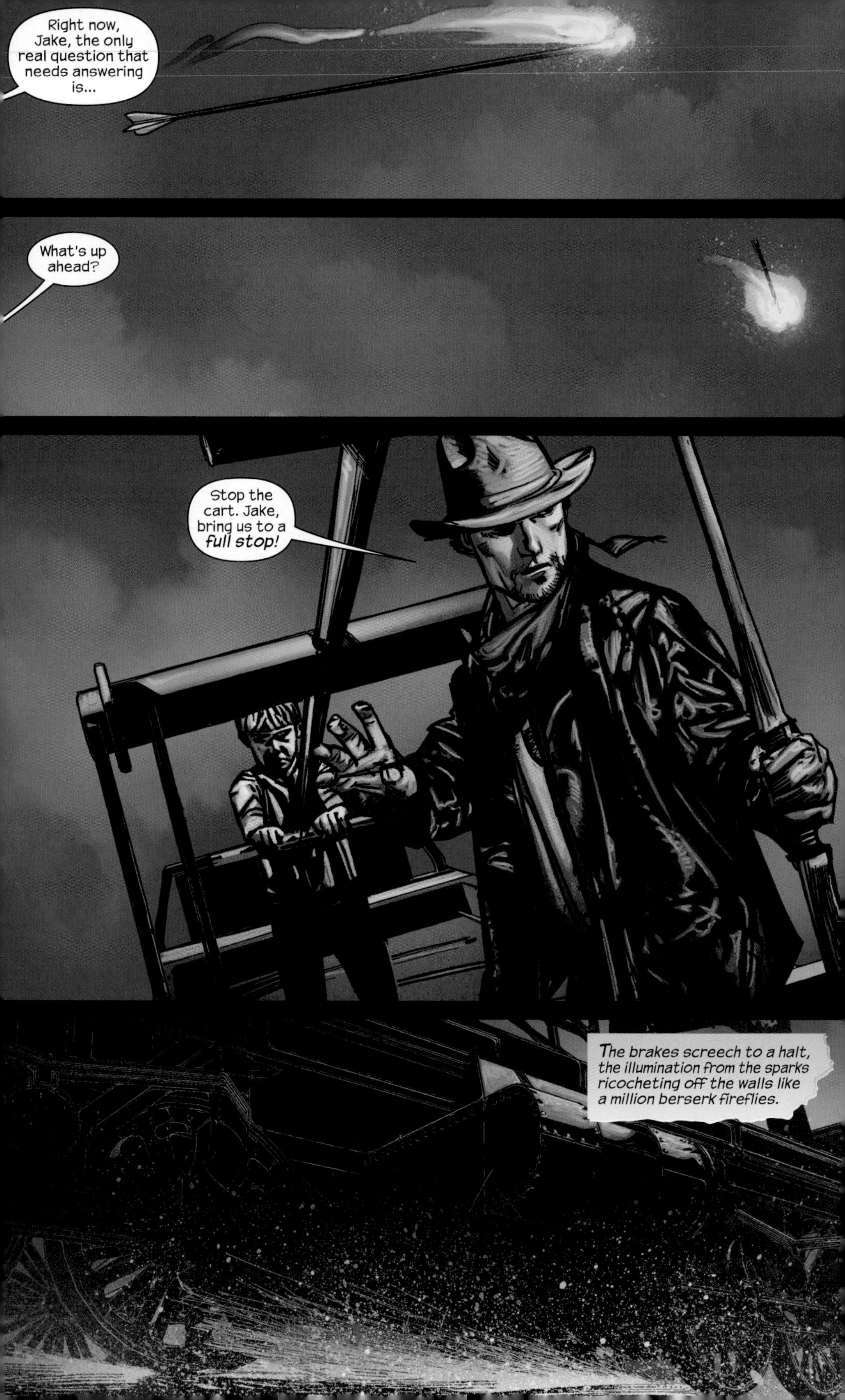
Right now, Jake, the only real question that needs answering is...
What's up ahead?
Stop the cart. Jake, bring us to a *full stop!*
The brakes screech to a halt, the illumination from the sparks ricocheting off the walls like a million berserk fireflies.

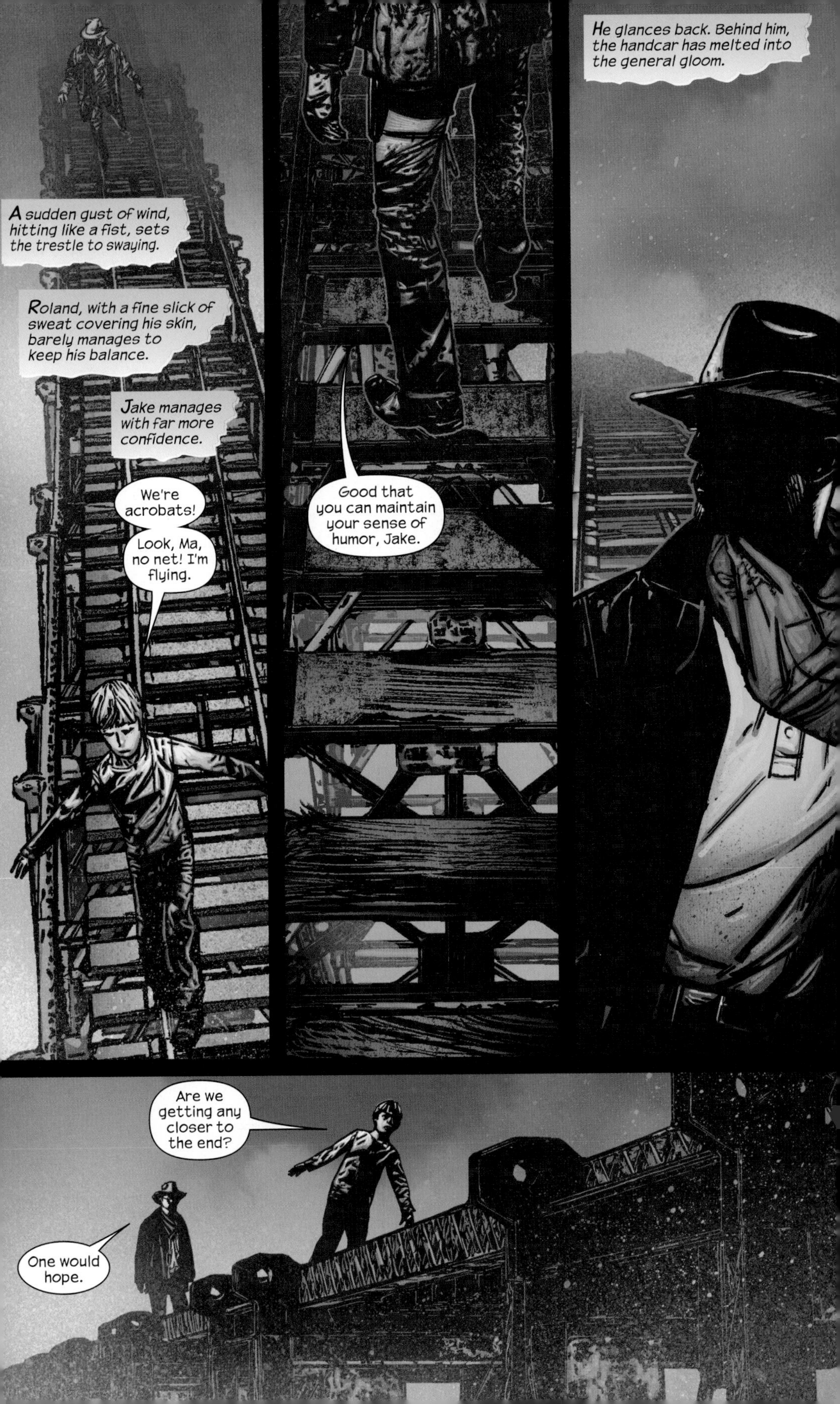
A sudden gust of wind, hitting like a fist, sets the trestle to swaying.
Roland, with a fine slick of sweat covering his skin, barely manages to keep his balance.
Jake manages with far more confidence.
We're acrobats!
Look, Ma, no net! I'm flying.
Good that you can maintain your sense of humor, Jake.
He glances back. Behind him, the handcar has melted into the general gloom.
Are we getting any closer to the end?
One would hope.

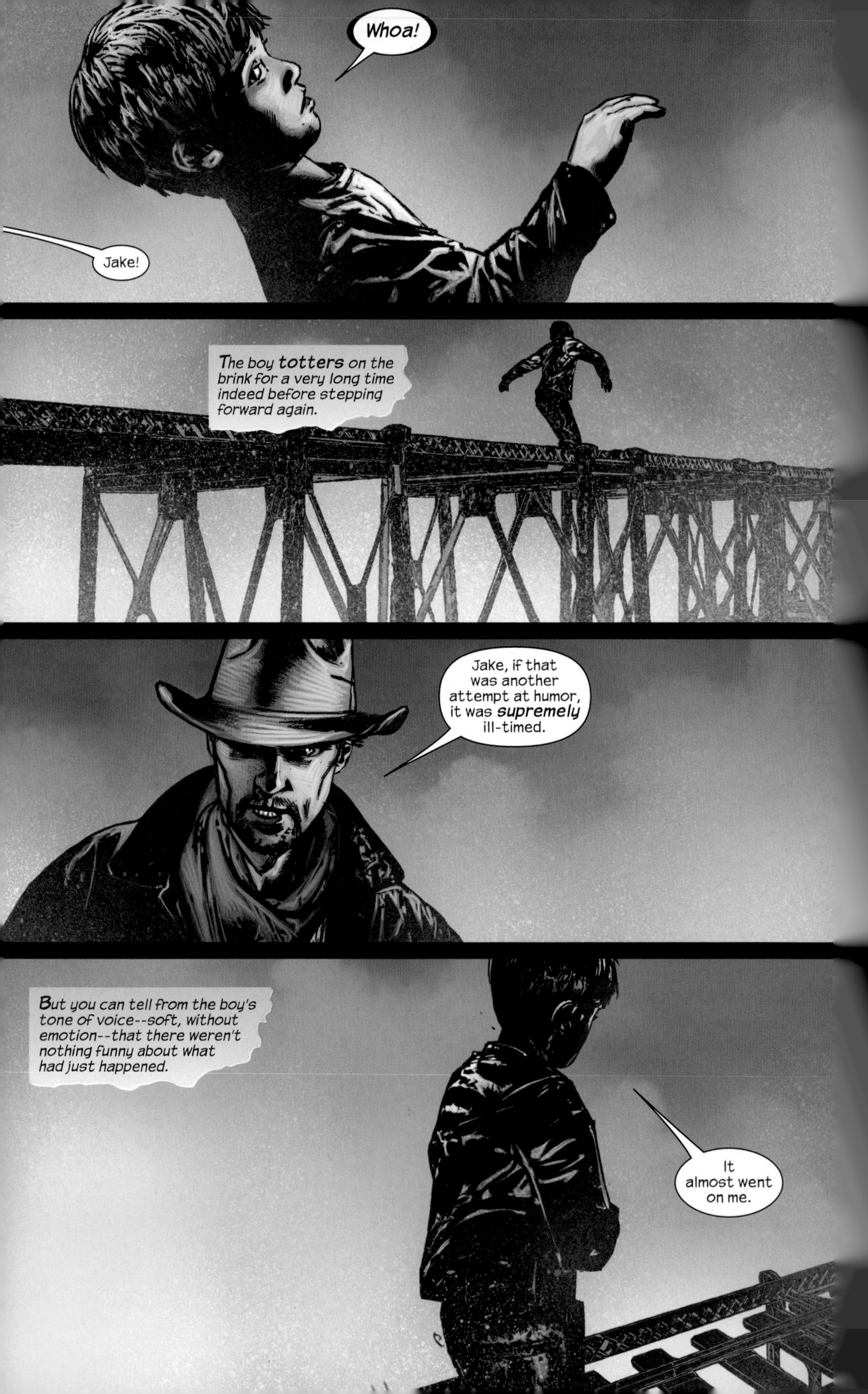
Whoa!
Jake!
The boy totters on the brink for a very long time indeed before stepping forward again.
Jake, if that was another attempt at humor, it was supremely ill-timed.
But you can tell from the boy's tone of voice--soft, without emotion--that there weren't nothing funny about what had just happened.
It almost went on me.

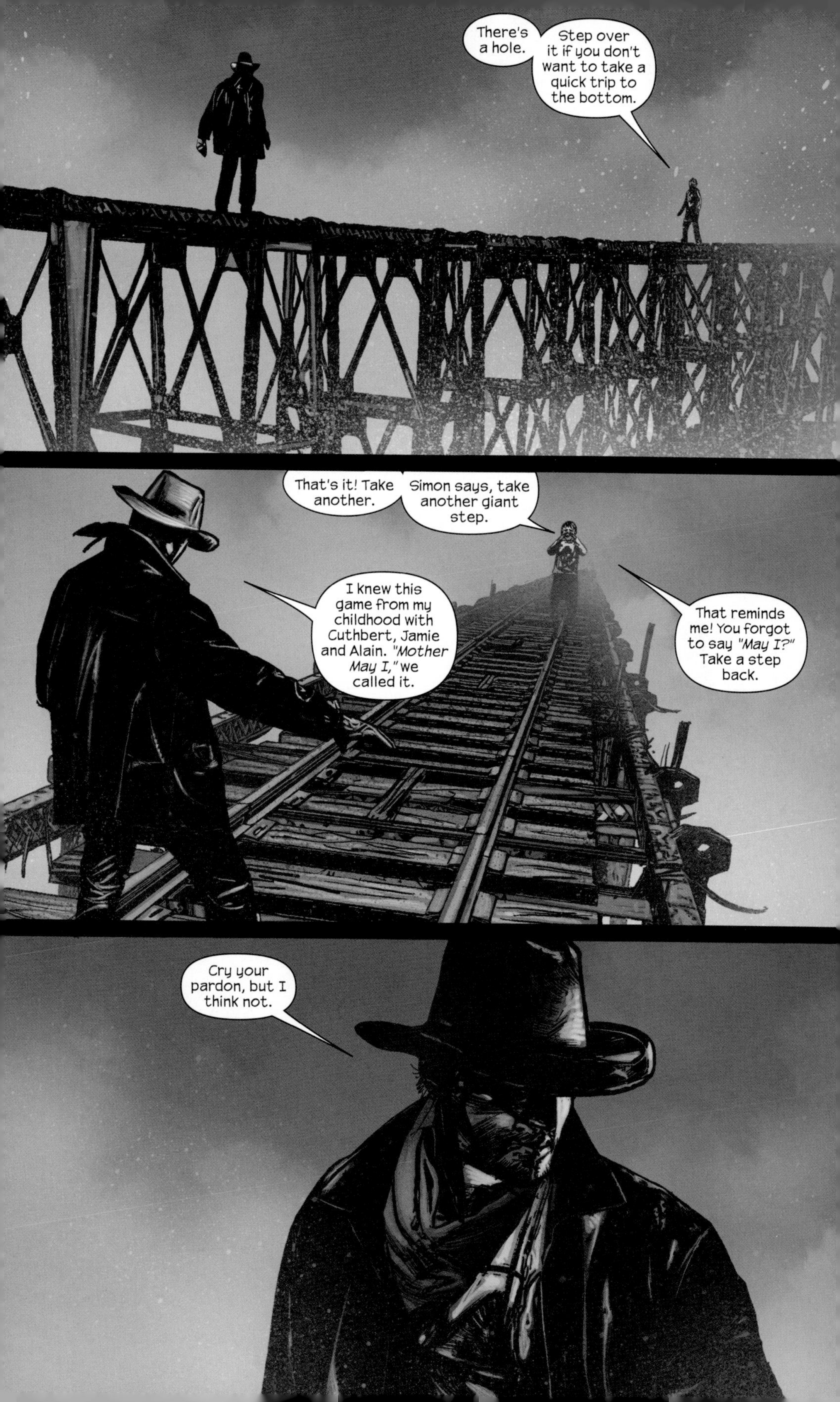
There's a hole.
Step over it if you don't want to take a quick trip to the bottom.
That's it! Take another.
Simon says, take another giant step.
I knew this game from my childhood with Cuthbert, Jamie and Alain. *"Mother May I,"* we called it.
That reminds me! You forgot to say *"May I?"* Take a step back.
Cry your pardon, but I think not.

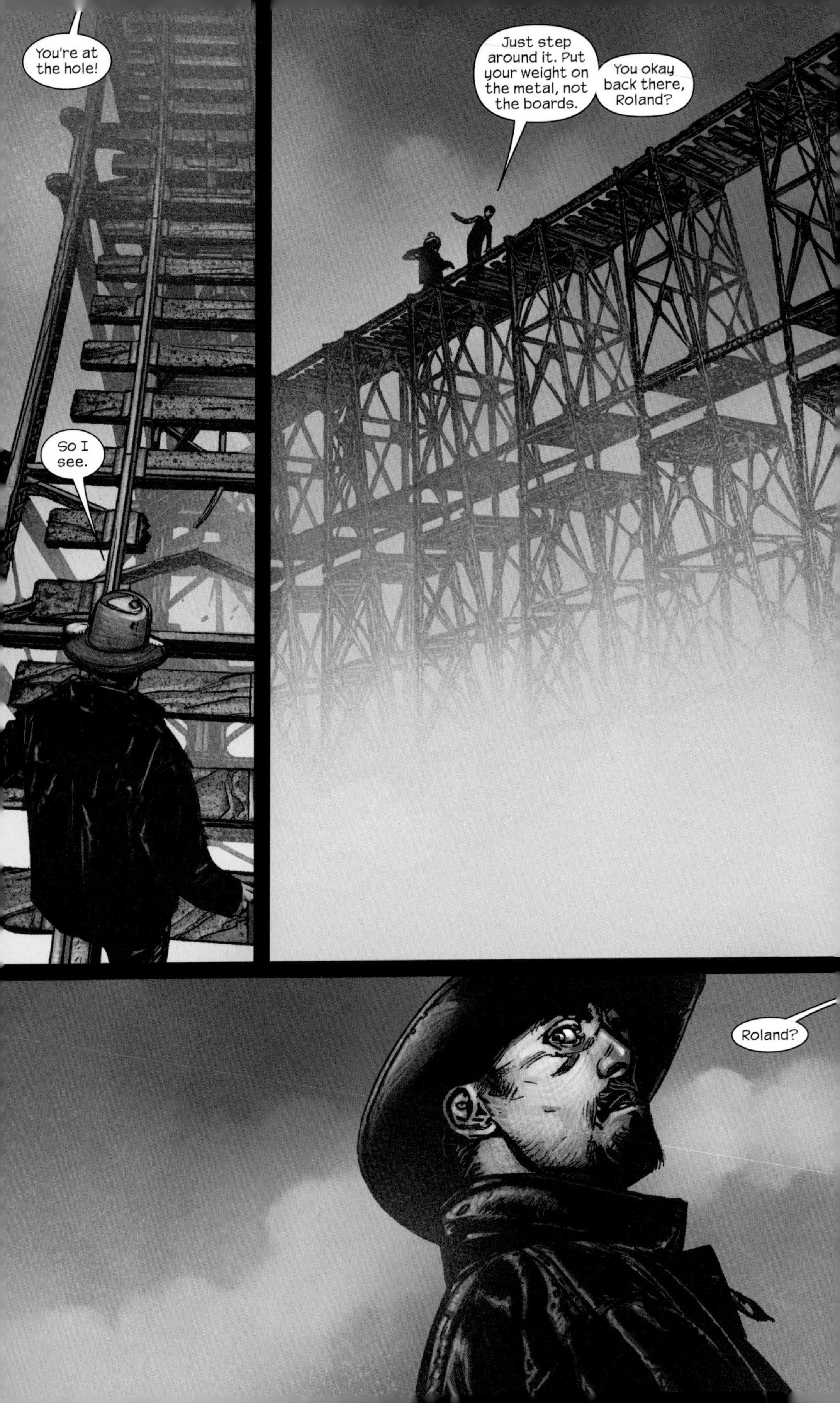
You're at the hole!
So I see.
Just step around it. Put your weight on the metal, not the boards.
You okay back there, Roland?
Roland?

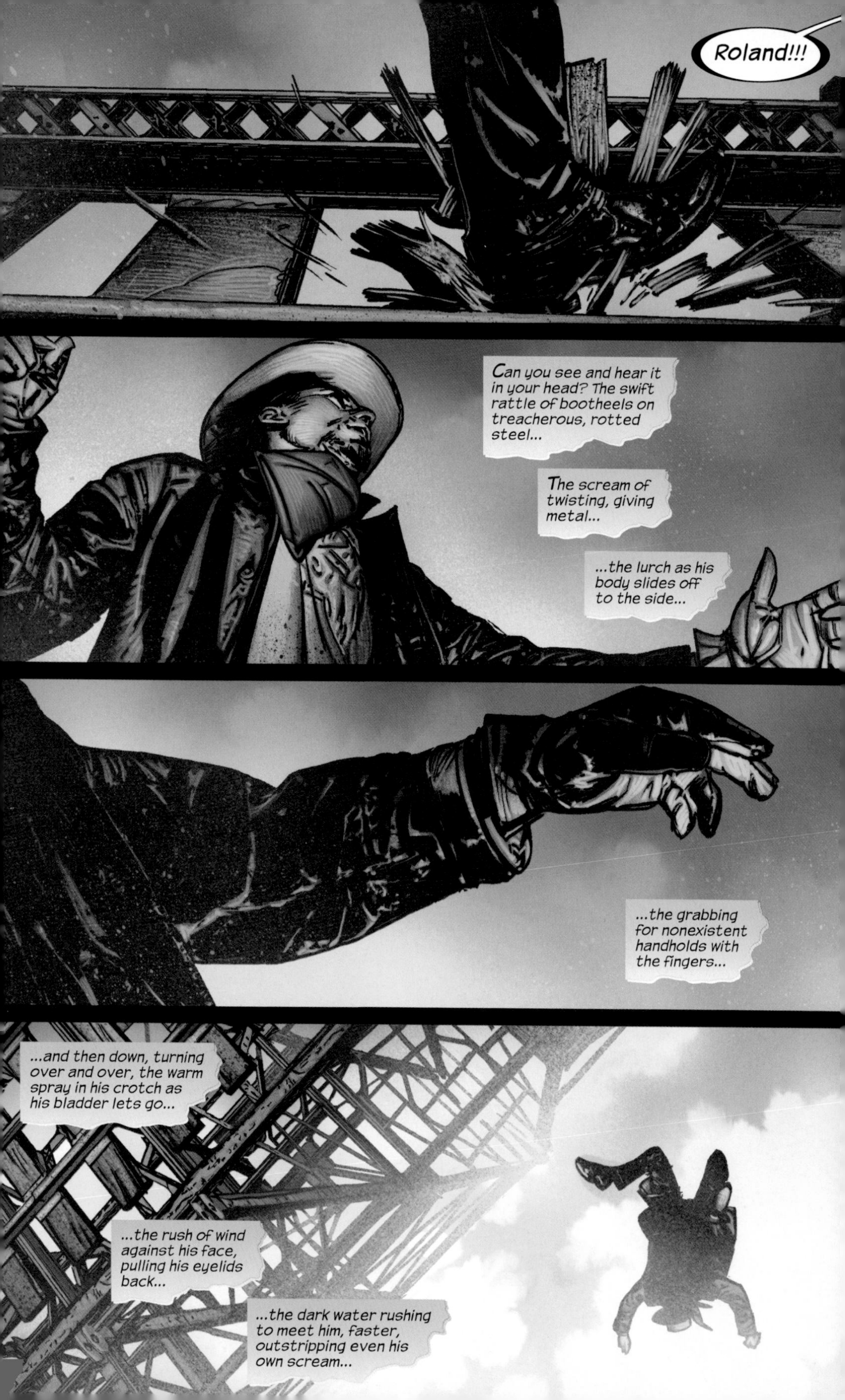
Roland!!!
Can you see and hear it in your head? The swift rattle of bootheels on treacherous, rotted steel...
The scream of twisting, giving metal...
...the lurch as his body slides off to the side...
...the grabbing for nonexistent handholds with the fingers...
...and then down, turning over and over, the warm spray in his crotch as his bladder lets go...
...the rush of wind against his face, pulling his eyelids back...
...the dark water rushing to meet him, faster, outstripping even his own scream...

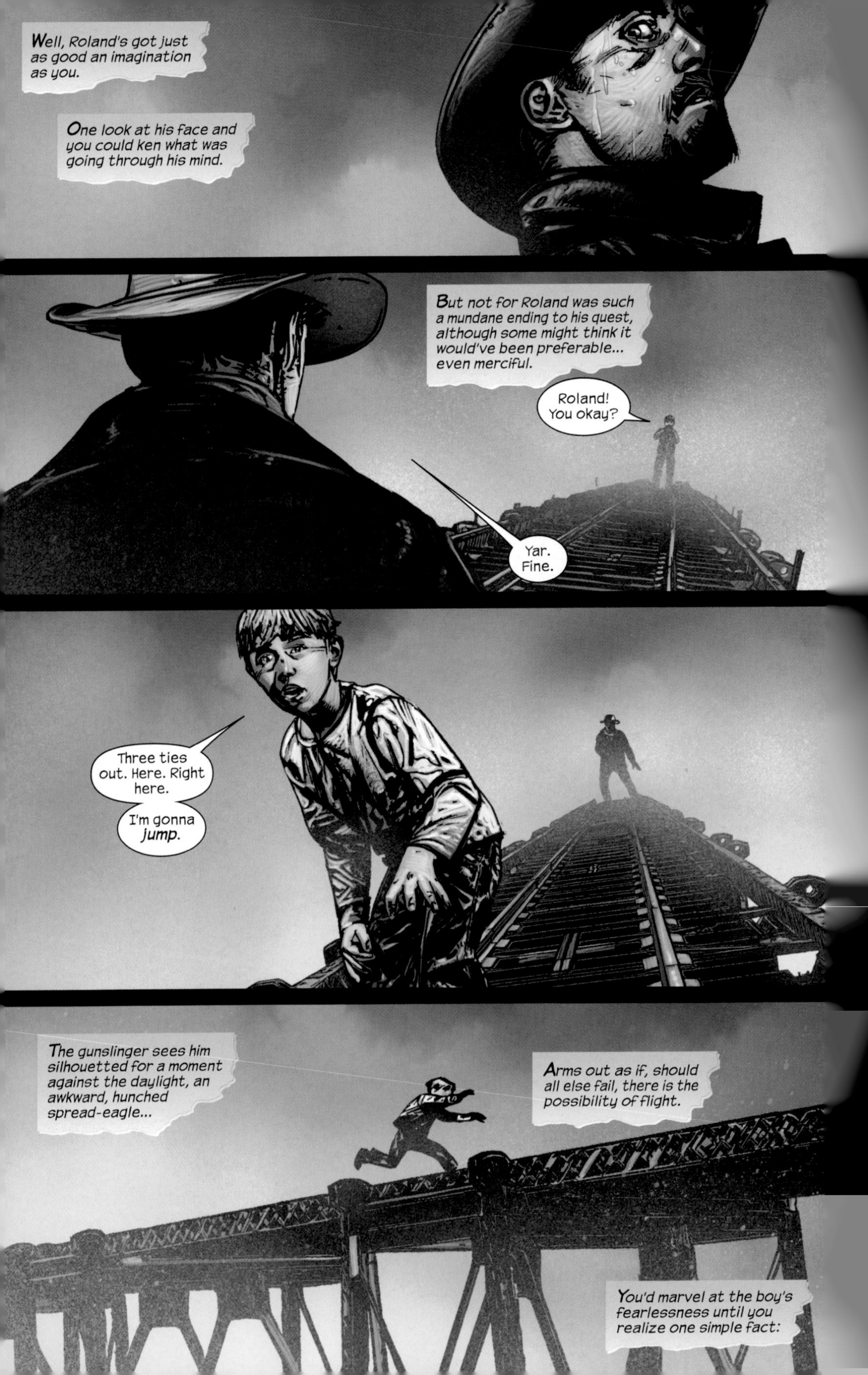
Well, Roland's got just as good an imagination as you.
One look at his face and you could ken what was going through his mind.
But not for Roland was such a mundane ending to his quest, although some might think it would've been preferable... even merciful.
Roland! You okay?
Yar. Fine.
Three ties out. Here. Right here.
I'm gonna *jump*.
The gunslinger sees him silhouetted for a moment against the daylight, an awkward, hunched spread-eagle...
Arms out as if, should all else fail, there is the possibility of flight.
You'd marvel at the boy's fearlessness until you realize one simple fact:

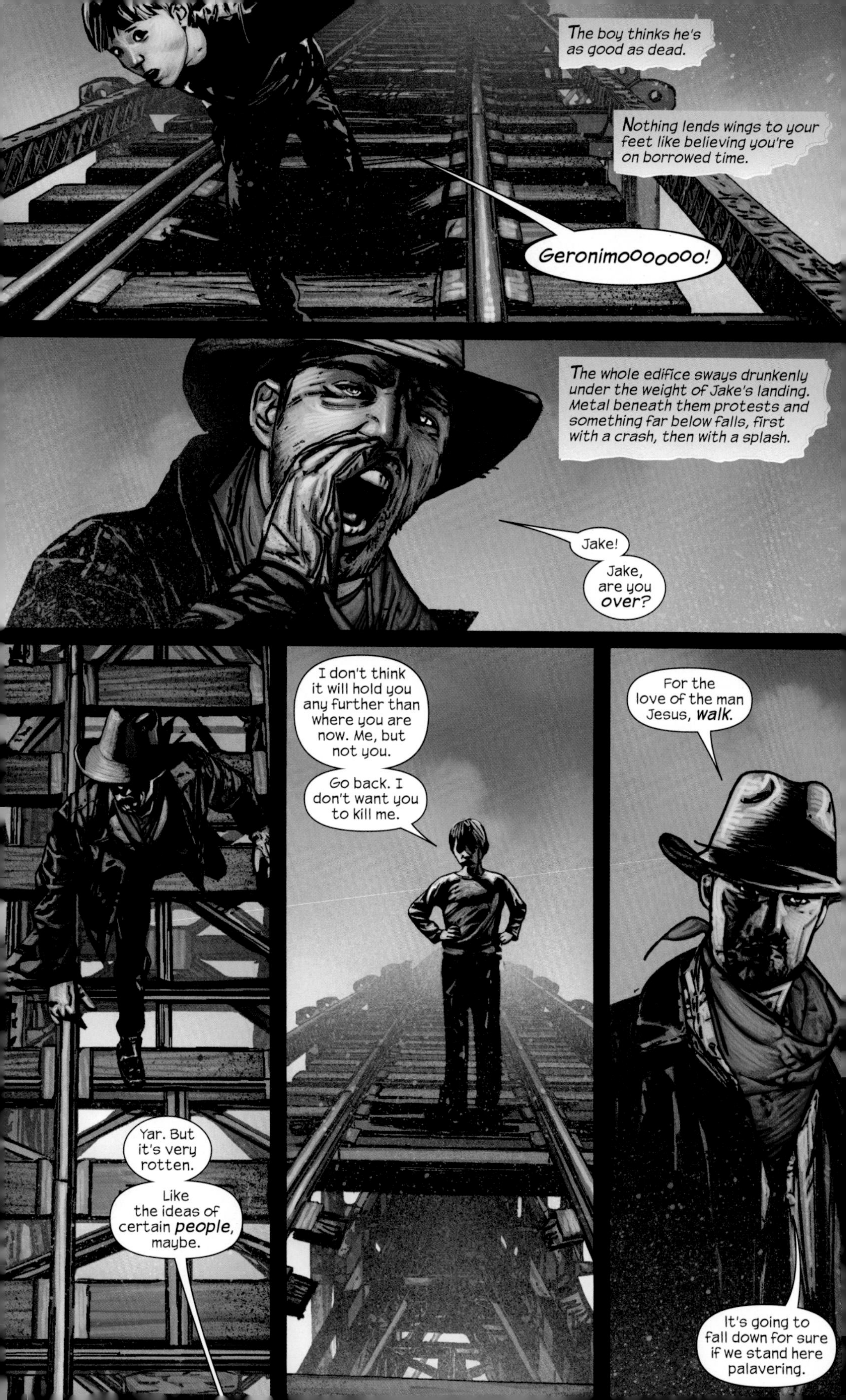

The boy thinks he's as good as dead.
Nothing lends wings to your feet like believing you're on borrowed time.
Geronimooooooo!
The whole edifice sways drunkenly under the weight of Jake's landing. Metal beneath them protests and something far below falls, first with a crash, then with a splash.
Jake!
Jake, are you *over?*
I don't think it will hold you any further than where you are now. Me, but not you.
Go back. I don't want you to kill me.
For the love of the man Jesus, *walk*.
Yar. But it's very rotten.
Like the ideas of certain *people*, maybe.
It's going to fall down for sure if we stand here palavering.

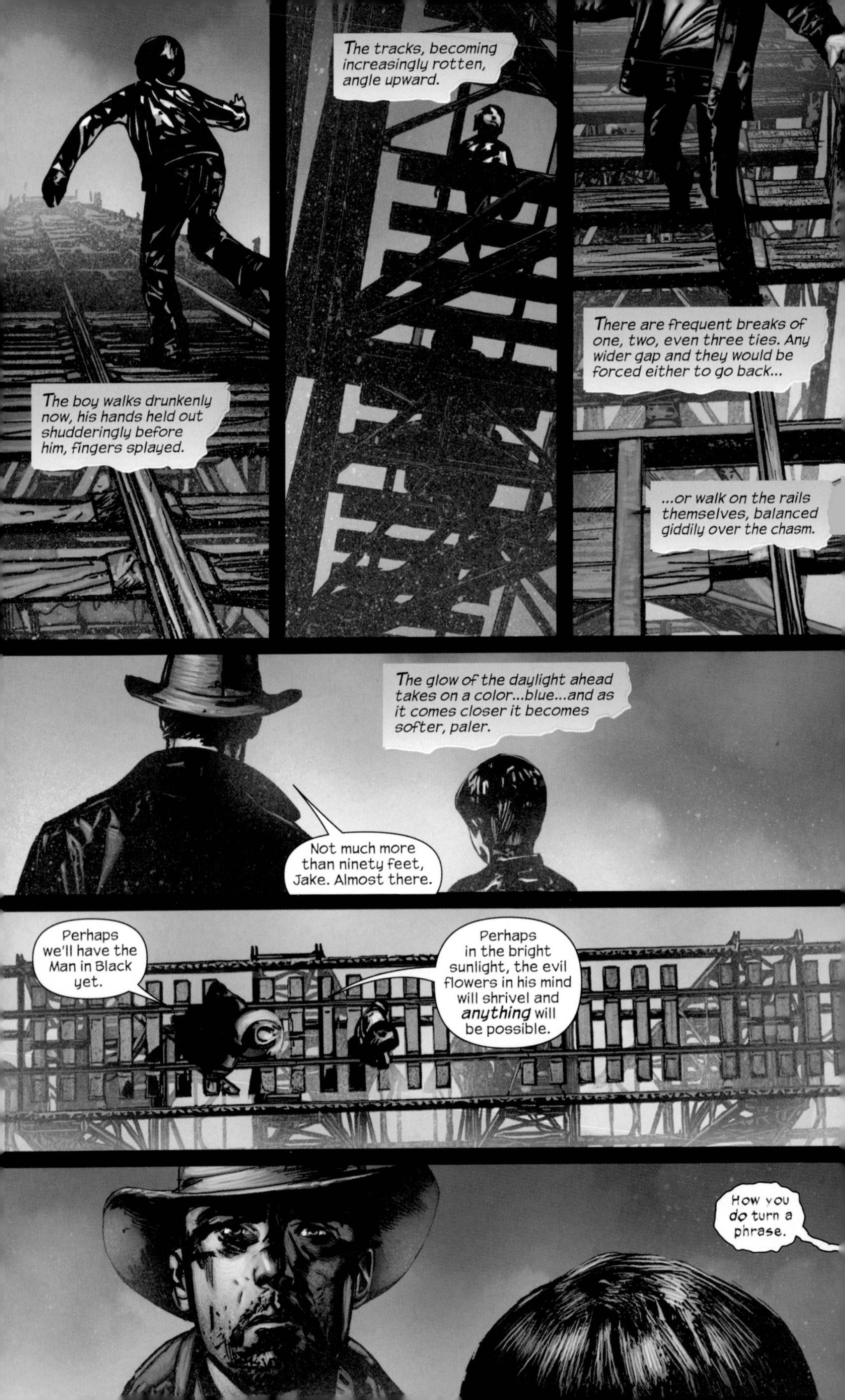
The boy walks drunkenly now, his hands held out shudderingly before him, fingers splayed.
The tracks, becoming increasingly rotten, angle upward.
There are frequent breaks of one, two, even three ties. Any wider gap and they would be forced either to go back...
...or walk on the rails themselves, balanced giddily over the chasm.
The glow of the daylight ahead takes on a color...blue...and as it comes closer it becomes softer, paler.
Not much more than ninety feet, Jake. Almost there.
Perhaps we'll have the Man in Black yet.
Perhaps in the bright sunlight, the evil flowers in his mind will shrivel and *anything* will be possible.
How you *do* turn a phrase.

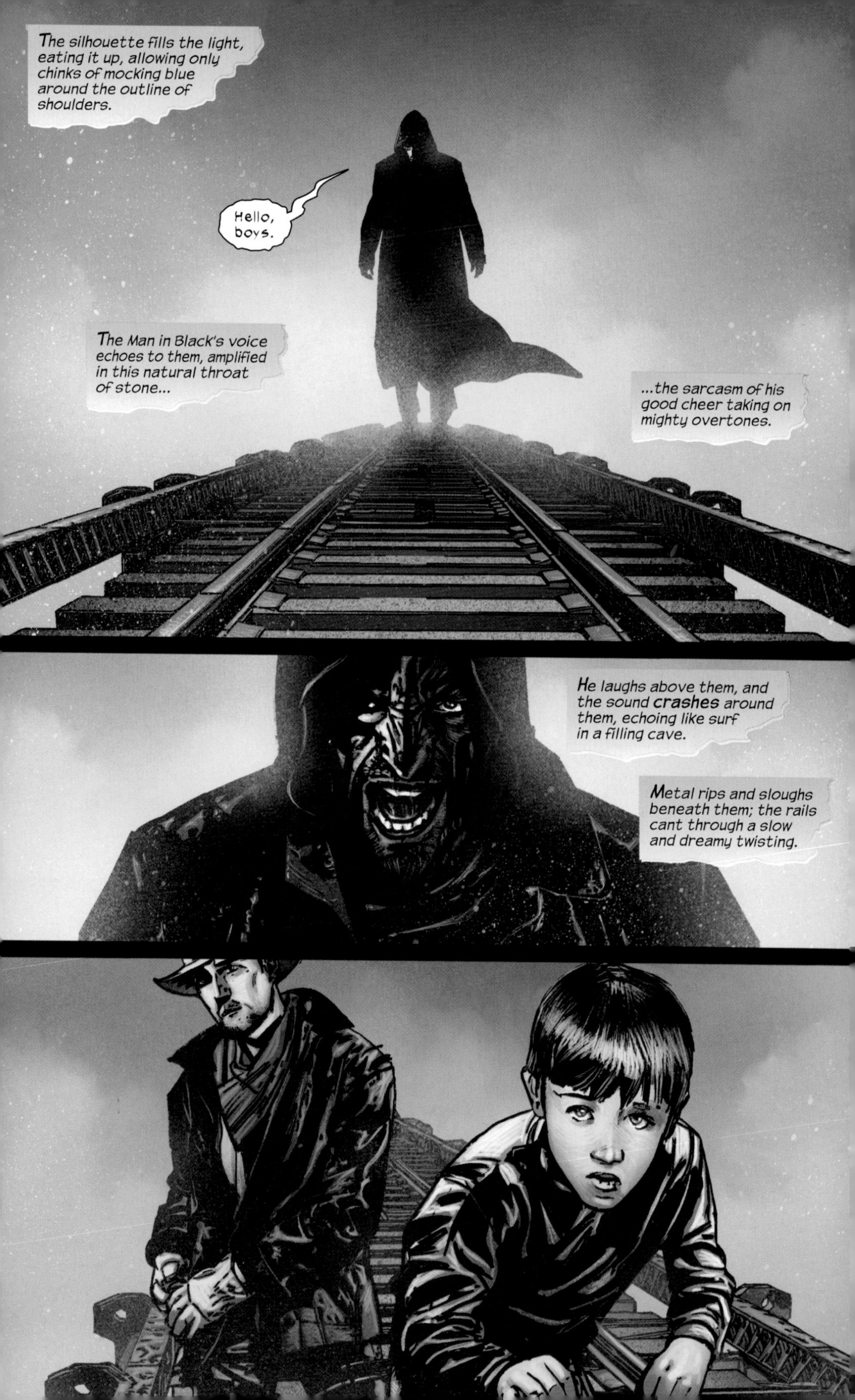
The silhouette fills the light, eating it up, allowing only chinks of mocking blue around the outline of shoulders.
Hello, boys.
The Man in Black's voice echoes to them, amplified in this natural throat of stone...
...the sarcasm of his good cheer taking on mighty overtones.
He laughs above them, and the sound crashes around them, echoing like surf in a filling cave.
Metal rips and sloughs beneath them; the rails cant through a slow and dreamy twisting.

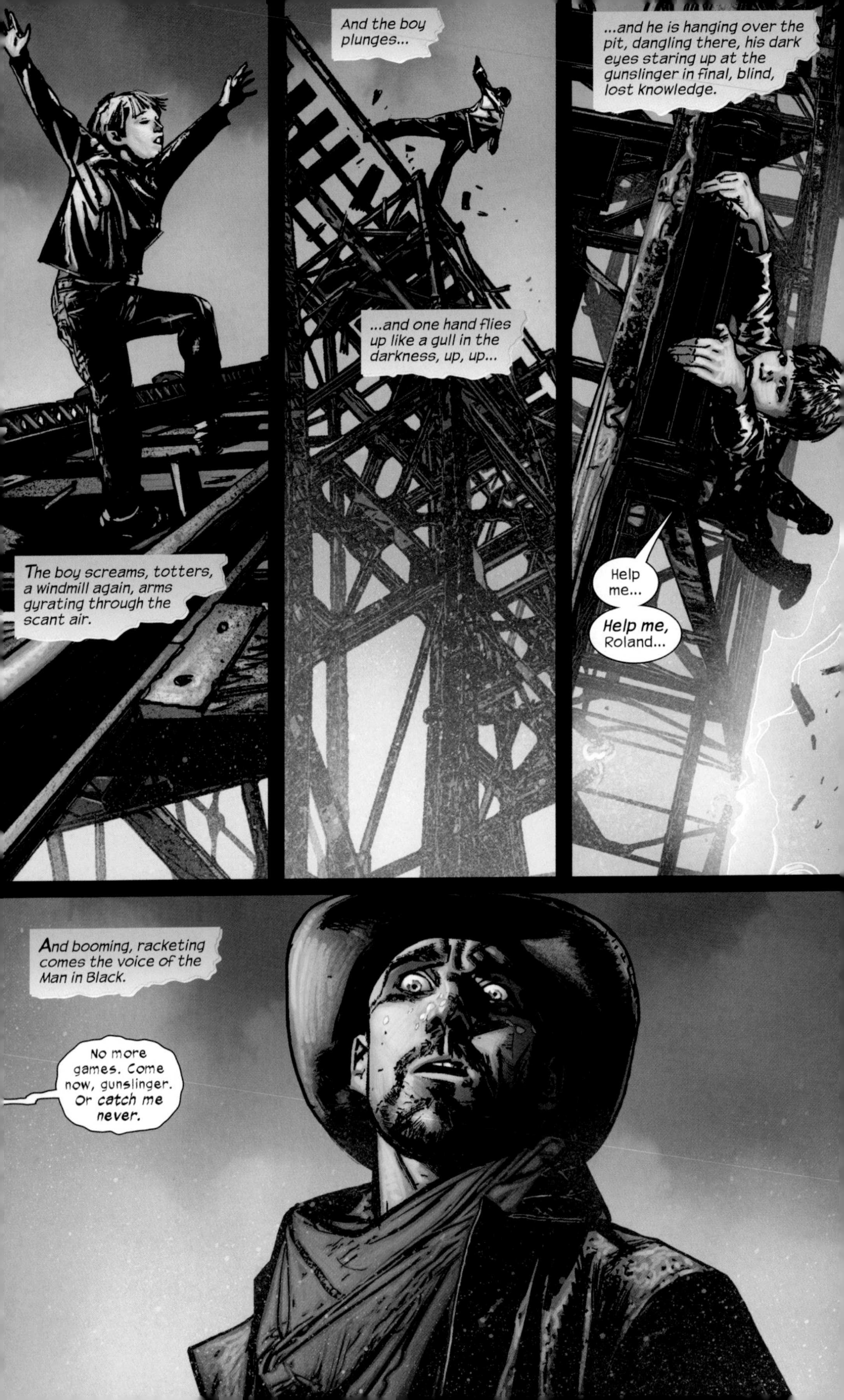
The boy screams, totters, a windmill again, arms gyrating through the scant air.
And the boy plunges...
...and one hand flies up like a gull in the darkness, up, up...
...and he is hanging over the pit, dangling there, his dark eyes staring up at the gunslinger in final, blind, lost knowledge.
Help me...
Help me, Roland...
And booming, racketing comes the voice of the Man in Black.
No more games. Come now, gunslinger. Or catch me never.

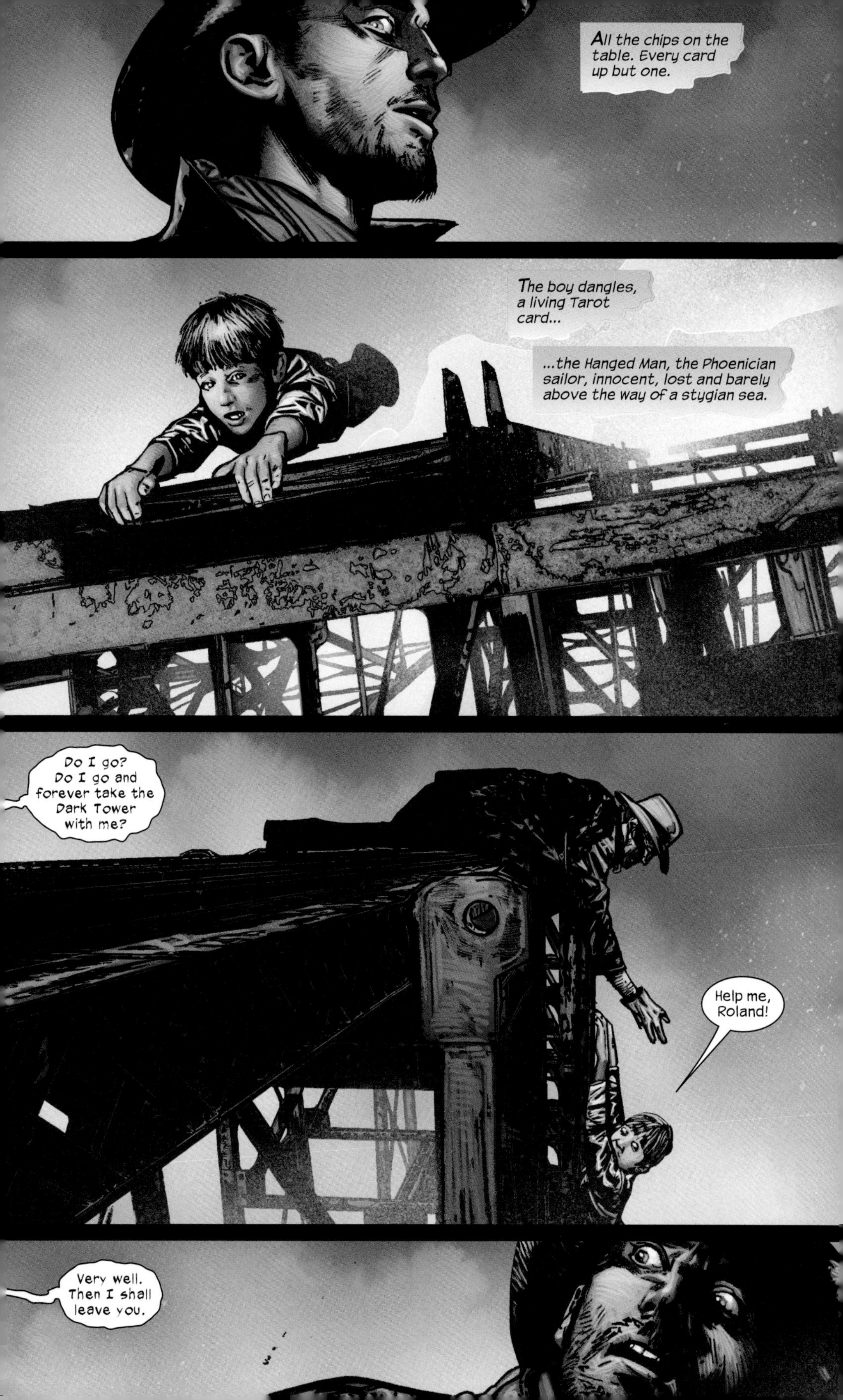
All the chips on the table. Every card up but one.
The boy dangles, a living Tarot card...
...the Hanged Man, the Phoenician sailor, innocent, lost and barely above the way of a stygian sea.
Do I go? Do I go and forever take the Dark Tower with me?
Help me, Roland!
Very well. Then I shall leave you.

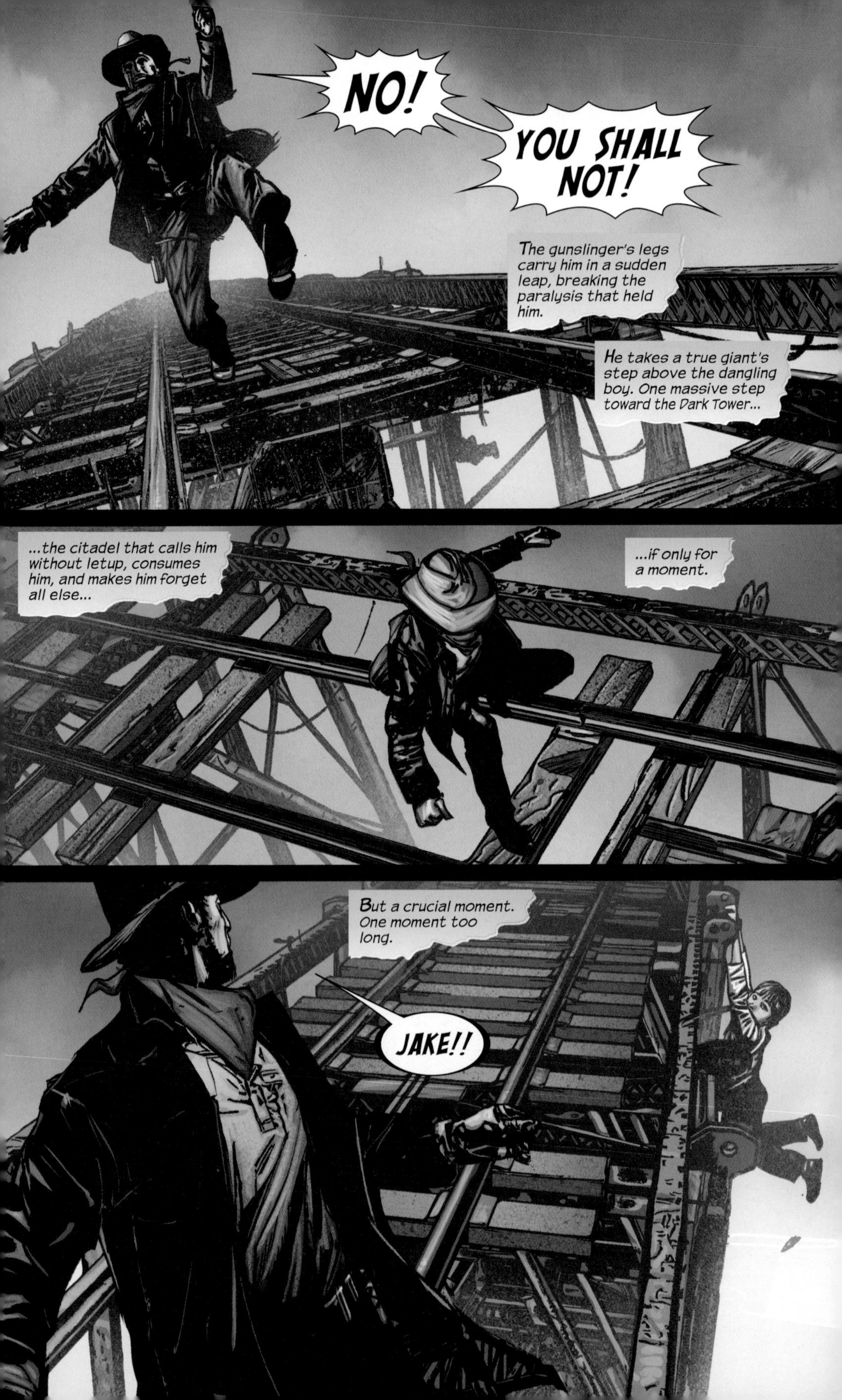
NO!
YOU SHALL NOT!
The gunslinger's legs carry him in a sudden leap, breaking the paralysis that held him.
He takes a true giant's step above the dangling boy. One massive step toward the Dark Tower...
...the citadel that calls him without letup, consumes him, and makes him forget all else...
...if only for a moment.
But a crucial moment. One moment too long.
JAKE!!

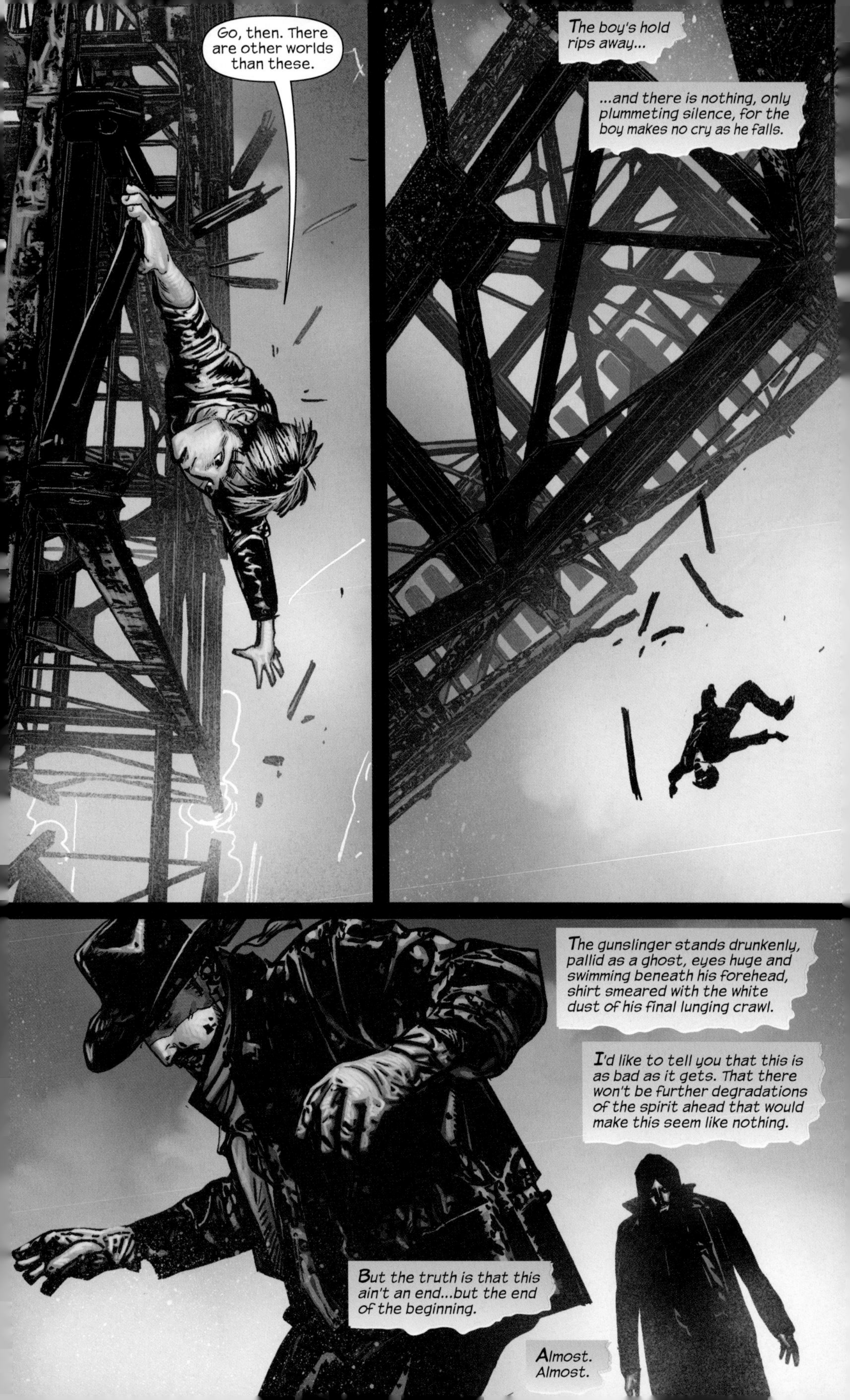
Go, then. There are other worlds than these.
The boy's hold rips away...
...and there is nothing, only plummeting silence, for the boy makes no cry as he falls.
The gunslinger stands drunkenly, pallid as a ghost, eyes huge and swimming beneath his forehead, shirt smeared with the white dust of his final lunging crawl.
I'd like to tell you that this is as bad as it gets. That there won't be further degradations of the spirit ahead that would make this seem like nothing.
But the truth is that this ain't an end...but the end of the beginning.
Almost. Almost.

STEPHEN KING

THE DARK TOWER
~ THE GUNSLINGER ~

THE MAN IN BLACK

CHAPTER FIVE

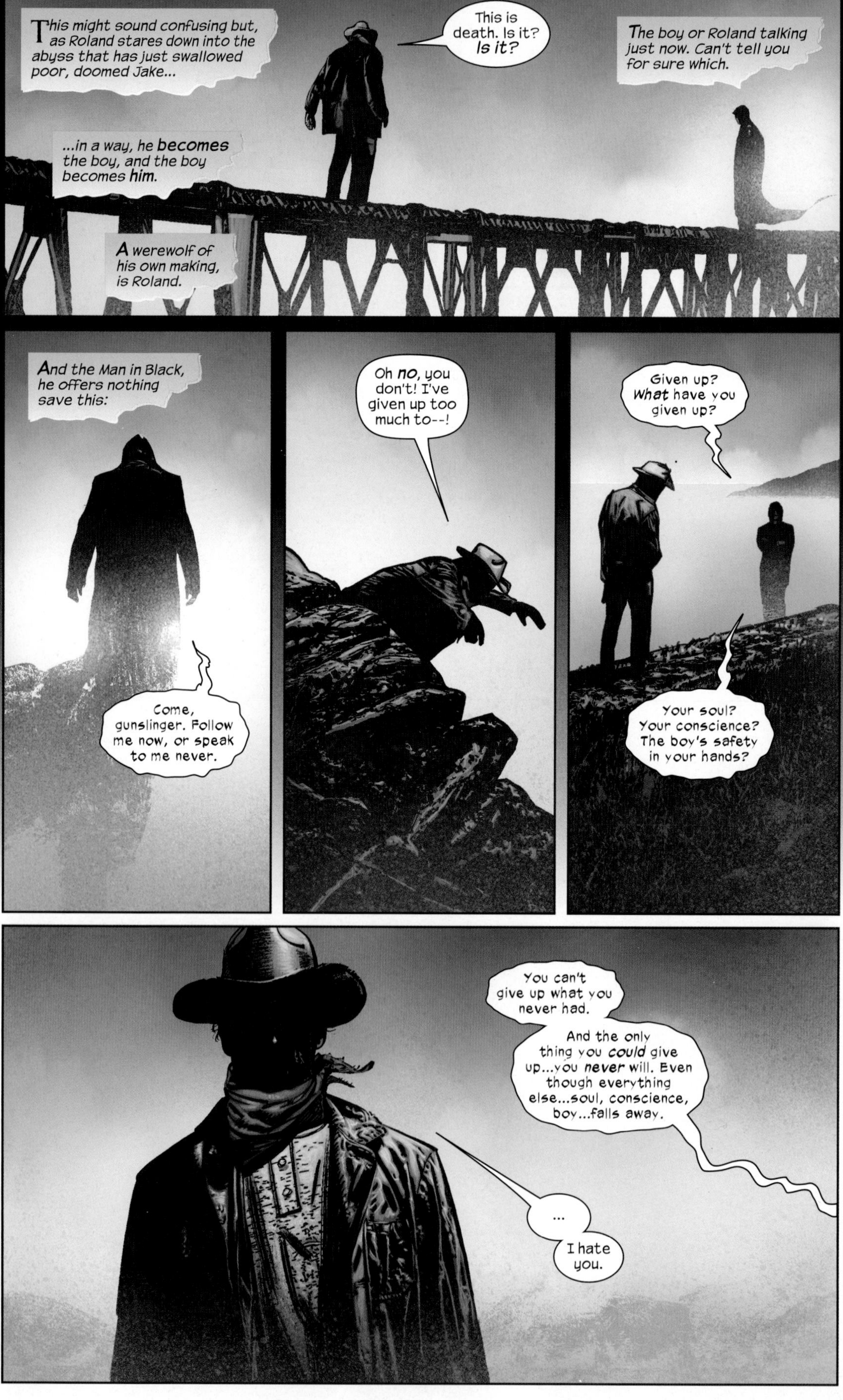
This might sound confusing but, as Roland stares down into the abyss that has just swallowed poor, doomed Jake...
This is death. Is it? Is it?
The boy or Roland talking just now. Can't tell you for sure which.
...in a way, he becomes the boy, and the boy becomes him.
A werewolf of his own making, is Roland.
And the Man in Black, he offers nothing save this:
Come, gunslinger. Follow me now, or speak to me never.
Oh no, you don't! I've given up too much to--!
Given up? What have you given up?
Your soul? Your conscience? The boy's safety in your hands?
You can't give up what you never had.
And the only thing you could give up...you never will. Even though everything else...soul, conscience, boy...falls away.
...
I hate you.

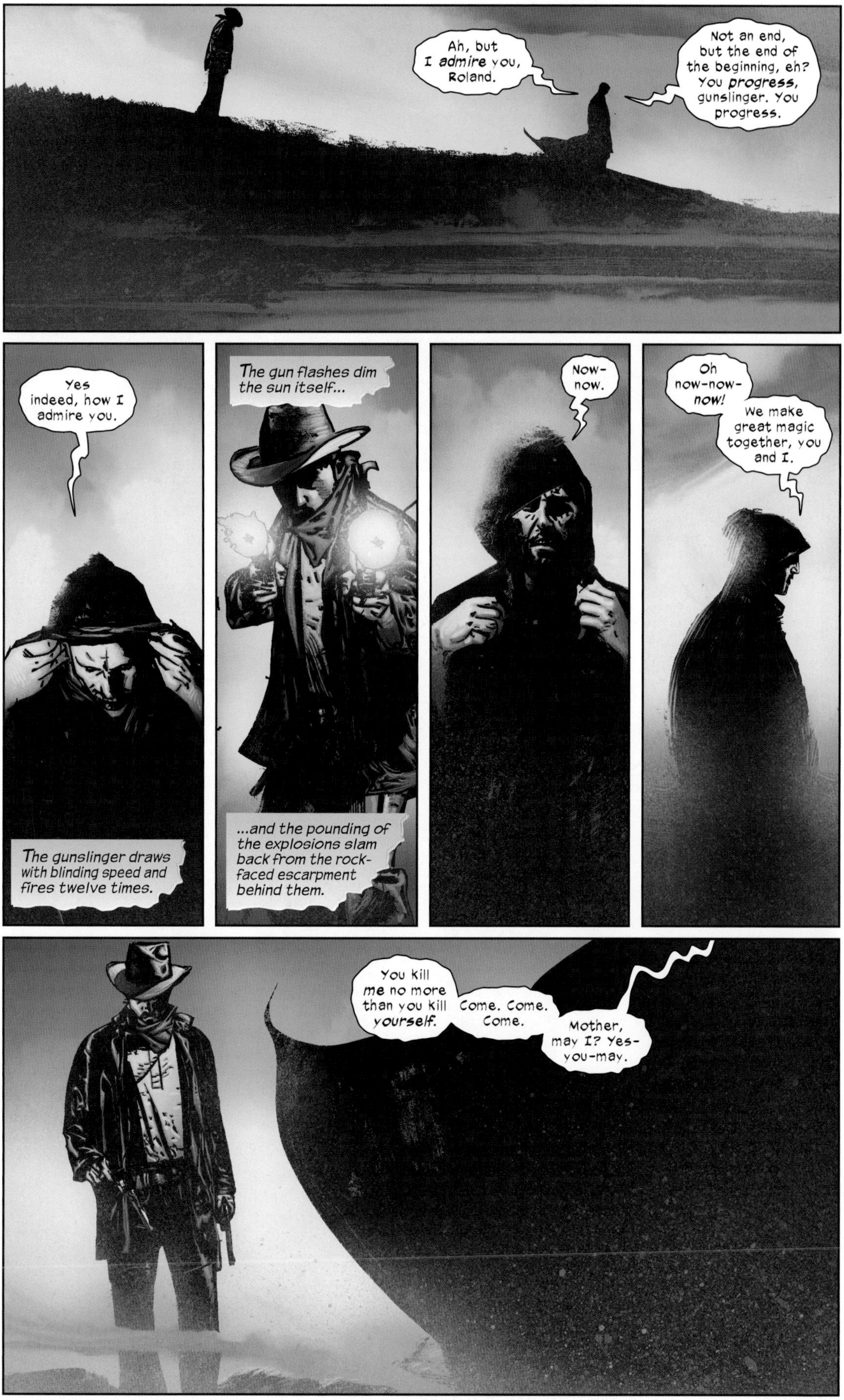

Ah, but I admire you, Roland.
Not an end, but the end of the beginning, eh? You progress, gunslinger. You progress.
Yes indeed, how I admire you.
The gunslinger draws with blinding speed and fires twelve times.
The gun flashes dim the sun itself...
...and the pounding of the explosions slam back from the rock-faced escarpment behind them.
Now-now.
Oh now-now-now!
We make great magic together, you and I.
You kill me no more than you kill yourself.
Come. Come. Come.
Mother, may I? Yes-you-may.

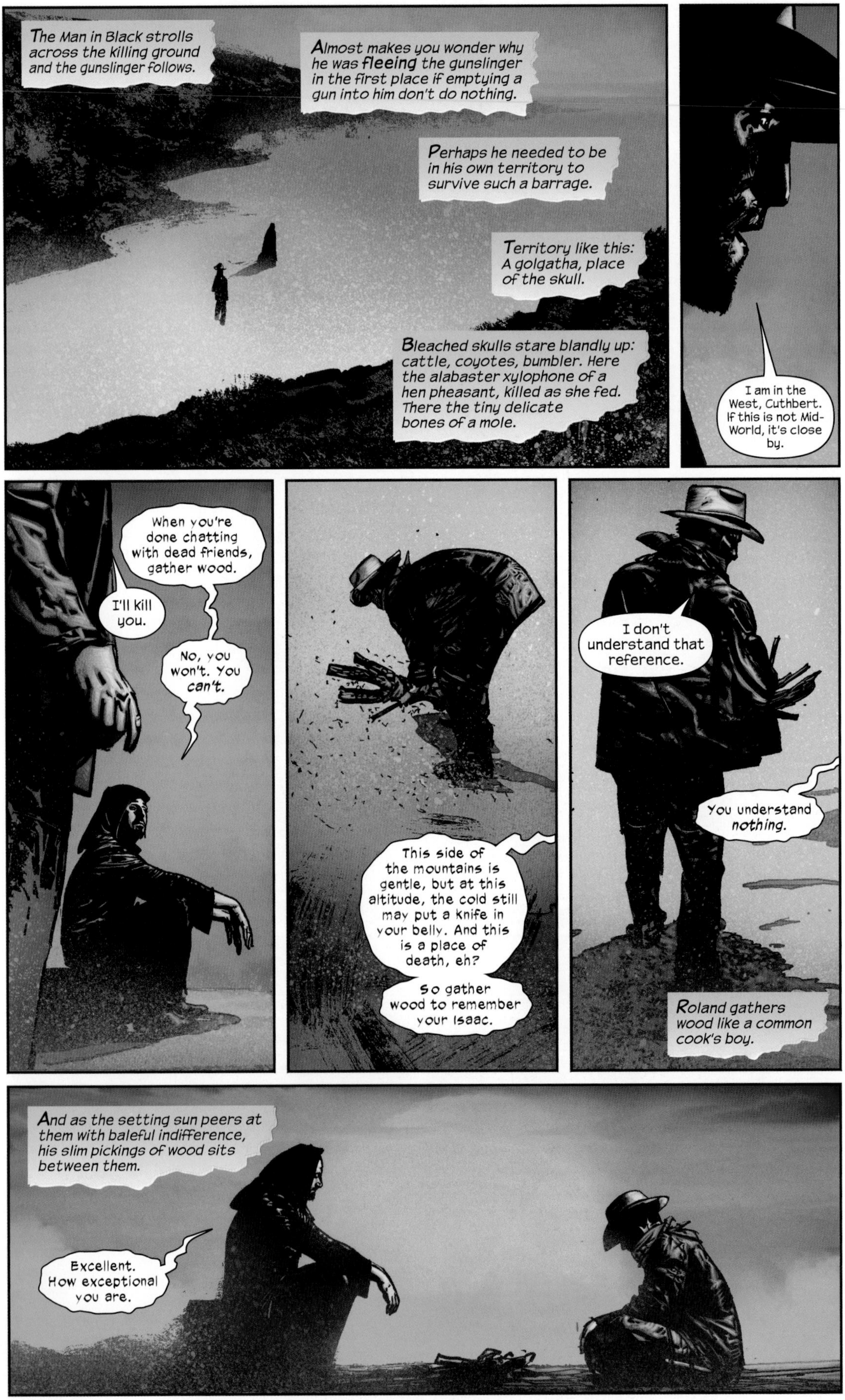

The Man in Black strolls across the killing ground and the gunslinger follows.
Almost makes you wonder why he was **fleeing** the gunslinger in the first place if emptying a gun into him don't do nothing.
Perhaps he needed to be in his own territory to survive such a barrage.
Territory like this: A golgatha, place of the skull.
Bleached skulls stare blandly up: cattle, coyotes, bumbler. Here the alabaster xylophone of a hen pheasant, killed as she fed. There the tiny delicate bones of a mole.
I am in the West, Cuthbert. If this is not Mid-World, it's close by.
When you're done chatting with dead friends, gather wood.
I'll kill you.
No, you won't. You *can't.*
This side of the mountains is gentle, but at this altitude, the cold still may put a knife in your belly. And this is a place of death, eh?
So gather wood to remember your Isaac.
I don't understand that reference.
You understand *nothing.*
Roland gathers wood like a common cook's boy.
And as the setting sun peers at them with baleful indifference, his slim pickings of wood sits between them.
Excellent. How exceptional you are.

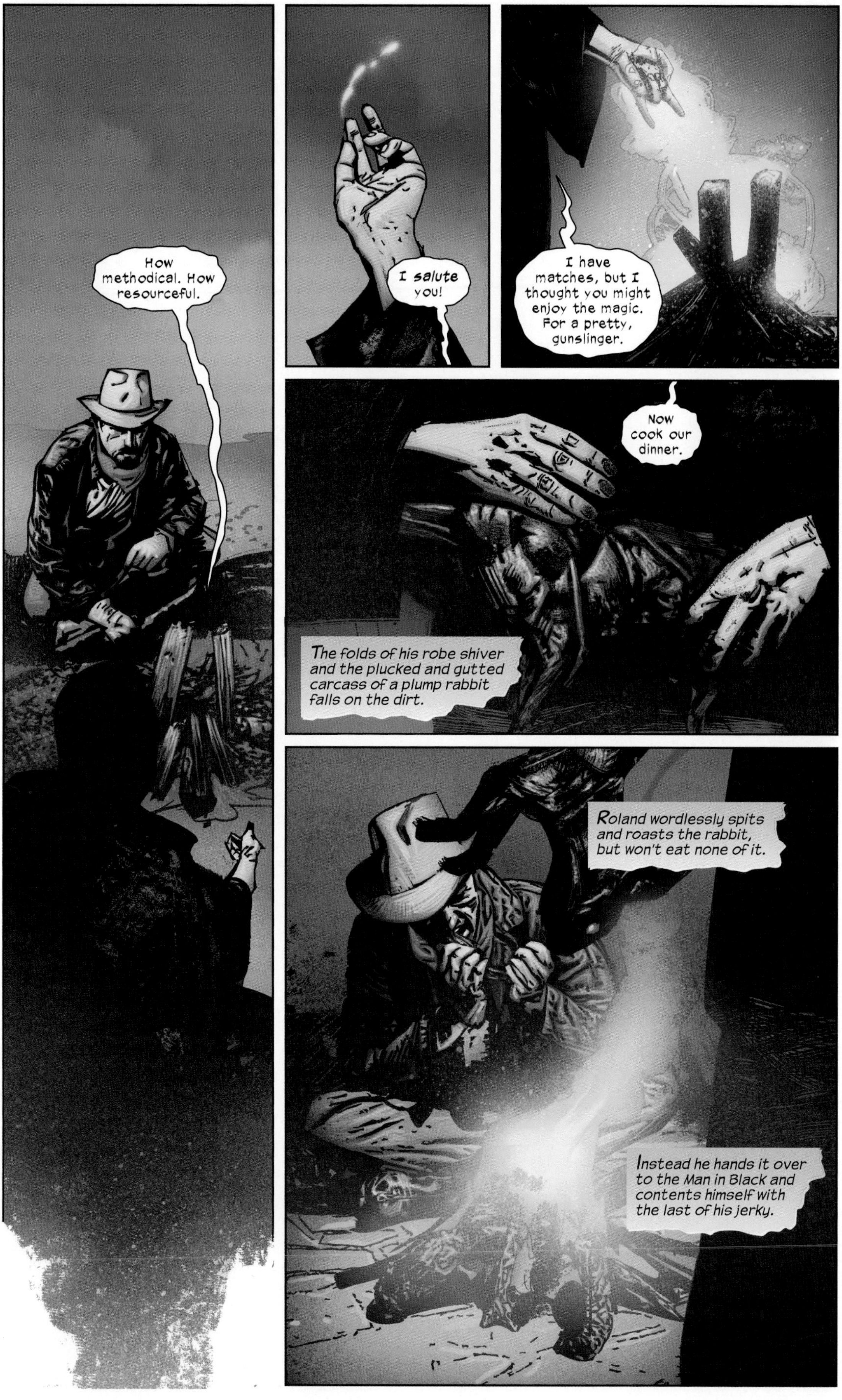
How methodical. How resourceful.
I salute you!
I have matches, but I thought you might enjoy the magic. For a pretty, gunslinger.
Now cook our dinner.
The folds of his robe shiver and the plucked and gutted carcass of a plump rabbit falls on the dirt.
Roland wordlessly spits and roasts the rabbit, but won't eat none of it.
Instead he hands it over to the Man in Black and contents himself with the last of his jerky.

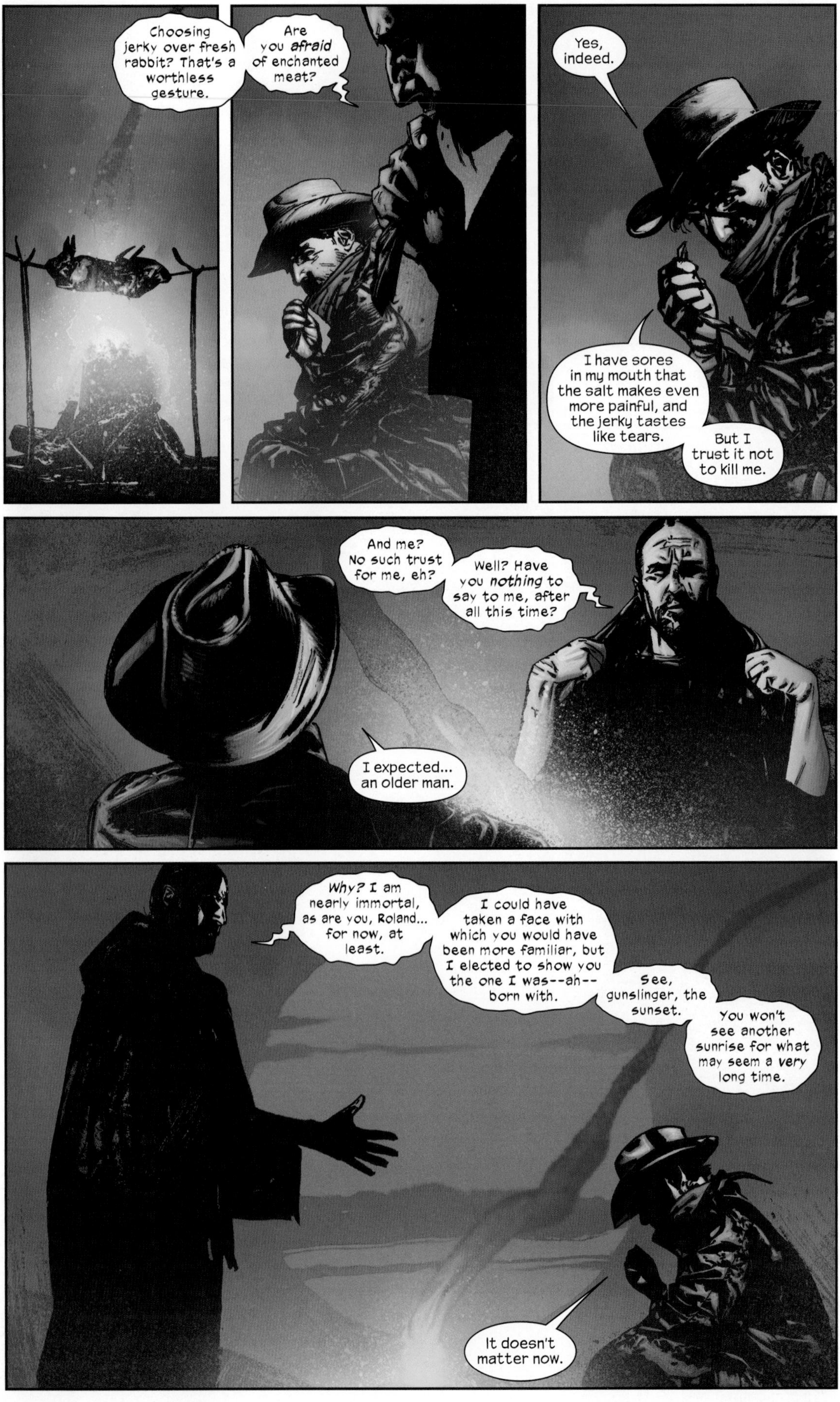
Choosing jerky over fresh rabbit? That's a worthless gesture.
Are you *afraid* of enchanted meat?
Yes, indeed.
I have sores in my mouth that the salt makes even more painful, and the jerky tastes like tears.
But I trust it not to kill me.
And me? No such trust for me, eh?
Well? Have you *nothing* to say to me, after all this time?
I expected... an older man.
Why? I am nearly immortal, as are you, Roland... for now, at least.
I could have taken a face with which you would have been more familiar, but I elected to show you the one I was--ah-- born with.
See, gunslinger, the sunset.
You won't see another sunrise for what may seem a *very* long time.
It doesn't matter now.

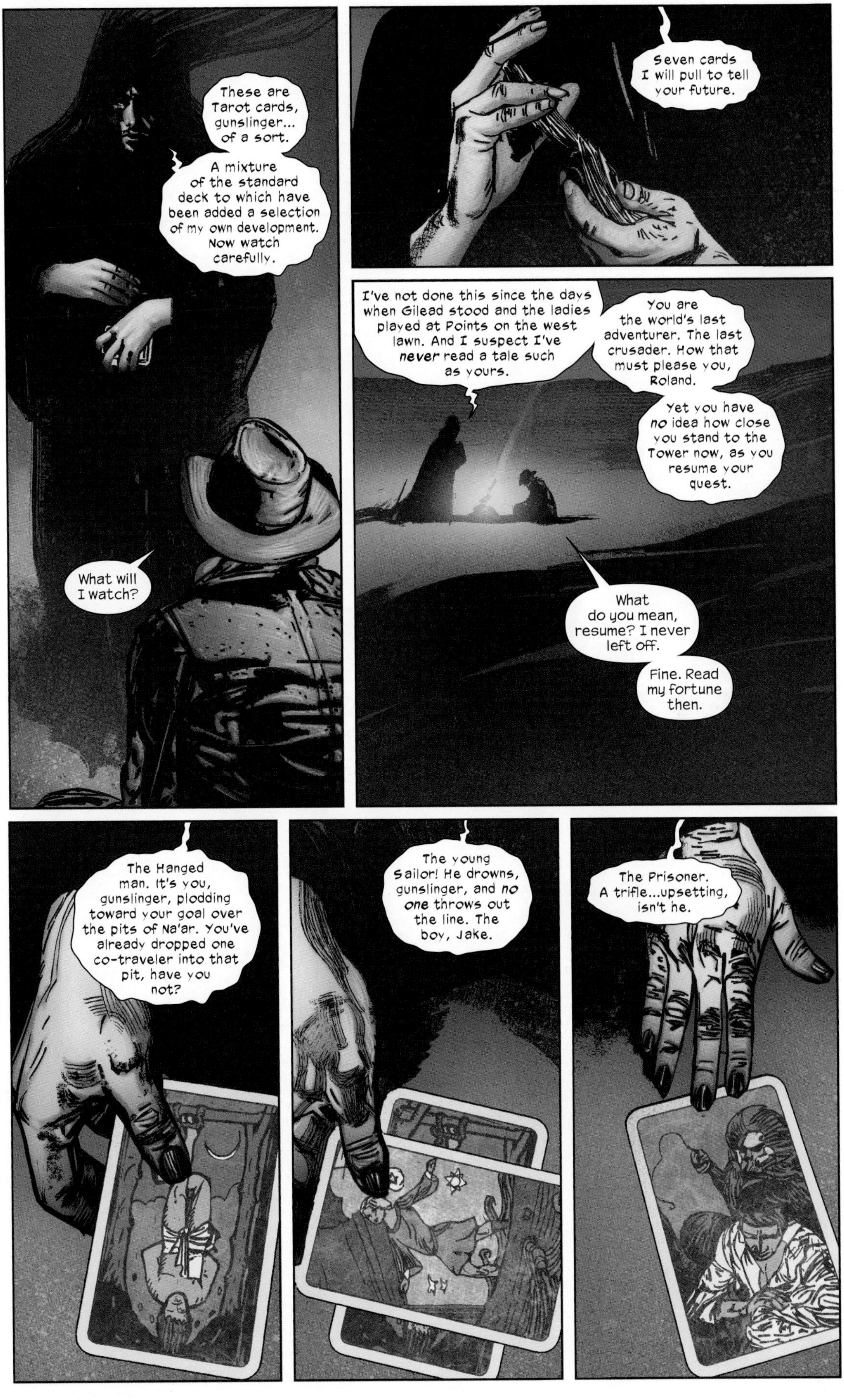
These are Tarot cards, gunslinger... of a sort.
A mixture of the standard deck to which have been added a selection of my own development. Now watch carefully.
What will I watch?
Seven cards I will pull to tell your future.
I've not done this since the days when Gilead stood and the ladies played at Points on the west lawn. And I suspect I've never read a tale such as yours.
You are the world's last adventurer. The last crusader. How that must please you, Roland.
Yet you have no idea how close you stand to the Tower now, as you resume your quest.
What do you mean, resume? I never left off.
Fine. Read my fortune then.
The Hanged man. It's you, gunslinger, plodding toward your goal over the pits of Na'ar. You've already dropped one co-traveler into that pit, have you not?
The young Sailor! He drowns, gunslinger, and no one throws out the line. The boy, Jake.
The Prisoner. A trifle...upsetting, isn't he.

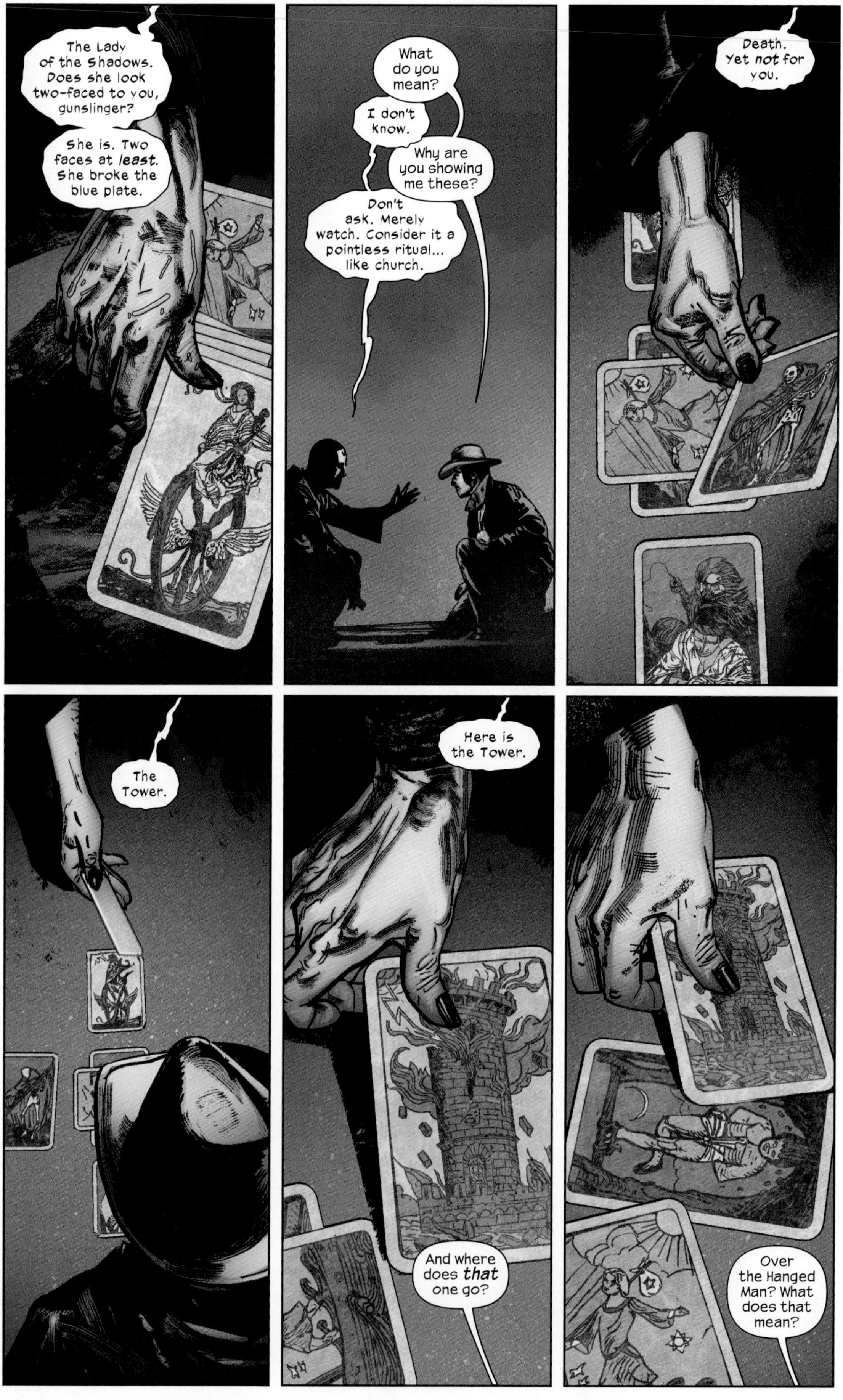
The Lady of the Shadows. Does she look two-faced to you, gunslinger?
She is. Two faces at *least*. She broke the blue plate.
What do you mean?
I don't know.
Why are you showing me these?
Don't ask. Merely watch. Consider it a pointless ritual... like church.
Death. Yet *not* for you.
The Tower.
Here is the Tower.
And where does *that* one go?
Over the Hanged Man? What does that mean?

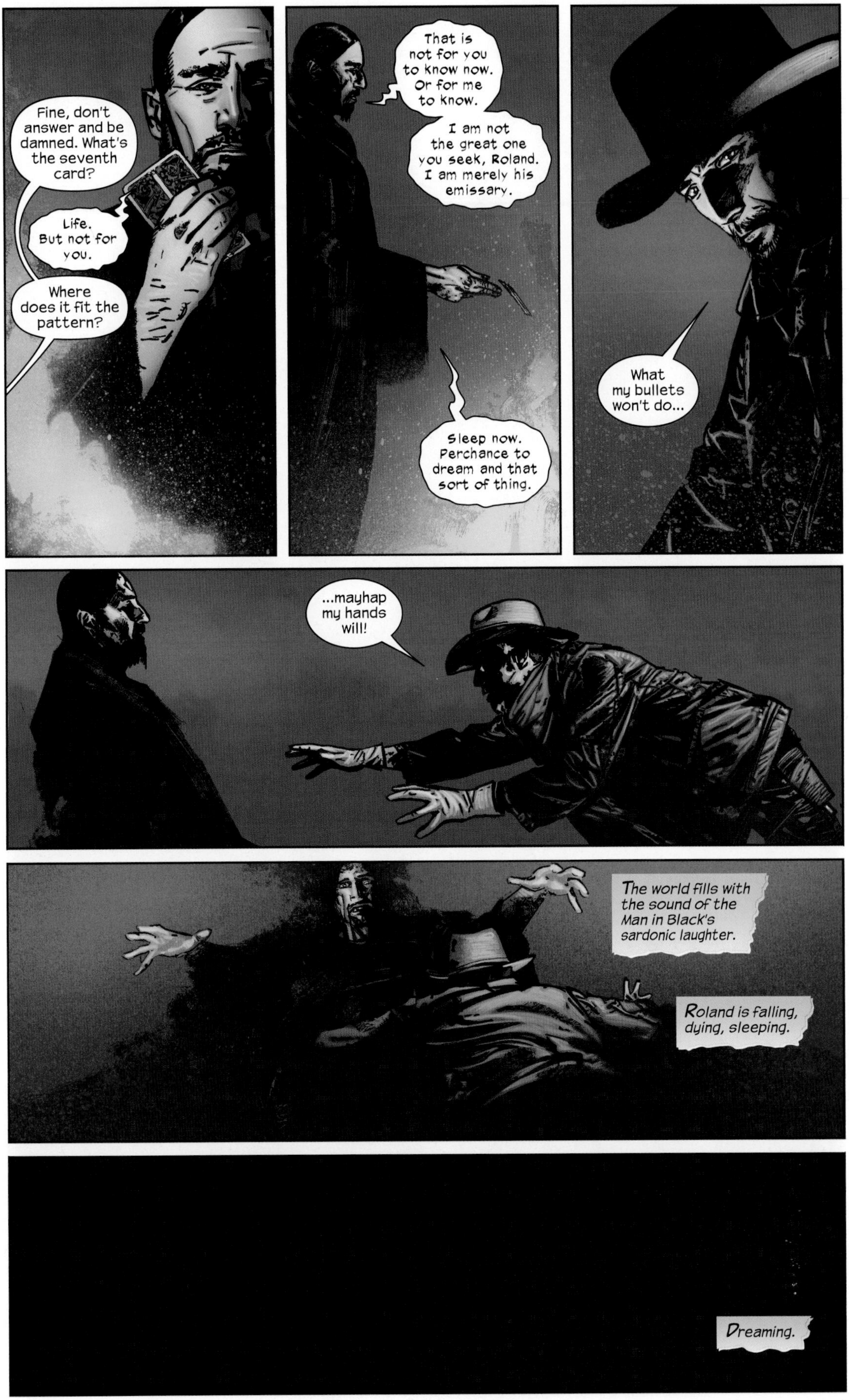
Fine, don't answer and be damned. What's the seventh card?
Life. But not for you.
Where does it fit the pattern?
That is not for you to know now. Or for me to know.
I am not the great one you seek, Roland. I am merely his emissary.
Sleep now. Perchance to dream and that sort of thing.
What my bullets won't do...
...mayhap my hands will!
The world fills with the sound of the Man in Black's sardonic laughter.
Roland is falling, dying, sleeping.
Dreaming.

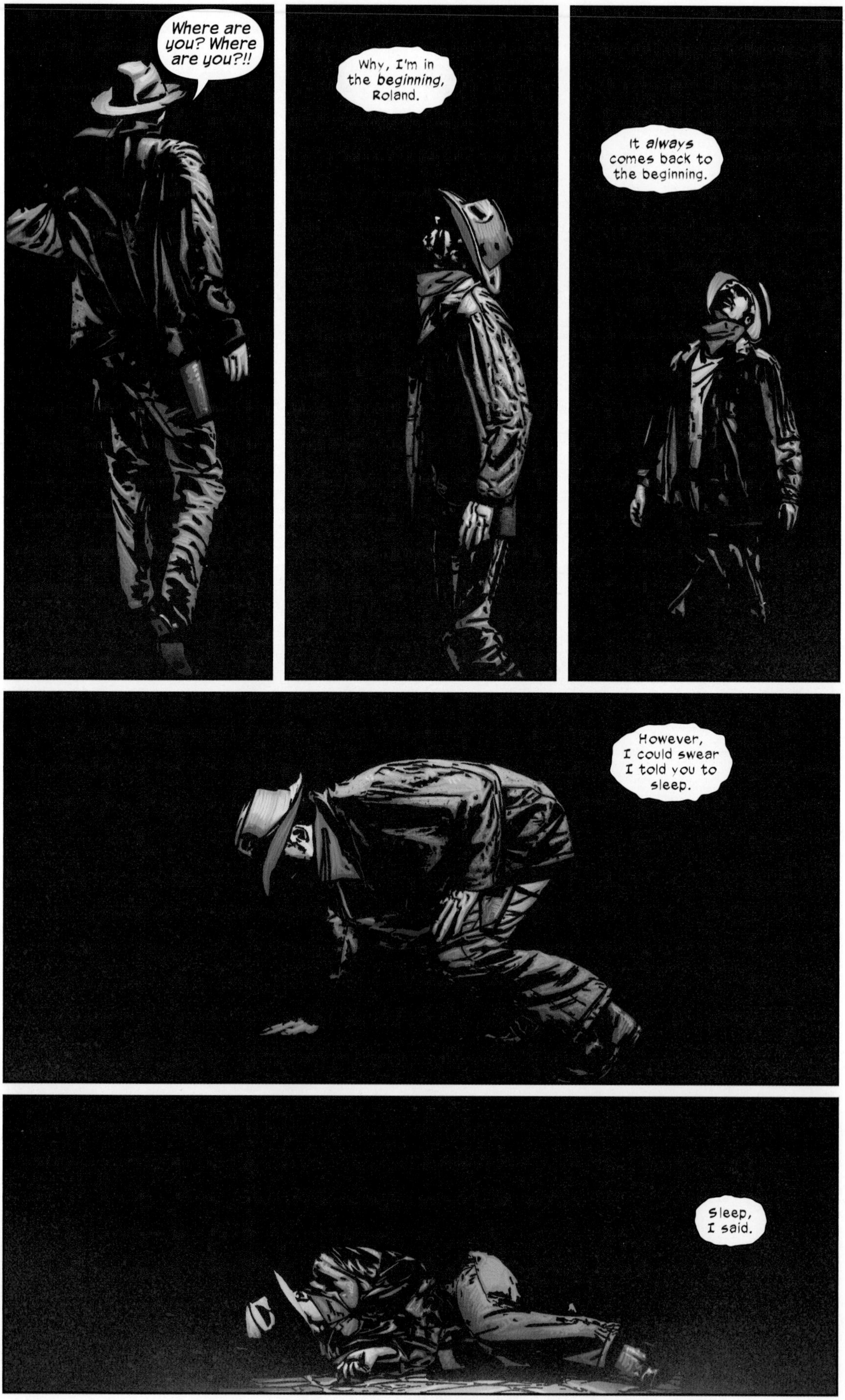
Where are you? Where are you?!!
Why, I'm in the *beginning*, Roland.
It *always* comes back to the beginning.
However, I could swear I told you to sleep.
Sleep, I said.

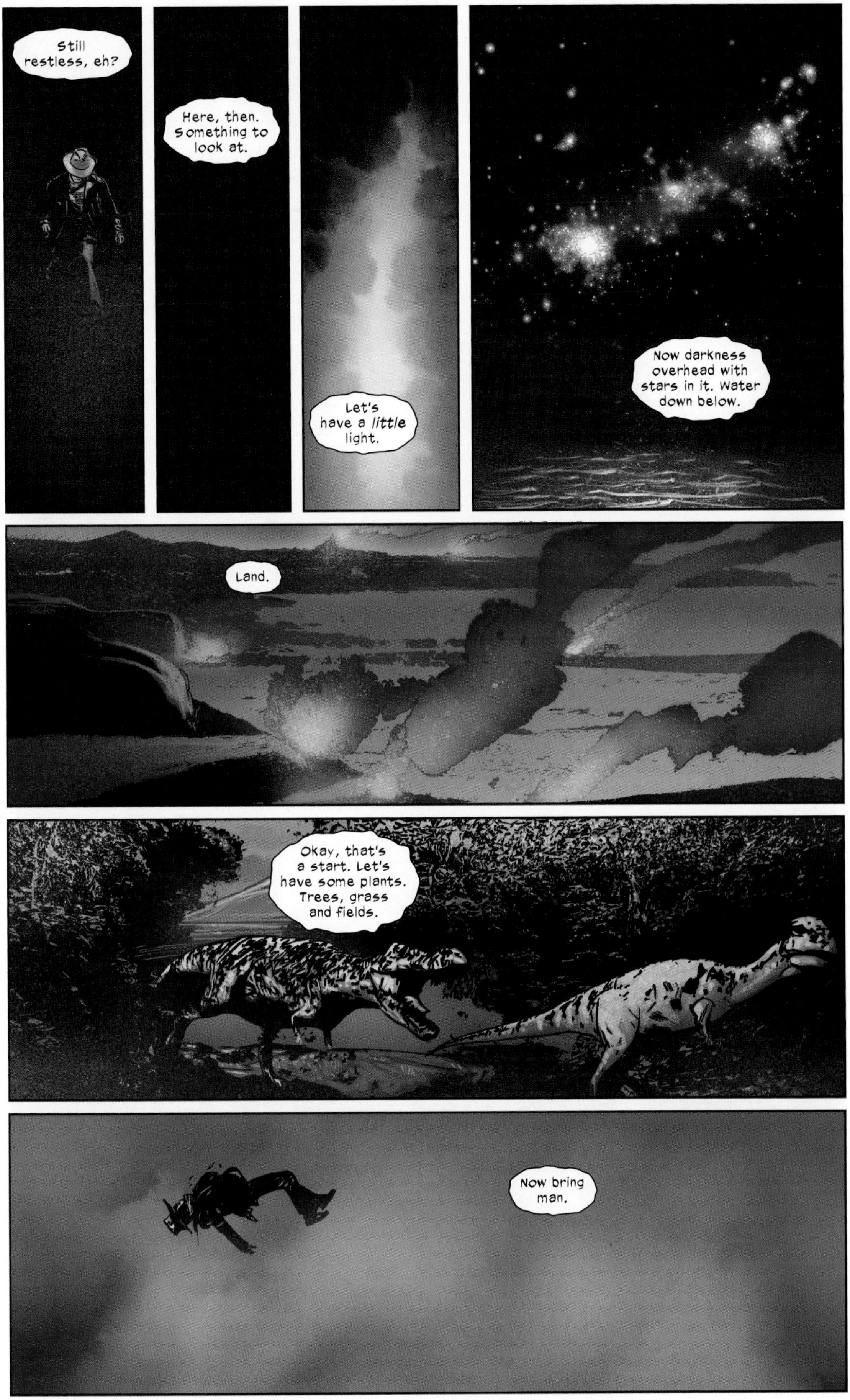
Still restless, eh?
Here, then. Something to look at.
Let's have a *little* light.
Now darkness overhead with stars in it. Water down below.
Land.
Okay, that's a start. Let's have some plants. Trees, grass and fields.
Now bring man.

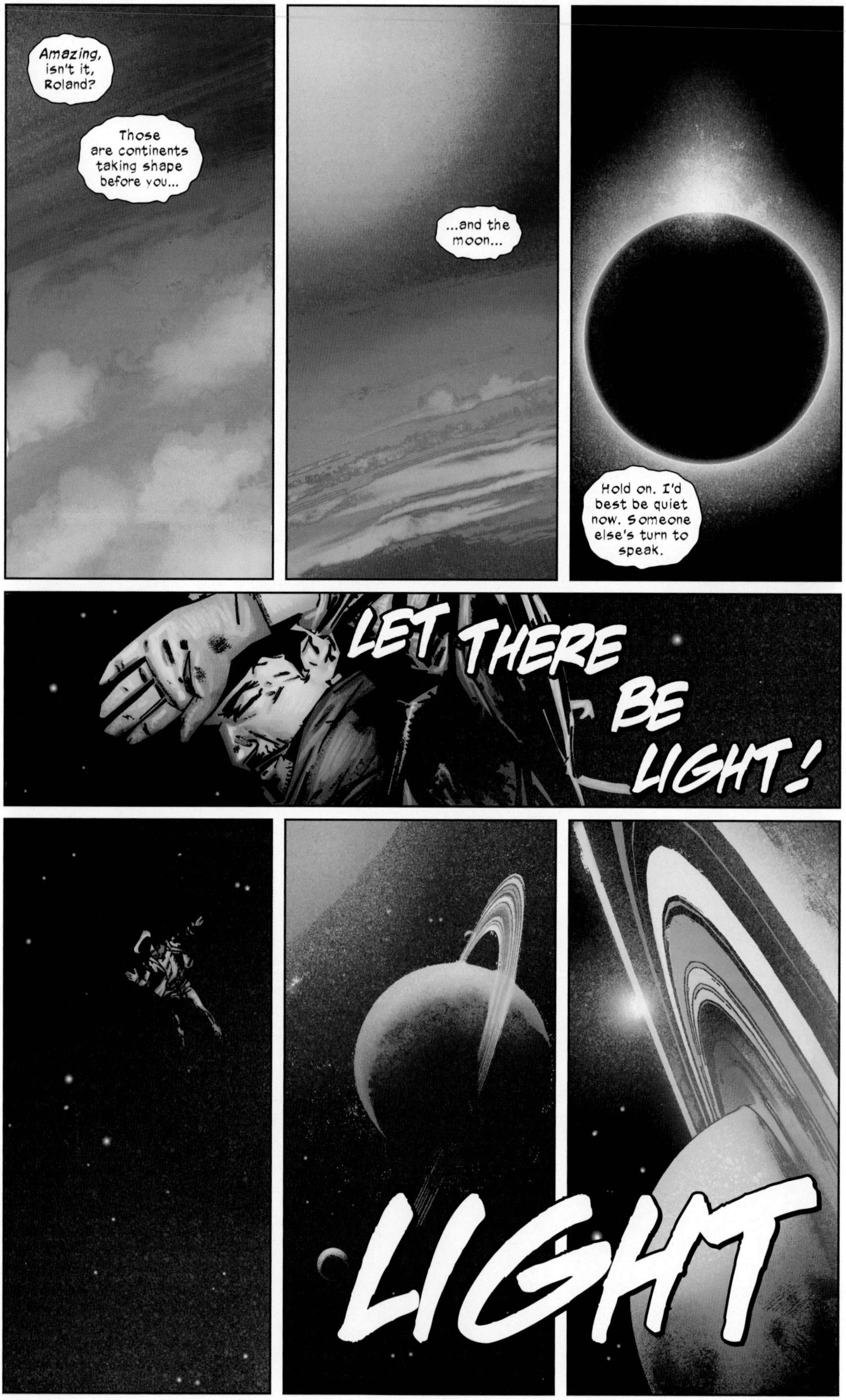
Amazing, isn't it, Roland?
Those are continents taking shape before you...
...and the moon...
Hold on. I'd best be quiet now. Someone else's turn to speak.
LET THERE BE LIGHT!
LIGHT

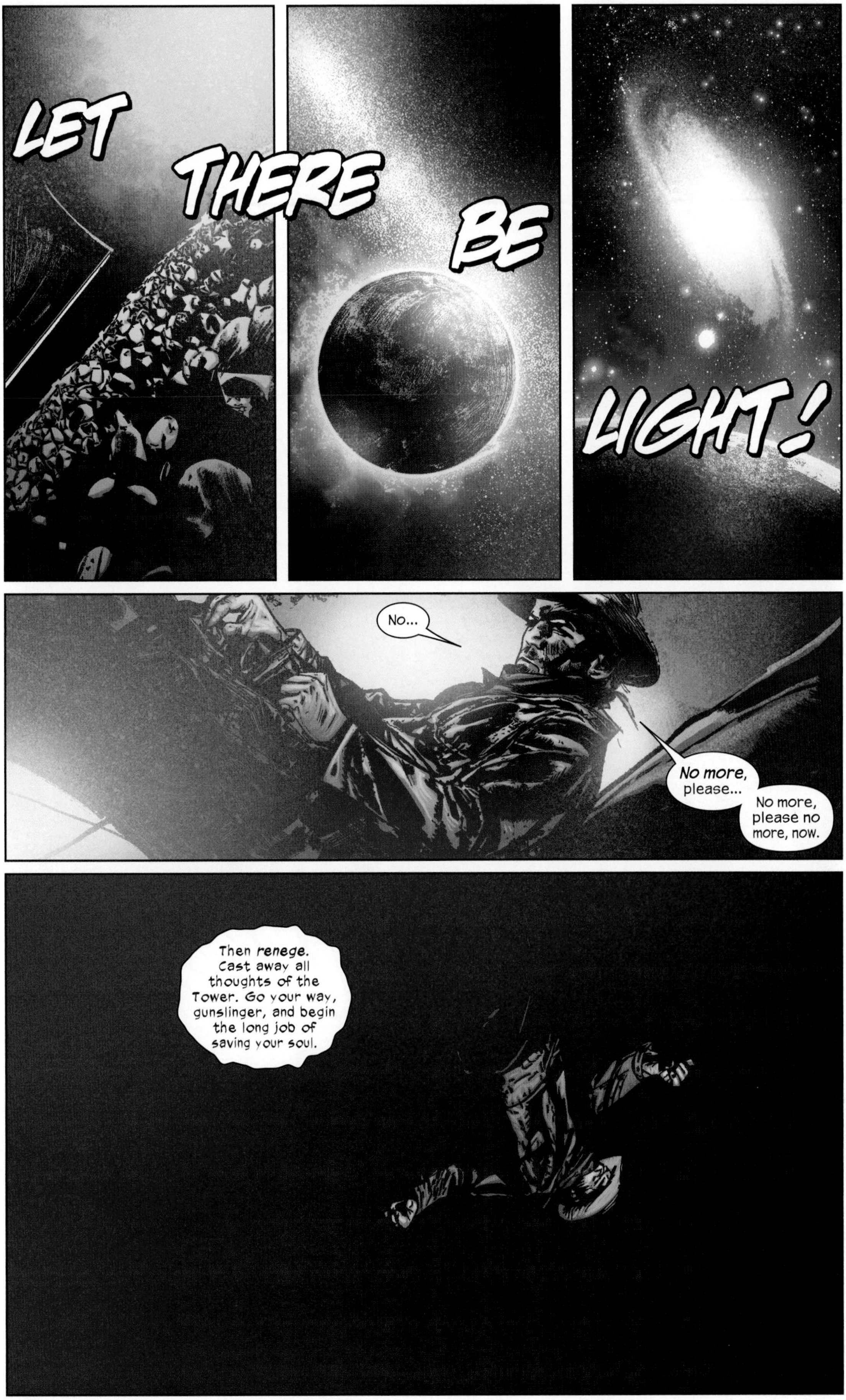

LET THERE BE LIGHT!
No...
No more, please...
No more, please no more, now.
Then renege. Cast away all thoughts of the Tower. Go your way, gunslinger, and begin the long job of saving your soul.

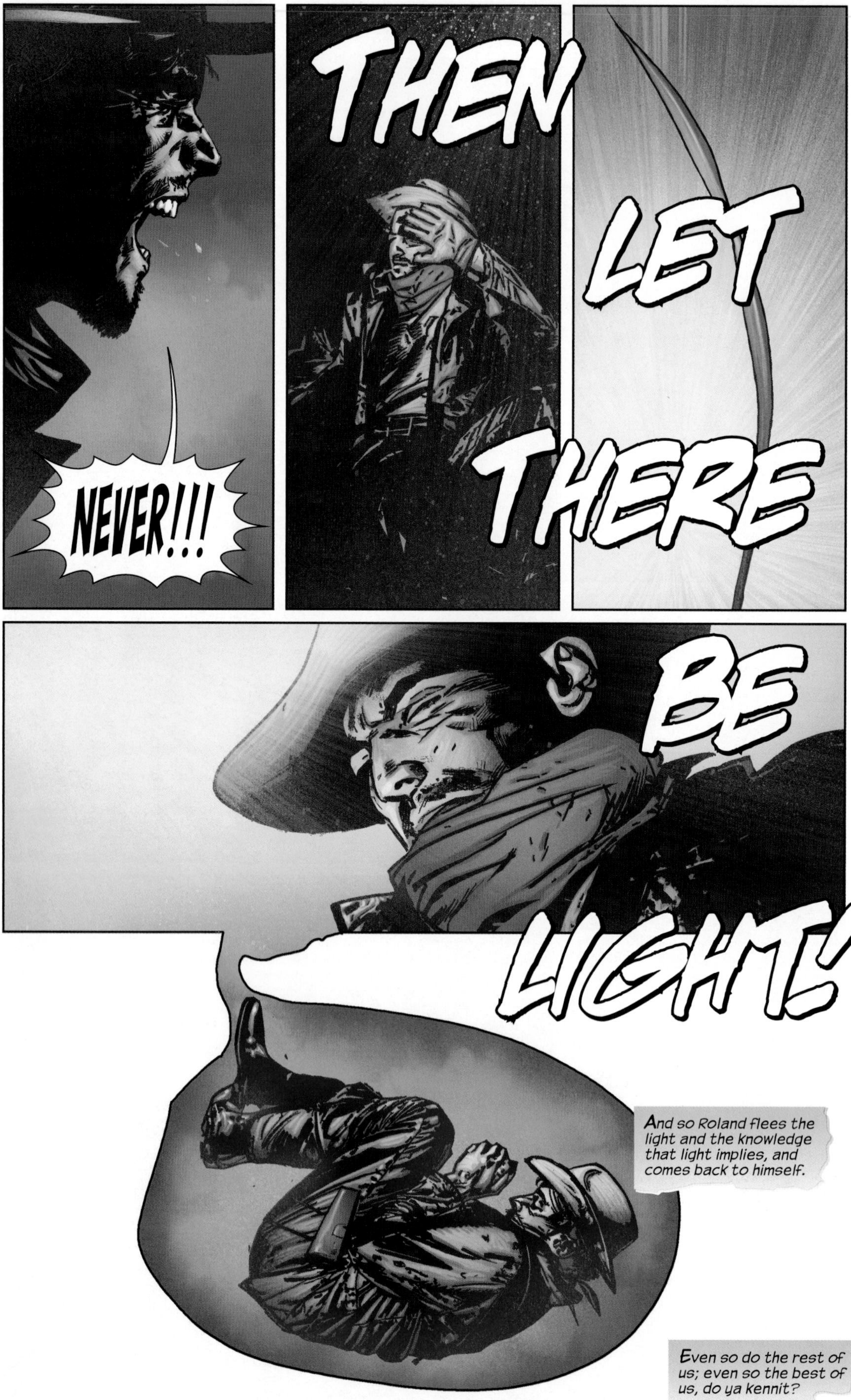

NEVER!!!
THEN
LET
THERE
BE
LIGHT!
And so Roland flees the light and the knowledge that light implies, and comes back to himself.
Even so do the rest of us; even so the best of us, do ya kennit?

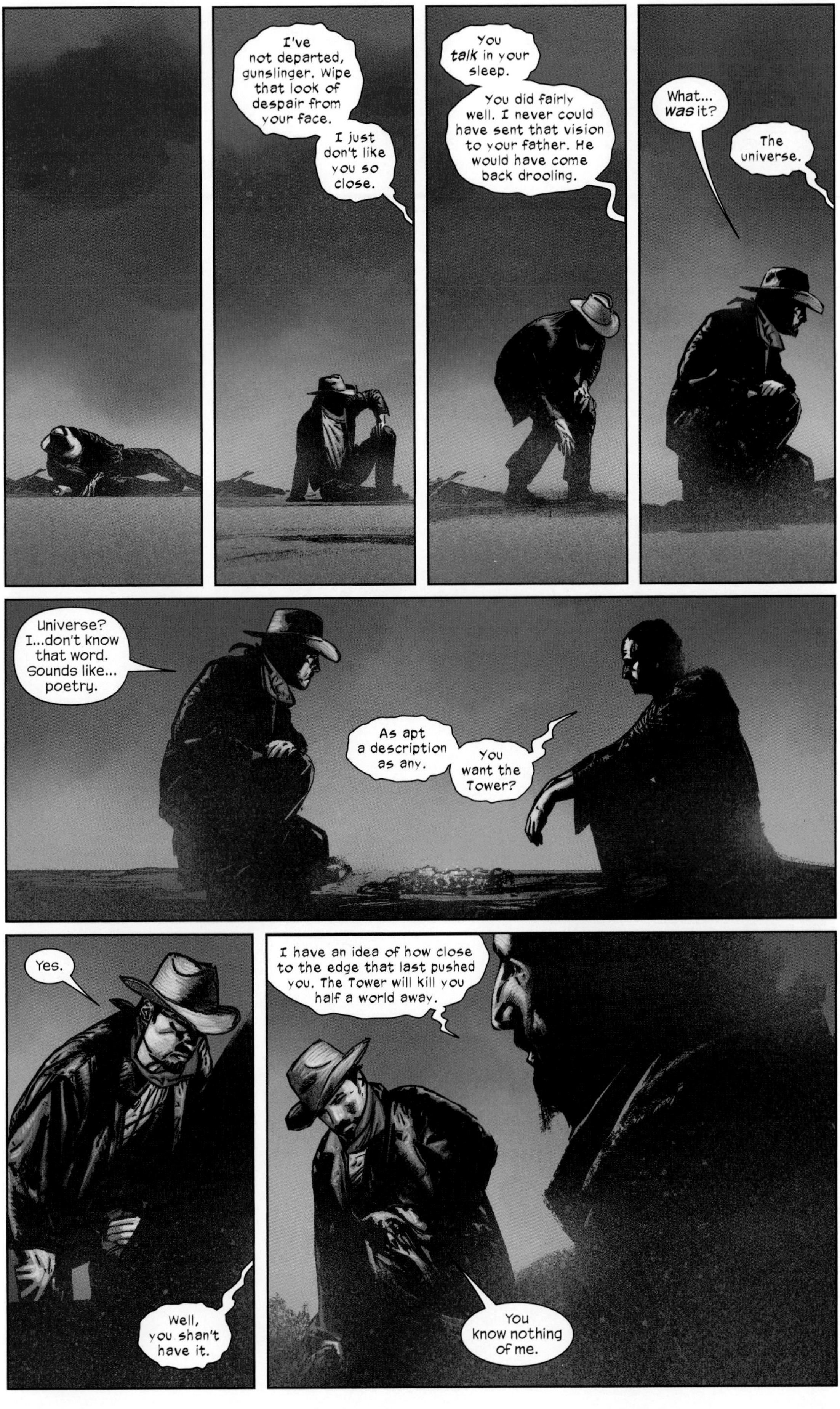
I've not departed, gunslinger. Wipe that look of despair from your face.
I just don't like you so close.
You *talk* in your sleep.
You did fairly well. I never could have sent that vision to your father. He would have come back drooling.
What... *was* it?
The universe.
Universe? I...don't know that word. Sounds like... poetry.
As apt a description as any.
You want the Tower?
Yes.
Well, you shan't have it.
I have an idea of how close to the edge that last pushed you. The Tower will kill you half a world away.
You know nothing of me.

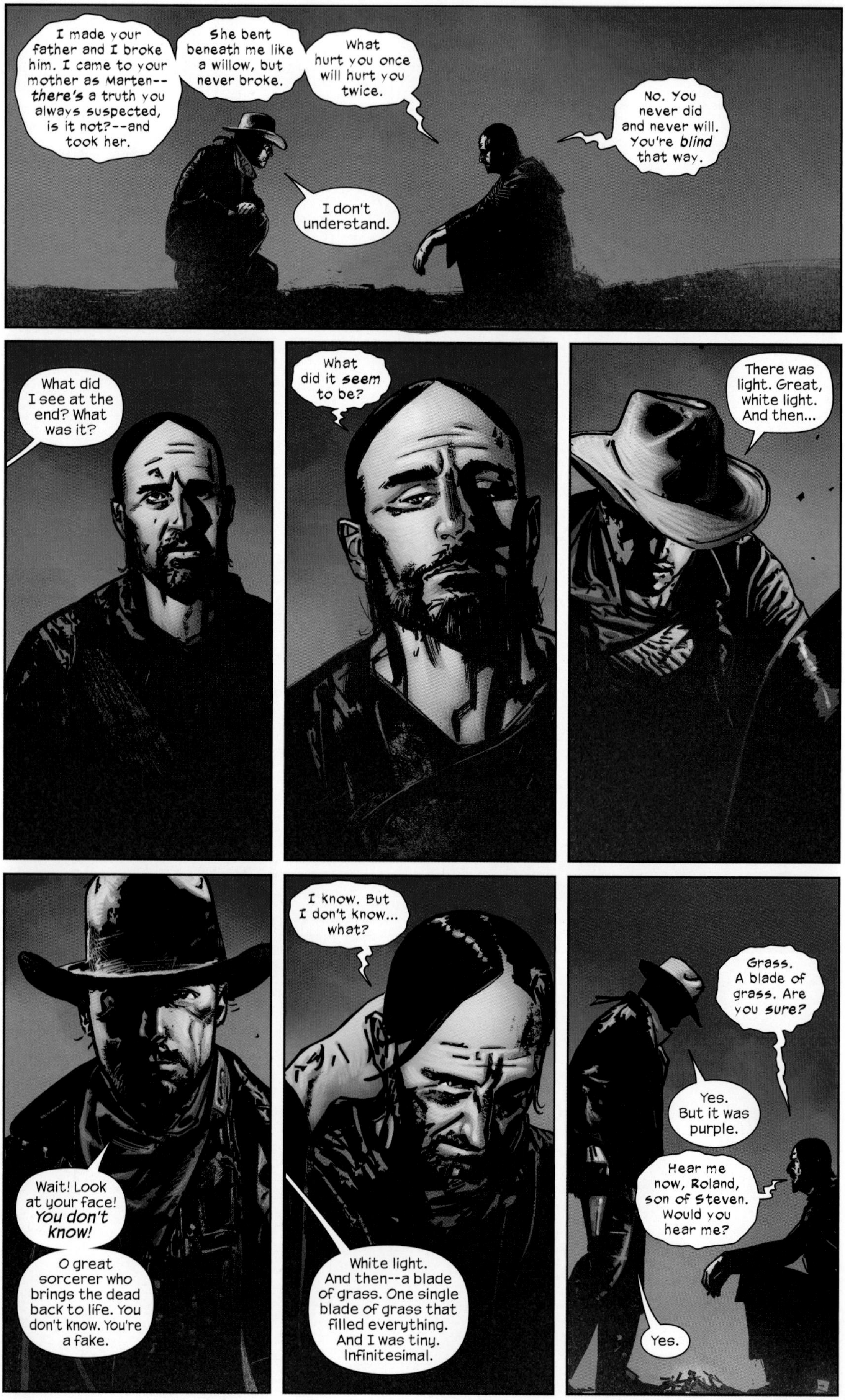
I made your father and I broke him. I came to your mother as Marten--*there's* a truth you always suspected, is it not?--and took her.
She bent beneath me like a willow, but never broke.
What hurt you once will hurt you twice.
I don't understand.
No. You never did and never will. You're *blind* that way.
What did I see at the end? What was it?
What did it *seem* to be?
There was light. Great, white light. And then...
Wait! Look at your face! *You don't know!*
O great sorcerer who brings the dead back to life. You don't know. You're a fake.
I know. But I don't know... what?
White light. And then--a blade of grass. One single blade of grass that filled everything. And I was tiny. Infinitesimal.
Grass. A blade of grass. Are you *sure?*
Yes. But it was purple.
Hear me now, Roland, son of Steven. Would you hear me?
Yes.

"The universe is the Great All, and offers a paradox too great for the finite mind to grasp.

"There was a time, yet a hundred generations before the world moved on, where mankind had achieved enough technical and scientific prowess to chip a few splinters from the great stone pillar of reality.

"Gunslinger, our many-times-great grandfathers *conquered* the disease-which-rots, which they called cancer, almost conquered aging, walked on the moon...

"...and one company, or cabal, led the way in this regard: *North Central Positronics*, it called itself.

"Yet despite a tremendous increase in available facts, there were remarkably *few* insights.

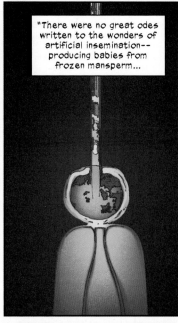

"There were no great odes written to the wonders of artificial insemination-- producing babies from frozen mansperm...

"...or to the cars that ran on power from the sun. They made the wondrous *mundane* and didn't appreciate the greatest mystery of the universe:

"Its size. Size encompasses life, and the Tower encompasses size. Size defeats us.

"For the fish, the lake in which he lives is the universe. What does the fish think...

"...when he is jerked up by the mouth through the silver limits of existence and into a new universe where the air drowns him and the light is blue madness?"

"Or one might take the tip of a pencil and *magnify* it. One reaches the point where a stunning realization strikes home...

"The pencil-tip is not solid; it is composed of atoms which whirl and revolve like a trillion demon planets.

"What seems solid to us is actually only a loose net held together by gravity.

"Viewed at their actual size, the distances between these atoms might become leagues, gulfs, aeons.

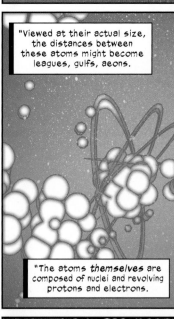

"The atoms *themselves* are composed of nuclei and revolving protons and electrons.

"One may step down further to subatomic particles, and then to what? Tachyons? Nothing? Of course not.

"Everything in the universe denies nothing; to suggest an ending is the *absurdity*.

"If you fell outward to the limit of the universe, you might find something hard and rounded, as the chick must see the egg from the inside.

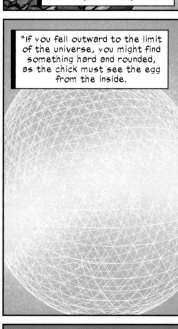

"And if you peck through that shell, what great and torrential light might shine through your opening at the end of space?

"Could it be that everything we can perceive, from the microscopic virus to the Horsehead Nebula, is contained in one blade of grass?

"And if a God watches over it all, does He mete out justice for a race of gnats among an infinitude of races of gnats?

"Imagine the sand of the Mohaine Desert, which you crossed to find me, and imagine a trillion universes-- not worlds, but universes-- encapsulated in each grain of that desert."

"Yet suppose *further*. Suppose that all worlds, all universes, met in a single nexus, a single pylon, a Tower.

"And within it, a stairway, perhaps rising to the Godhead itself.

"Would you *dare* climb to the top, gunslinger? Could it be that somewhere above all of endless reality, there exists a Room...?

"You dare not."

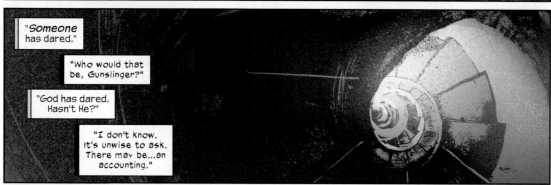

"*Someone* has dared."

"Who would that be, Gunslinger?"

"God has dared. Hasn't He?"

"I don't know. It's unwise to ask. There may be...an accounting."

The fire. I'm cold.

Build it up yourself. It's the butler's night off.

When is the sun rising?

You seek the light so soon?

I was made for light.

So you were. But this night will go on for as long as my king and master wills it.

Who *is* this king?

He comes to me in my dreams, yet I have never seen him. But *you* must.

But before you meet him, you must *first* meet the Ageless Stranger and slay him.

And this Stranger, does he have a name?

Oh, he is named. His name is Legion.

Yet I do not think that is what you wished to ask, gunslinger. It is not your nature to think so far ahead.

This Stranger is a minion of the Tower? Like yourself?

Yar. He *darkles*. He *tincts*. He is in all times. Yet there is one greater than he.

Who?

Ask me no more! I *know not*. I do not *wish* to know. To speak of the things in End-World is to speak of the ruination of one's own soul. Now ask what you wish to ask.

Will I succeed? Will I win through?

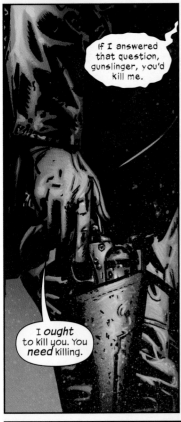

If I answered that question, gunslinger, you'd kill me.

I *ought* to kill you. You *need* killing.

Those do not open doors, gunslinger; those only close them forever.

Where must I go?

Start west. Go to the sea. Where the world ends is where you must begin.

There was a man who gave you advice. The man you bested so long ago...

Yes, Cort. What of it?

"The advice was to wait. It was bad advice. For even then my plans against your father had proceeded. He sent you away and, well...you *know* what happened to your mother when you returned.

"Marten, meanwhile, had gone west, to join the rebels. So all said, anyway, and so you believed. Yet he and a certain witch left you a trap and you fell into it. Good boy!"

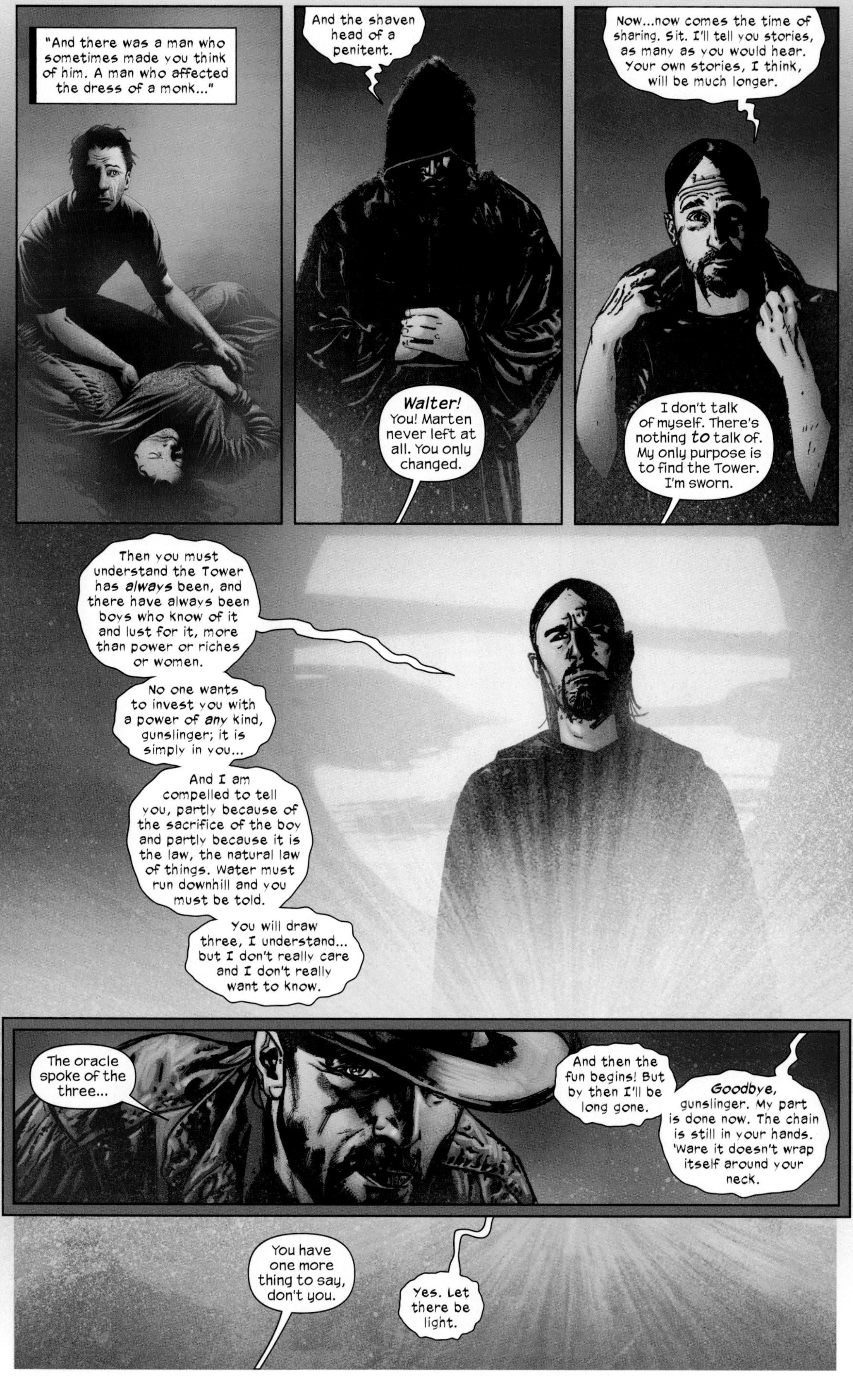
"And there was a man who sometimes made you think of him. A man who affected the dress of a monk..."
And the shaven head of a penitent.
Walter! You! Marten never left at all. You only changed.
Now...now comes the time of sharing. Sit. I'll tell you stories, as many as you would hear. Your own stories, I think, will be much longer.
I don't talk of myself. There's nothing to talk of. My only purpose is to find the Tower. I'm sworn.
Then you must understand the Tower has always been, and there have always been boys who know of it and lust for it, more than power or riches or women.
No one wants to invest you with a power of any kind, gunslinger; it is simply in you...
And I am compelled to tell you, partly because of the sacrifice of the boy and partly because it is the law, the natural law of things. Water must run downhill and you must be told.
You will draw three, I understand... but I don't really care and I don't really want to know.
The oracle spoke of the three...
And then the fun begins! But by then I'll be long gone.
Goodbye, gunslinger. My part is done now. The chain is still in your hands. 'Ware it doesn't wrap itself around your neck.
You have one more thing to say, don't you.
Yes. Let there be light.

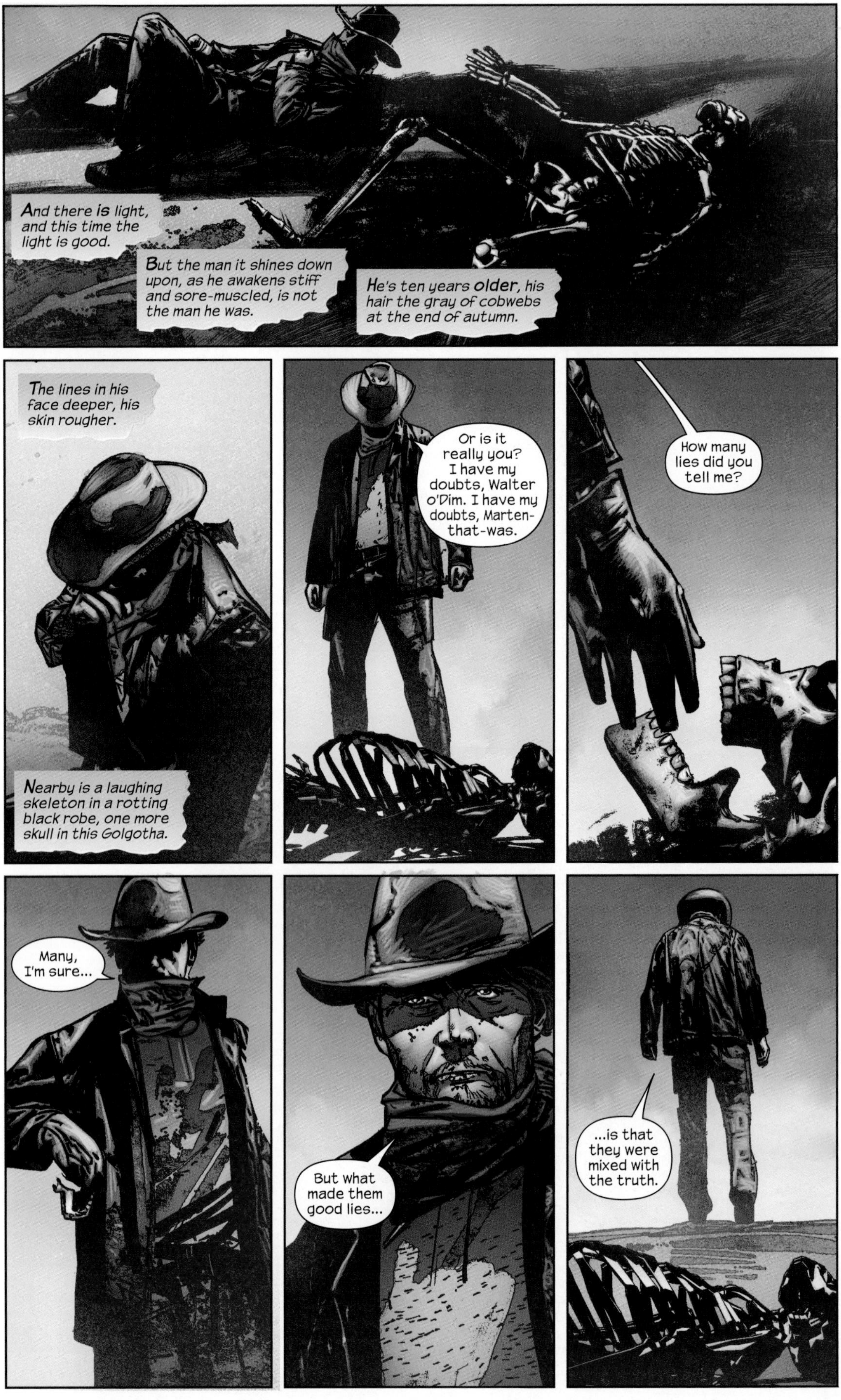

And there is light, and this time the light is good.
But the man it shines down upon, as he awakens stiff and sore-muscled, is not the man he was.
He's ten years older, his hair the gray of cobwebs at the end of autumn.
The lines in his face deeper, his skin rougher.
Nearby is a laughing skeleton in a rotting black robe, one more skull in this Golgotha.
Or is it really you? I have my doubts, Walter o'Dim. I have my doubts, Marten-that-was.
How many lies did you tell me?
Many, I'm sure...
But what made them good lies...
...is that they were mixed with the truth.

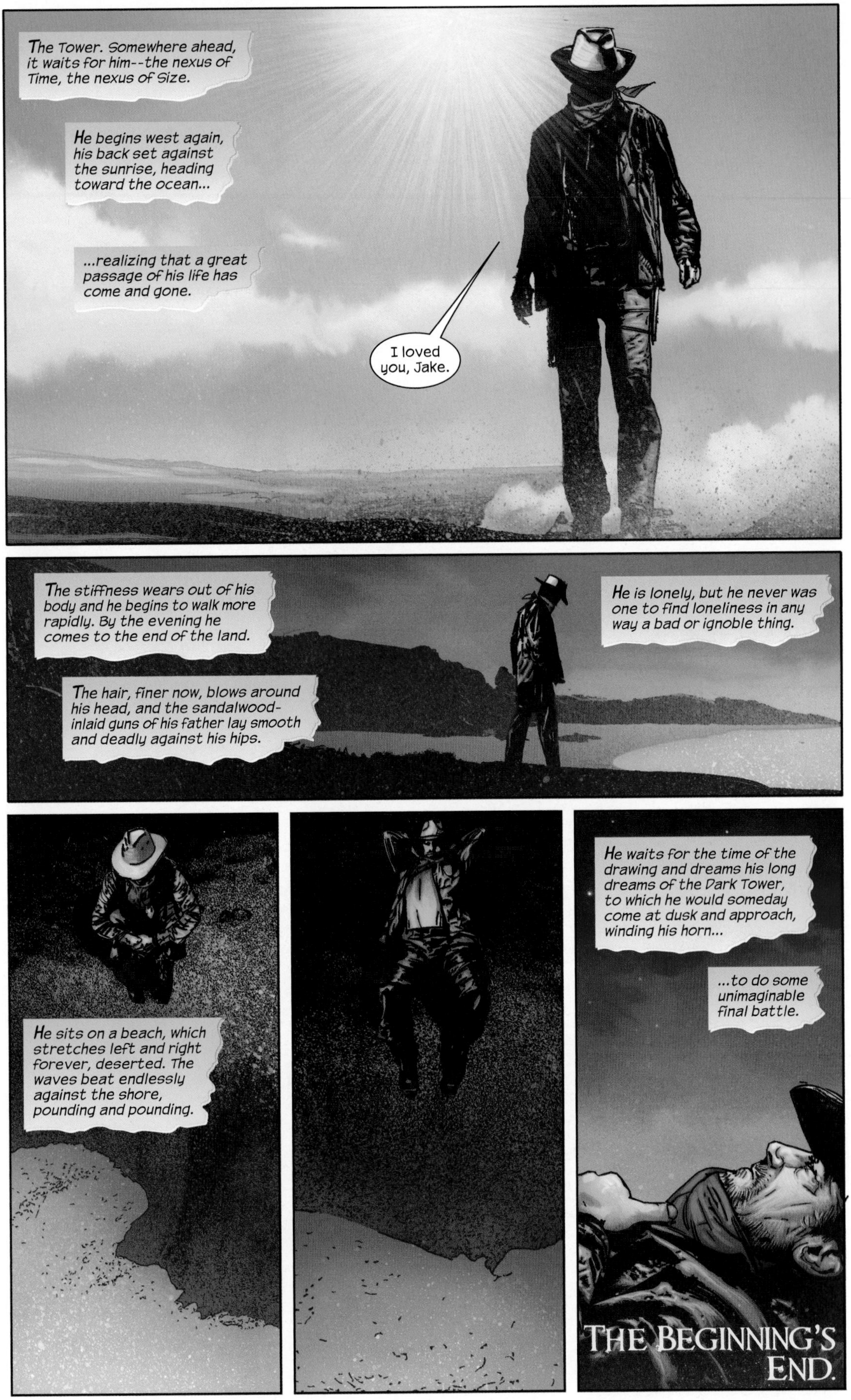
The Tower. Somewhere ahead, it waits for him--the nexus of Time, the nexus of Size.
He begins west again, his back set against the sunrise, heading toward the ocean...
...realizing that a great passage of his life has come and gone.
I loved you, Jake.
The stiffness wears out of his body and he begins to walk more rapidly. By the evening he comes to the end of the land.
The hair, finer now, blows around his head, and the sandalwood-inlaid guns of his father lay smooth and deadly against his hips.
He is lonely, but he never was one to find loneliness in any way a bad or ignoble thing.
He sits on a beach, which stretches left and right forever, deserted. The waves beat endlessly against the shore, pounding and pounding.
He waits for the time of the drawing and dreams his long dreams of the Dark Tower, to which he would someday come at dusk and approach, winding his horn...
...to do some unimaginable final battle.
THE BEGINNING'S END.

The story continues in *Dark Tower: The Gunslinger — Sheemie's Tale*

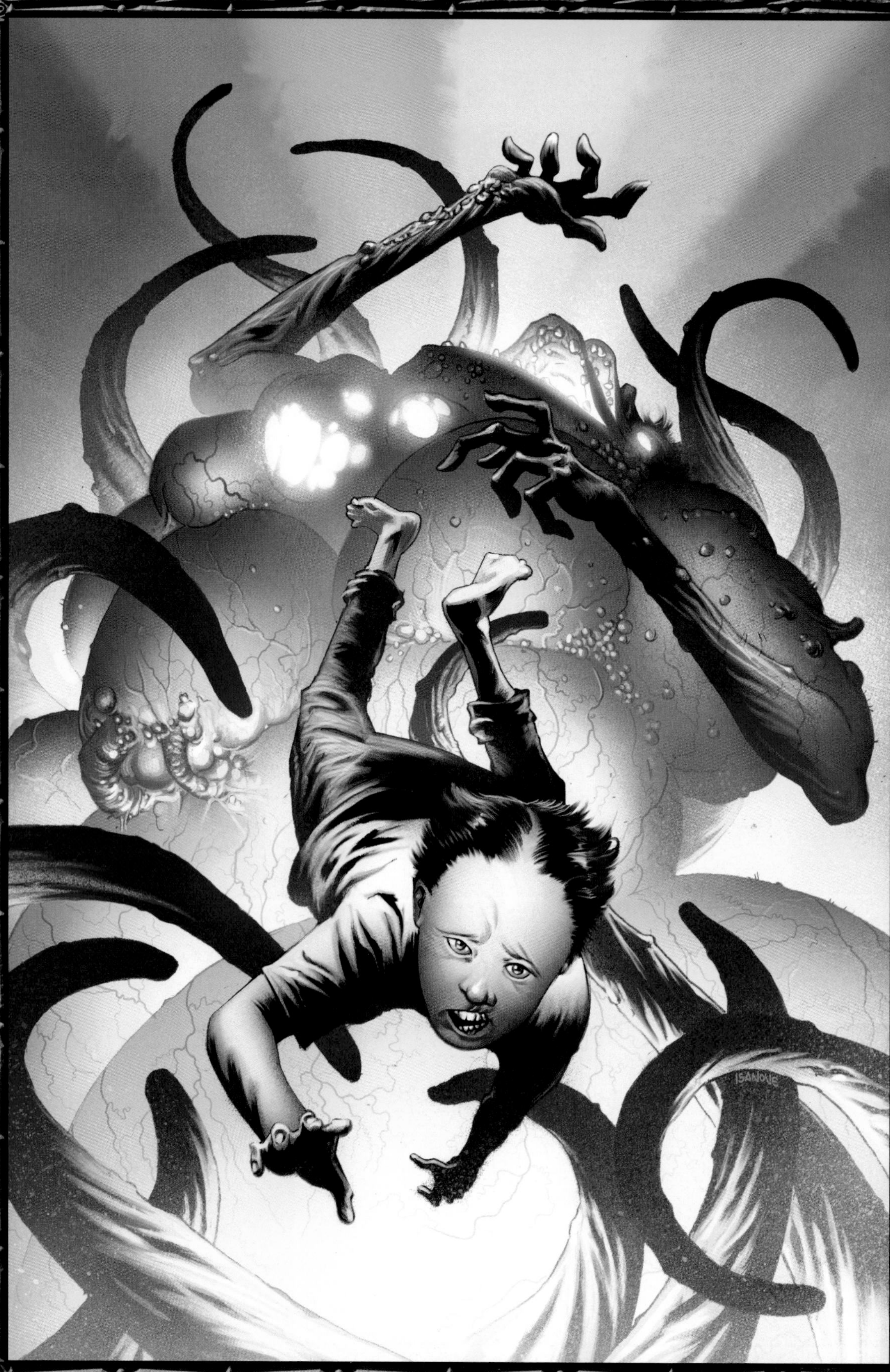
ISANOVE

The Dark Tower: The Gunslinger — The Man in Black #1 **Cover by Alex Maleev**

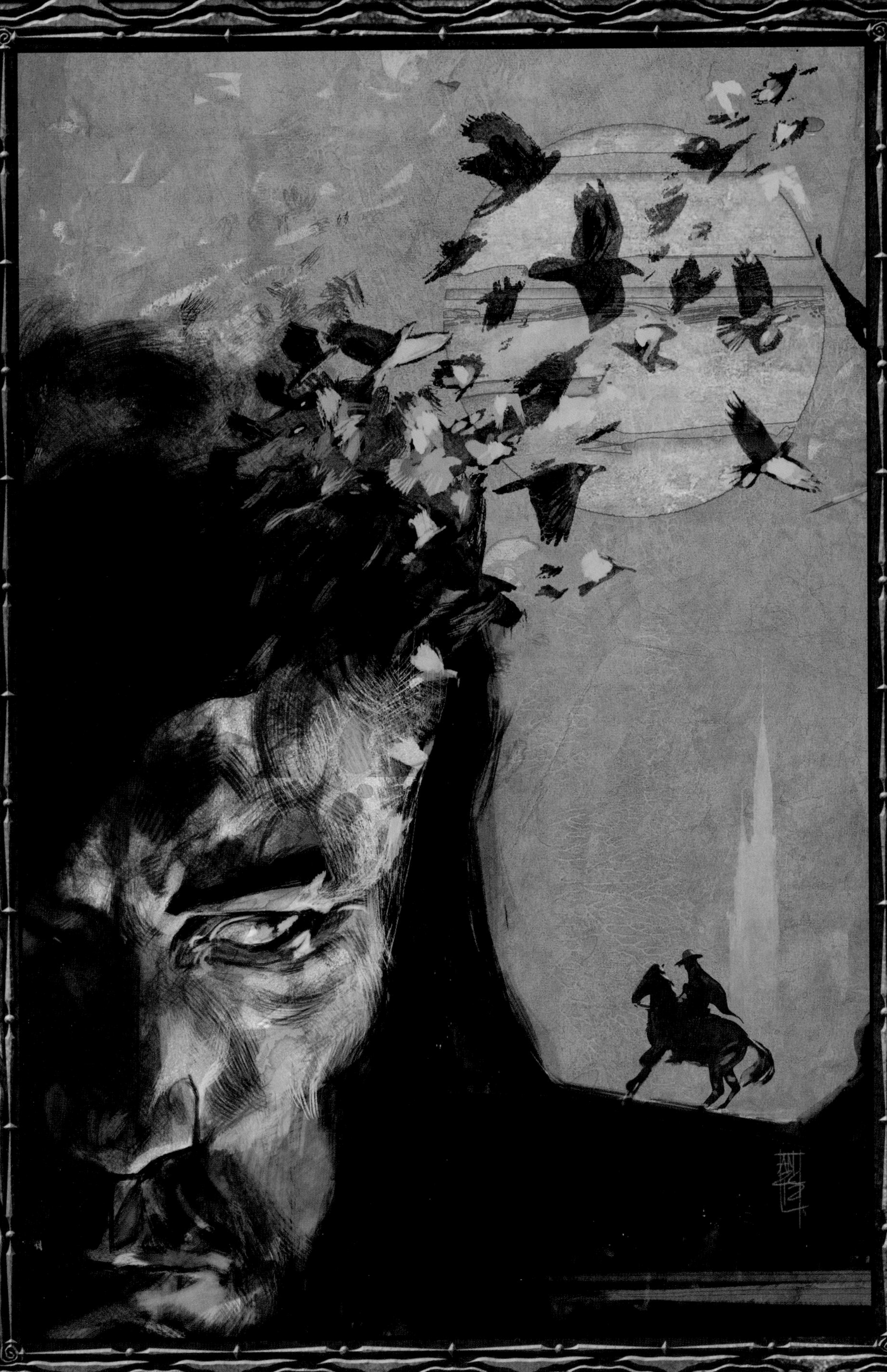

The Dark Tower: The Gunslinger — The Man in Black #2 **Cover by Alex Maleev**

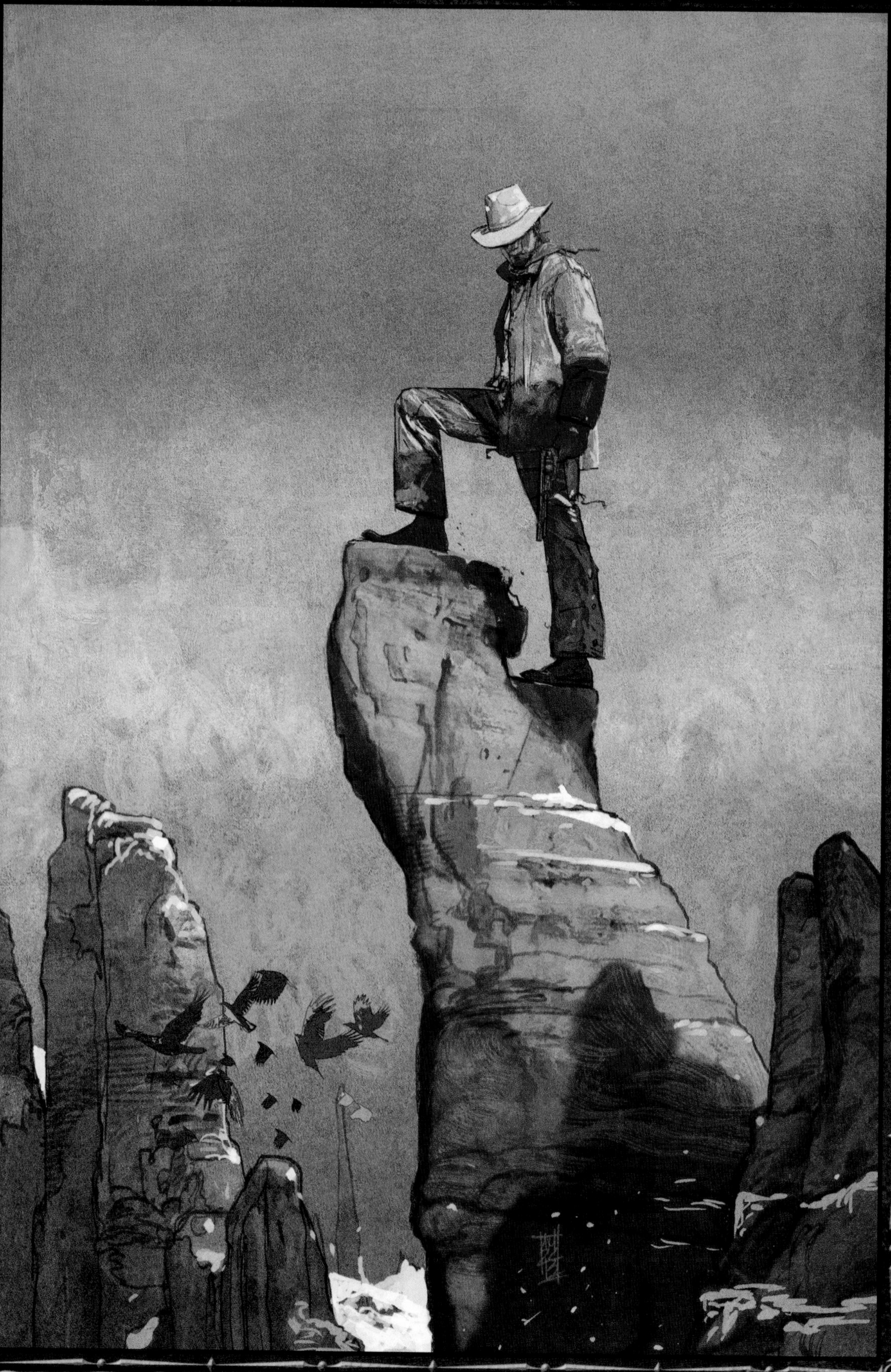

The Dark Tower: The Gunslinger — The Man in Black #3 **Cover by Alex Maleev**

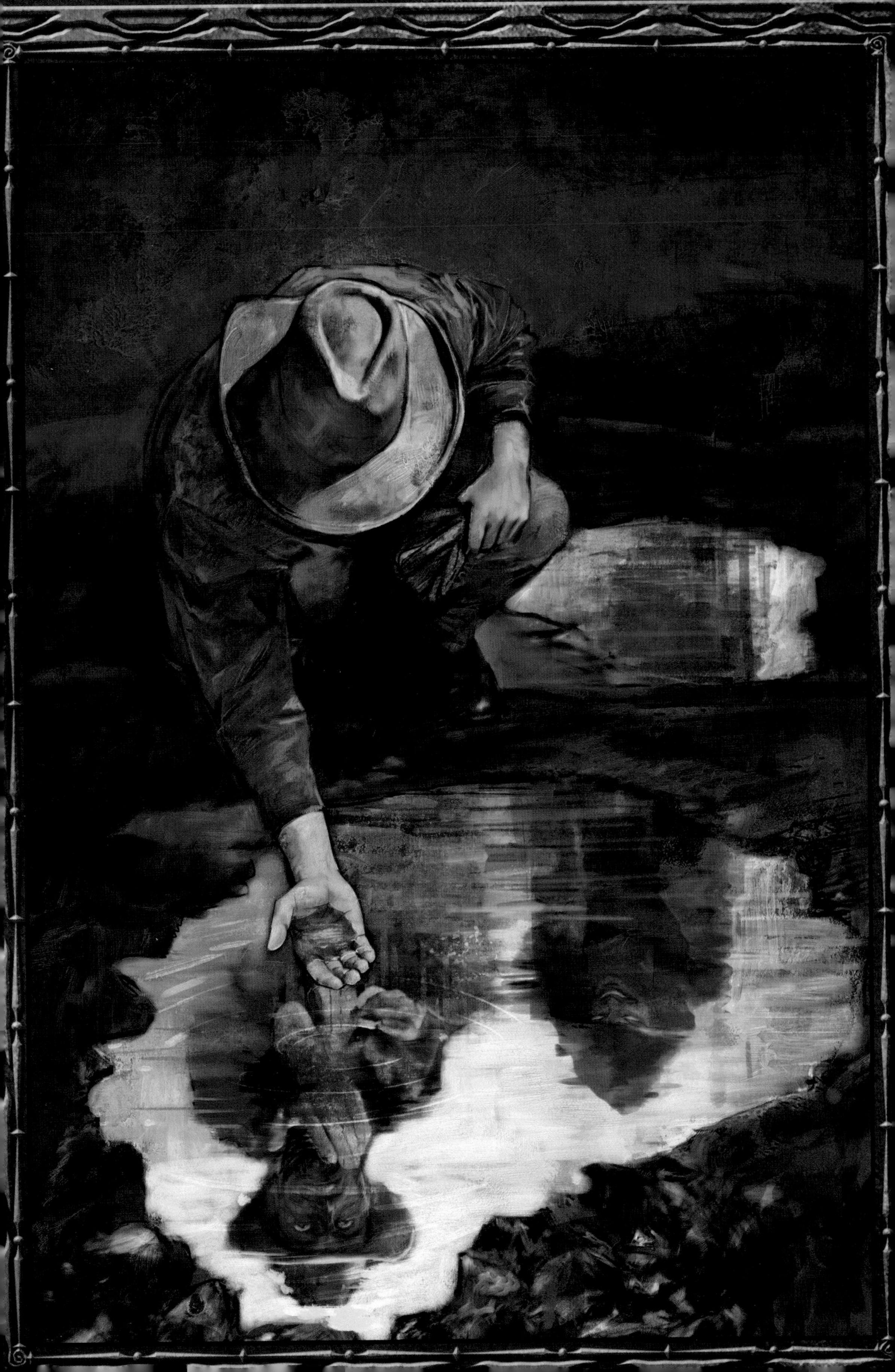

The Dark Tower: The Gunslinger — The Man in Black #4 **Cover by Alex Maleev**

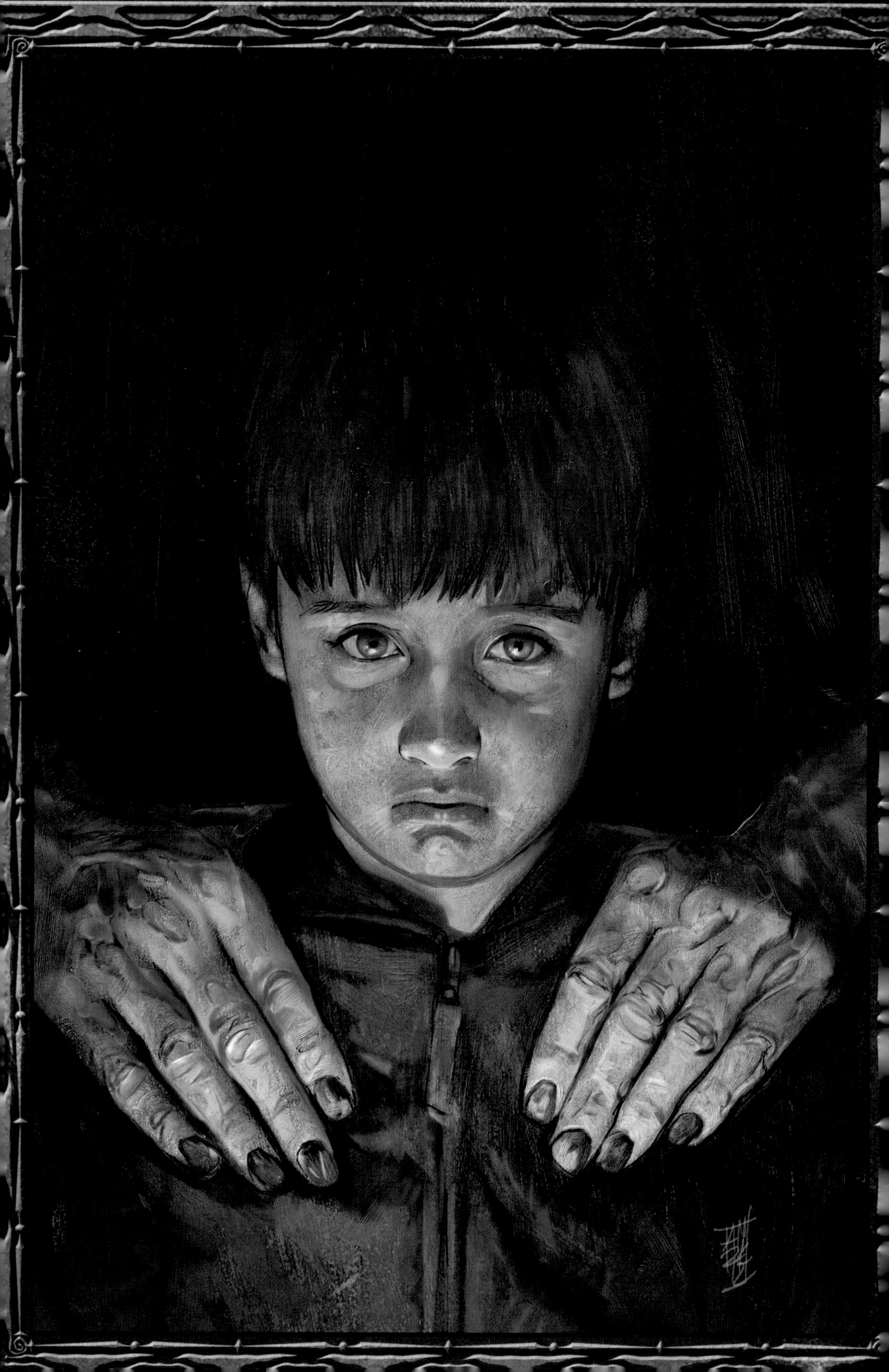

The Dark Tower: The Gunslinger — The Man in Black #5 **Cover by Alex Maleev**

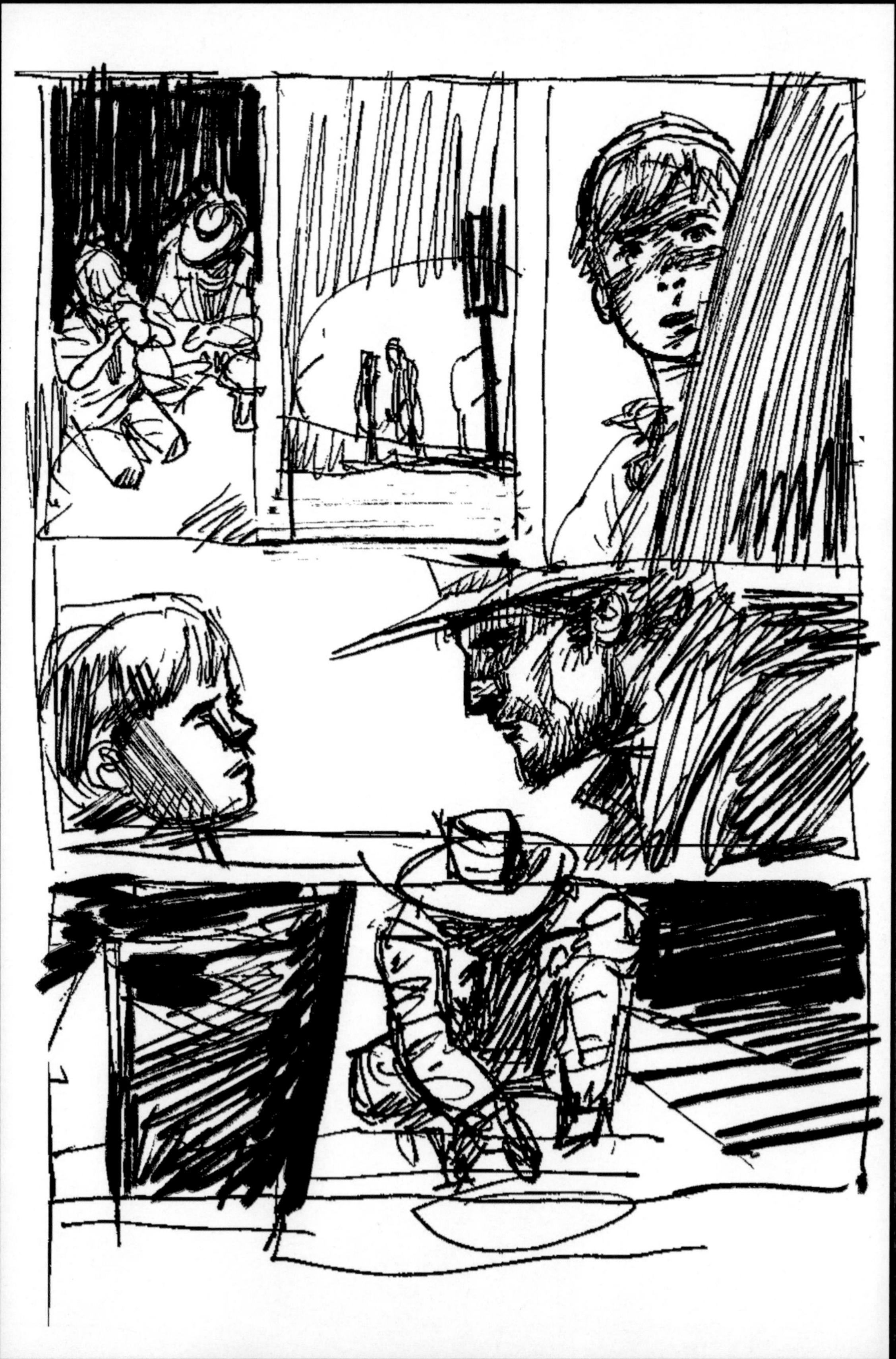

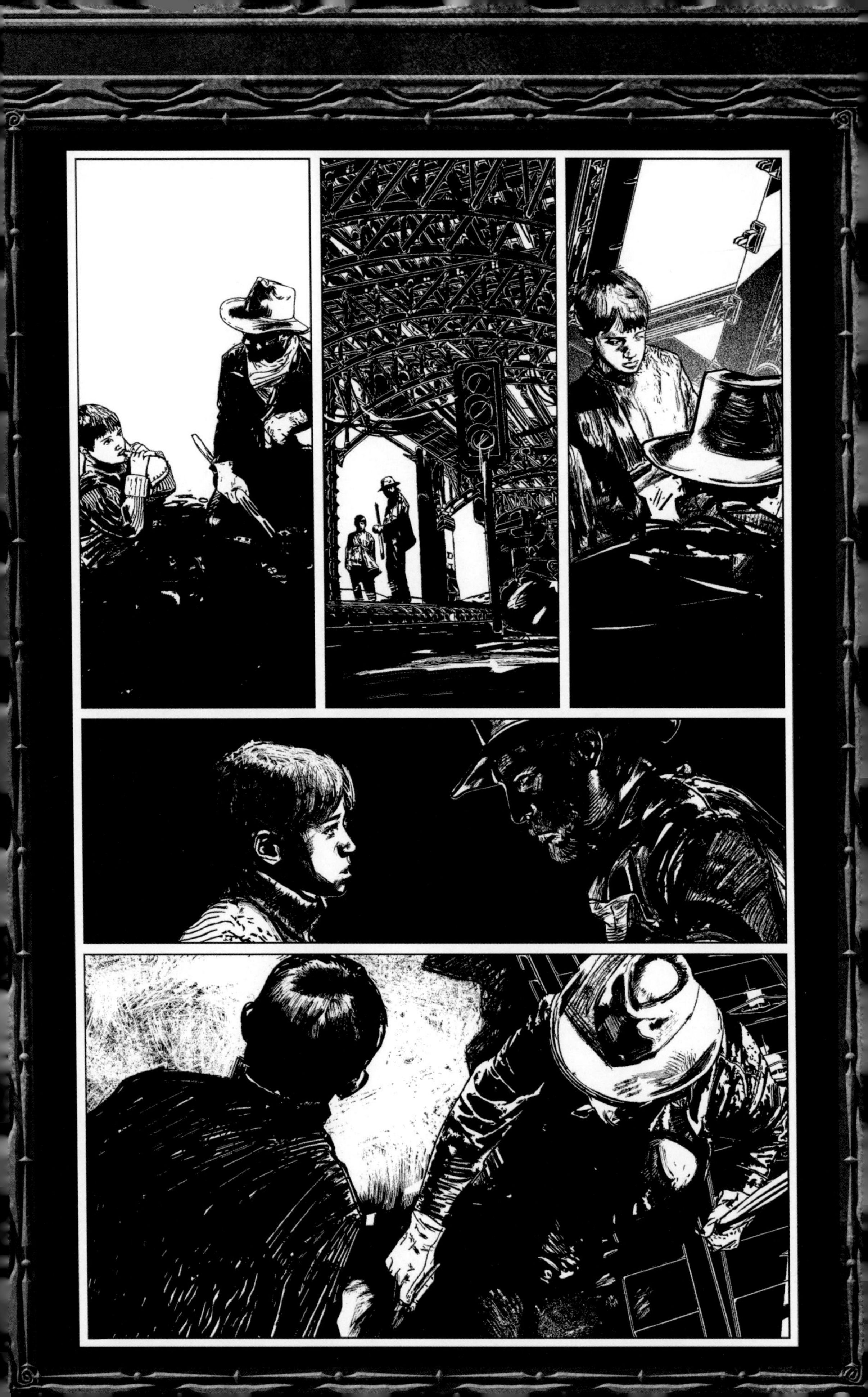

THE DARK TOWER READING CHRONOLOGY

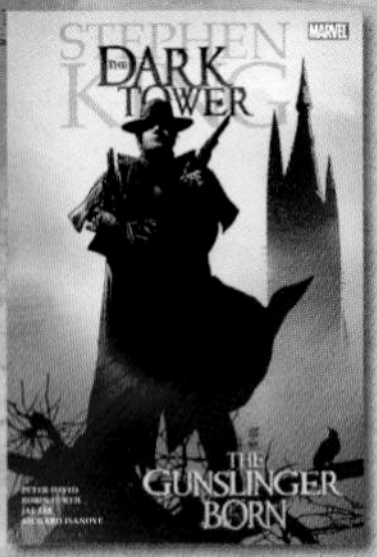
STEPHEN KING
DARK TOWER
MARVEL
THE GUNSLINGER BORN

THE DARK TOWER THE GUNSLINGER BORN

BOOK 1

ISBN: 978-0-7851-2144-2

A man's quest begins with a boy's test. The world of Roland Deschain — the world of the Dark Tower — has been a thirty-year obsession for Stephen King. And now, King carries his masterwork of fantasy to Marvel, bringing stunning new textures to his epic story! *The Gunslinger Born* seamlessly integrates the wonder of Mid-World and the story of its hard-bitten cast of characters into the finest Marvel Comics storytelling tradition.

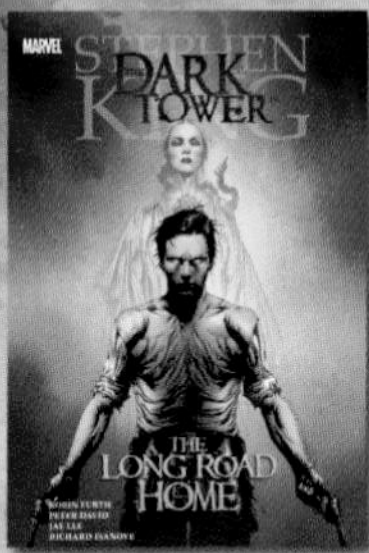
MARVEL
STEPHEN KING
DARK TOWER
THE LONG ROAD HOME

THE DARK TOWER THE LONG ROAD HOME

BOOK 2

ISBN: 978-0-7851-2709-3

The gunslinger is born into a harsh world of mystery and violence. Susan Delgado is dead. Clay Reynolds and the vestiges of the Big Coffin Hunters are in pursuit. The ka-tet fragments as evil abounds. It will be a long road home. With Roland seemingly lost inside the haunted world of Maerlyn's Grapefruit, and the dark forces therein tugging at his soul, it will take all the courage of his ka-tet to get him out of Hambry and back home. But as the Dogan stirs, portending an evil of which Roland and his ka-tet have no ken, it may very well be that the gunslinger born walks a long road home to death.

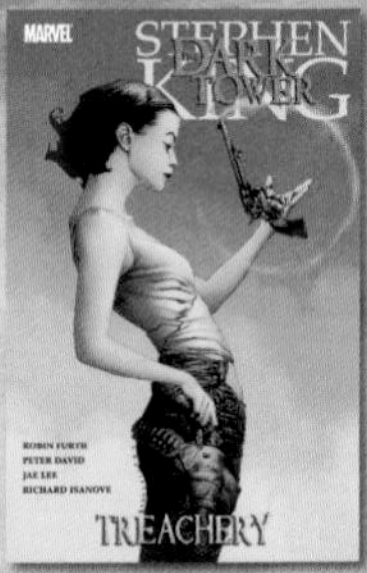
MARVEL
STEPHEN KING
DARK TOWER
TREACHERY

THE DARK TOWER TREACHERY

BOOK 3

ISBN: 978-0-7851-3574-6

From the creative team that brought Roland's early adventures to life in *Dark Tower: The Gunslinger Born* and *Dark Tower: The Long Road Home* comes the third chapter of this dark saga of friendship, betrayal and a cosmic quest as conceived by master storyteller Stephen King.

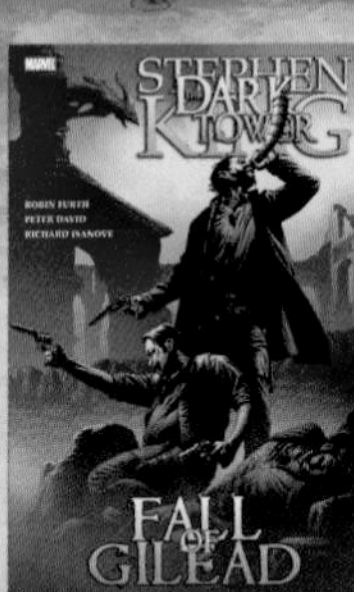
STEPHEN KING
DARK TOWER
FALL OF GILEAD

THE DARK TOWER FALL OF GILEAD

BOOK 4

ISBN: 978-0-7851-29516

How could you have done it, Roland? How could you have killed your own mother? That's what everyone in Gilead's asking — even your grieving father. But you know the answer: Marten Broadcloak and one of them evil grapefruits. That's how. And while you rot in jail, the plot your matricide was only one small part of is wrapping its bloody and black tendrils around Gilead. Your town — the home of the Gunslingers — is the prize possession of the great enemy of the land, John Farson. And he means to have it. Gilead will fall, it will. And it will fall to the death of a thousand cuts. It started with your mother, yes, but it won't end there.

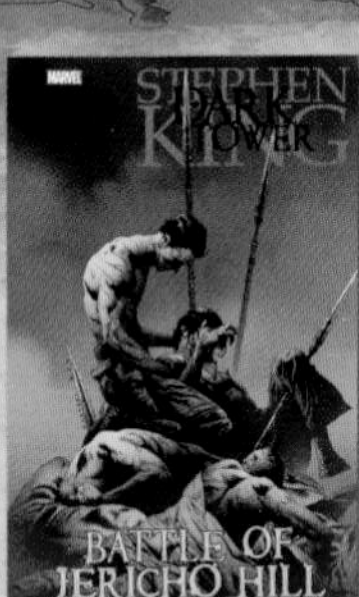
STEPHEN KING
DARK TOWER
BATTLE OF JERICHO HILL

THE DARK TOWER BATTLE OF JERICHO HILL

BOOK 5

ISBN: 978-0-7851-2953-0

A brand-new story featuring Roland Deschain and his beleaguered ka-tet as they go on the run following the complete destruction of their beloved city of Gilead! And when such as Gilead falls, the pillars of reality itself — the six beams holding all of existence together — begins to crumble. The satanic plan of the Crimson King to return all of existence to the primal state of chaos is nigh.

THE DARK TOWER READING CHRONOLOGY

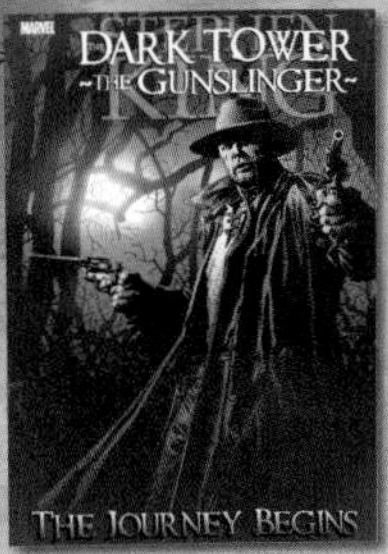
DARK TOWER
THE GUNSLINGER
THE JOURNEY BEGINS

THE DARK TOWER THE GUNSLINGER
THE JOURNEY BEGINS

ISBN: 978-0-7851-4709-1

The Barony of Gilead has fallen to the forces of the evil John Farson, as the Gunslingers are massacred at the Battle of Jericho Hill. But one Gunslinger rises from the ashes: Roland Deschain. As Deschain's limp body is tossed onto a funeral pyre…he's not dead yet. Roland escapes; as the last of the Gunslingers, he sets out in search of the mysterious Dark Tower — the one place where he can set the events of his out-of-synch world right. Along the way, Roland will battle the Not-Men, the Slow Mutants and more as he trails the Man in Black, the sorcerer who holds the key to Roland's finding the Dark Tower.

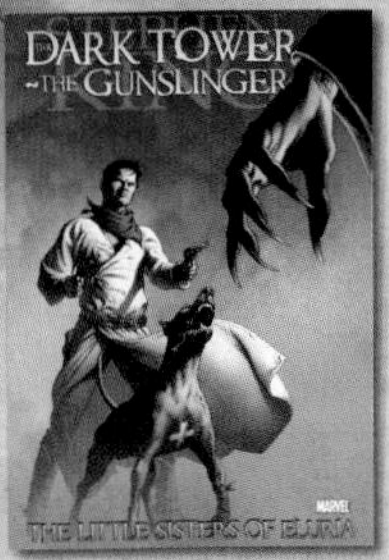
DARK TOWER
THE GUNSLINGER
THE LITTLE SISTERS OF ELURIA

THE DARK TOWER THE GUNSLINGER
THE LITTLE SISTERS OF ELURIA

ISBN: 978-0-7851-4931-6

Near death from an attack by slow mutants, Roland Deschain is taken in by a group of nuns who specialize in anything but the healing arts. These hideous, corpse-like creatures — the Little Sisters of Eluria — have murder on their twisted minds. And in his current condition, there's almost nothing the last Gunslinger can do to prevent their tender mercies from taking hold

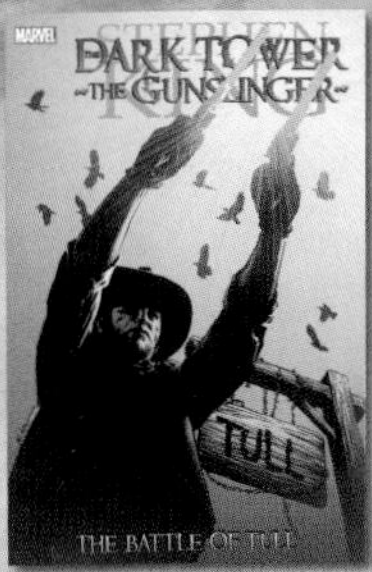
DARK TOWER
THE GUNSLINGER
TULL
THE BATTLE OF TULL

THE DARK TOWER THE GUNSLINGER
THE BATTLE OF TULL

ISBN: 978-0-7851-4933-0

Roland Deschain continues his epic search for the Man in Black. Instead, he finds Tull, the last stop of civilization. A town of devil grass, desert sand and despair It may seem Tull is on the very edge of the world, with nothing past the horizon but a steep fall to oblivion. But Roland believes otherwise: that beyond the limits of Tull lies a hidden truth that means everything to the fate of Mid-World. The Man in Black holds the key to that mystery, and Roland is going to keep following him — even through a trap set in Tull — to unlock it.

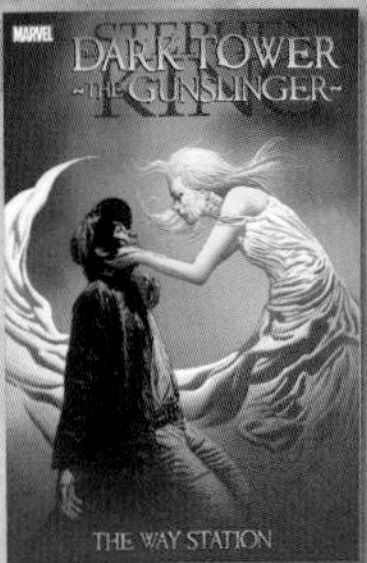
DARK TOWER
THE GUNSLINGER
THE WAY STATION

THE DARK TOWER THE GUNSLINGER
THE WAY STATION

ISBN: 978-0-7851-4935-4

Roland continues his pursuit of the elusive Man in Black across the endless Mohaine desert. Taking refuge in the Way Station, he finds a boy who has lost his memory. But are those lost memories about Roland's world — or ours? Young Jake Chambers, murdered by the Man in Black, becomes part of Roland's hunt in Mid-World. But as Roland and Jake travel toward the Dark Tower, dangers lurk in the mountains — planning a horrible fate for the gunslinger and his companion. Are Roland and Jake any closer to the Man in Black — or just closer to their own demise?

COLLECTING THE FIRST FIVE VOLUMES OF THE *NEW YORK TIMES* BEST-SELLING SERIES IN ONE OMNIBUS HARDCOVER

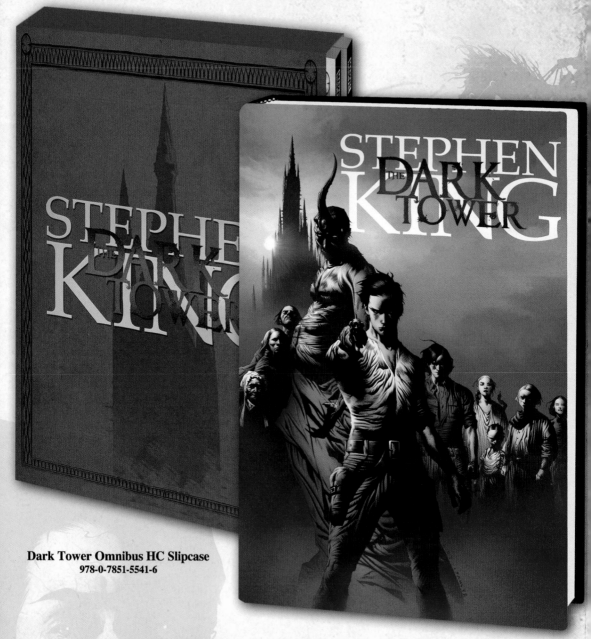

Dark Tower Omnibus HC Slipcase
978-0-7851-5541-6

"Marvel's Dark Tower series, with Robin Furth and Peter David and a team of exceptional artists travelling a path that is more than I imagined, ends here with this book of wonders. It's terrific!" – *Stephen King*

On Sale Now

741.
597
DAV

David, Peter.

The dark tower The
gunslinger

DUE DATE **MCN** 01/13 24.99
